The Information
Professional's Guide to

CAREER
DEVELOPMENT
ONLINE

*The Information
Professional's Guide to*

CAREER
DEVELOPMENT
ONLINE

Sarah L. Nesbeitt
and
Rachel Singer Gordon

 Information Today, Inc.

Medford, New Jersey

The Information Professional's Guide to Career Development Online

Library of Congress Cataloging-in-Publication Data

Nesbeitt, Sarah L., 1969-
    The information professional's guide to career development online / Sarah L. Nesbeitt and Rachel Singer Gordon.
    p. cm.
    Includes bibliographical references and index.
    ISBN 1-57387-124-9
    1. Library science--Vocational guidance. 2. Information science--Vocational guidance. 3. Library science--Computer network resources. 4. Information science--Computer network resources. 5. Career development--Computer network resources. I. Gordon, Rachel Singer. II. Title.

    Z682.35.V62 N47 2001
    020'.23--dc21

                          2001039469

Printed and bound in the United States of America

Publisher: Thomas H. Hogan, Sr.
Editor-in-Chief: John B. Bryans
Managing Editor: Deborah R. Poulson
Copy Editor: Dorothy J. Pike
Production Manager: M. Heide Dengler
Book Designer: Kara Mia Jalkowski
Cover Designer: Lisa Boccadutre
Indexer: Lori Lathrop

Table of Contents

List of Figures ix

Foreword xiii

The Career Development Online
Web Site xv

Acknowledgments xvii

Introduction 1

Part 1: Learning and Growing Online

Chapter 1—Getting Connected 7
Librarianship Transformed 8
Connecting to the Internet 9
Learning More About the Internet 17

Chapter 2—Networking Online 21
E-Mail 22
Forums 41
Chat 45

Chapter 3—Current Awareness 51
How the Internet Has Changed Current Awareness 53
Purposes of Current Awareness Services in the Field 56
Types of Current Awareness Services 57
Handling Information Overload 68
Additional Sources for Current Awareness Information ... 70

Part 2: Professional Involvement

Chapter 4—Professional Associations 79
Why Join an Association? 80
Professional Associations vs. Library Consortia 82

Exploring Professional Associations Using the Internet . . . 84
Getting Involved in Person 102

Chapter 5—Learning About and Participating in Conferences . . 105
Conferences Sponsored by Organizations 106
Conferences Sponsored by Publishers 107
Connecting with Vendors at Conferences 108
Conference Presentations and Poster Sessions 110
Best Online Conference Listings 113
Registering for Conferences and Housing Online 117
Print Journals and Journal Web Pages 120

Chapter 6—Your Online Presence 121
Web Sites 122
Weblogs 133
E-Mail Discussion Lists and Newsletters 136
Promoting Your Online Resource 142

Chapter 7—Professional Literature: Reading and Contributing Online 145
Locating Publishing Opportunities 148
Query Submission 159
Researching Your Topic Online 166
Additional Online Advantages 171
Reading Professional Literature Online 175

Part 3: Education
Chapter 8—Education Decisions 179
Locating LIS Programs 180
The MLS Decision Process 186
Finding Continuing Education Opportunities 192
Acquiring Certification 195
Locating a Ph.D. Program 199

Chapter 9—Distance Education 203
Why Online? 205

Formats and Requirements of Online Coursework 207
Earning an MLS Degree Online 212
Continuing Education Opportunities Online 223
Disadvantages of Online Coursework 229

**Chapter 10—Show Me the Money!
Scholarships, Grants, and
Awards** 235
Scholarships 236
Grants 243
Awards 248

Part 4: Employment

Chapter 11—Your Electronic Resume 253
Why Create an Electonic Resume? 255
Resume Formats 257
Posting Your Resume on the Web 272
When To Send Your Resume Electronically 277
Web Sites for Electronic Resume Help 279

**Chapter 12—Library Job Hunting
Online** 281
Pros and Cons of the Online Job Search 282
Online Job Listings for Librarians 287
Sources for Nontraditional Library Positions 302
The Application Process 305
Job-Hunting Advice and Interview Questions 309

**Chapter 13—Researching Employment
Situations** 311
Career Planning and Self-Assessment 311
Employer Background 313
Salary Information 322
Moving and Relocation 323
Summary 324

Conclusion—Putting It All Together 327

Part 5: Appendices

Appendix A—Professional Organizations and Conferences with an Online Presence 333

National Associations in the U.S. 333
National (English-Language) Associations
  Outside the U.S. 338
U.S. State and Regional Associations 338
Canadian Provincial and Regional Associations 343
International Associations 344

Appendix B—English-Language Library- Related Publishing Outlets with an Online Presence 345

Monographs 345
National and International Journals 348
Peer-Reviewed Journals (With a Print Counterpart) 352
Electronic Journals and Newsletters
  (General and Refereed) 358
Related Publications Outside the Library Field 361
Reviewing Opportunities 361
State/Local Journals 363

Appendix C—Recommended Reading 365

General Sources for Librarianship, Career Development,
  and the Internet 365
Chapters 1–3: Learning and Growing Online 367
Chapters 4–7: Professional Involvement 370
Chapters 8–10: Education 372
Chapters 11–13: Employment 374

About the Authors 377

Index 379

List of Figures

Figure 1.1   "The List" of Internet Service Providers 12
Figure 1.2   Cybercafes.com, Internet Cyber Cafés Guide . 15

Figure 2.1   Web4Lib E-Mail Discussion List Archives 27
Figure 2.2   Library-Oriented Lists & Electronic Serials,
             Subject Listing 33
Figure 2.3   Chicago Library System Online Discussion
             Group Entrance Page 44
Figure 2.4   SLA Chat Lobby 48

Figure 3.1   How Much Information?, University of
             California, Berkeley, School of Information
             Management and Systems 54
Figure 3.2   Emerald E-Mail Alert Service 59
Figure 3.3   LISNews.com: Library and Information
             Science News, Web-Based Current Awareness
             Service (Blake Carver) 66
Figure 3.4   Mind-It Web Page Update Notification
             Service 68

Figure 4.1   Web Page for NELINET, the New England
             Library and Information Network 83
Figure 4.2   Michigan Library Association Web Page 89
Figure 4.3   American Library Association Home Page 93
Figure 4.4   New Members Round Table (Part of the
             American Library Association) 97

Figure 5.1   Information Today, Inc. Conference Page
             Describing the InfoToday Conference 108
Figure 5.2   ISIS2000 (Information Services in Schools)
             Online Conference Page 115

Figure 6.1 Marylaine.com 126
Figure 6.2 Web Publishing Guidelines from
Bridgewater State College, Mass. 132
Figure 6.3 librarian.net Weblog, Maintained by
Jessamyn West 135
Figure 6.4 The Bookdragon Review, Maintained by
Melanie C. Duncan 139
Figure 6.5 Yahoo! Groups E-Mail List Setup Screen 141

Figure 7.1 *InPrint: Publishing Opportunities for
College Librarians* E-Book 149
Figure 7.2 Haworth Press Sample Journal Issue
Program 151
Figure 7.3 ALA Editions Writers Only Section 153
Figure 7.4 Index Morganagus: Library-Related
Electronic Serials Full-Text Index 168

Figure 8.1 World List of Departments and Schools
of Information Studies, Information
Management, Information Systems, Etc. 185
Figure 8.2 Bertram C. Bruce Faculty Page,
UIUC GSLIS 188
Figure 8.3 Indiana SLIS Alumni Profiles 190
Figure 8.4 DuPage Library System (Ill.) *Miscellany*
Newsletter, Local Workshops, Seminars,
Meetings, etc. 194

Figure 9.1 Is Online Learning for Me? From
OnlineCSU 211
Figure 9.2 The LEEP Experience from the
UIUC GSLIS 220
Figure 9.3 ARL Online Lyceum 226

Figure 10.1 SLA Scholarship Program 237
Figure 10.2 OCLC Visiting Scholar Program 246
Figure 10.3 Syracuse University's 21st-Century
Librarian Award 249

Figure 11.1 Sample Resume in Microsoft Word Format
(Download full version at http://www.
lisjobs.com/careerdev/demoresume.doc.) . . 260
Figure 11.2 Sample Resume in ASCII (Text Only)
Format, Created with Microsoft Notepad
(View full version at http://www.lisjobs.
com/careerdev/demoresume.txt) 263
Figure 11.3 Sample Resume in HTML, as Viewed in
Web Browser (View complete, full-color
version online at http://www.lisjobs.com/
careerdev/demoresume.htm) 267

Figure 12.1 Library Job Postings on the Internet
(Sarah Nesbeitt) 282
Figure 12.2 Lisjobs.com's Job Postings Page (Rachel
Singer Gordon) 283
Figure 12.3 New England Jobline, Simmons Graduate
School of Library & Information Science 297

Figure 13.1 Libweb, Index to Library Web Pages
Around the World (Berkeley Digital Library
SunSITE) 314
Figure 13.2 Washington-Centerville Public Library
Home Page (Centerville, Ohio) 315

Foreword

Sarah L. Nesbeitt and Rachel Singer Gordon's book, *The Information Professional's Guide to Career Development Online*, is a must-read for information professionals, MLS students, prospective students, and anyone who wishes to use technology more effectively to develop his or her career. It is indispensable for those considering an education or career in library or information science. Even if you have been in the profession for years, this book will help you use online resources to shape your career, grow professionally, and maximize your time. You will find information to help you connect to the Internet, network online, stay aware of current news and trends, get involved in professional associations and attend conferences, maintain an online presence, read and contribute to professional literature, make education decisions, pursue a distance education program, apply for scholarships and grants, create an electronic resume, hunt for a job, and research a prospective employer online.

The authors have done extensive legwork to pull a huge number of resources into one place. The book contains clear explanations, practical advice, and exhaustive lists of electronic resources. Technical topics are explained clearly for those unfamiliar with technology, but even the most technically advanced information professional will learn something new from this book.

Several features make *The Information Professional's Guide to Career Development Online* unique. Within the book, readers will find extensive lists of Web sites and other online resources, and the glossaries of terms interspersed throughout will be helpful to those unfamiliar with technical jargon. Of particular interest are the comprehensive appendices listing professional organizations and publishing outlets. The chapters on locating scholarships online and distance education are especially useful—these chapters will be helpful to prospective MLS students, current students, new and experienced librarians, Ph.D. candidates, and those struggling to finance professional travel. Another helpful and current chapter includes information on creating and using electronic resumes. The companion Web site, which will be updated regularly, is an invaluable added resource.

Nesbeitt and Gordon bring a great deal of expertise and interest to this topic. Both maintain heavily used library employment Web sites. The authors have also surveyed librarians about career issues and written articles on the topic, and Gordon's electronic newsletter, *Info Career Trends*, offers practical career advice to new professionals. The authors are professionally active leaders in the field who are devoted to helping other librarians build successful careers. As their book demonstrates, they both use technology to network effectively—in fact, I have never met them in person, but we have developed a friendship through e-mail.

The Information Professional's Guide to Career Development Online should be recommended to all prospective and current library and information science students. While the book is especially helpful to those new to the profession, it is equally valuable to librarians and information professionals at any stage of a career. Also, while it is specifically tailored to the information professional, the advice and information here will be of use to those in other fields.

This is an invaluable book. Read it now, and consult it whenever your interests, experience, and career goals change.

Priscilla K. Shontz
Past President, ALA NMRT
May 2001

Priscilla Shontz served as president of ALA NMRT in 1999-2000, and is active in ALA, Texas Library Association, and NASIG. She is the author of *Jump Start Your Career in Library and Information Science* (Scarecrow, 2001) and has written extensively on career issues for newer librarians. Shontz is currently the Branch Librarian at the Aldine Branch Library of the Harris County Public Library System, Houston, Texas.

The Career Development Online Web Site

All Internet-connected information professionals are aware that the content on the Web is always changing, and that new resources are constantly being added.

To help readers of *The Information Professional's Guide to Career Development Online* combat this problem and make more effective use of the online resources recommended in this book, we have created a companion Web site. The site provides direct links to each Web address mentioned, organized by chapter. All links are checked on a semiannual basis. You will also find on this site the complete contents of Appendices A and B, which provide access, respectively, to library association Web pages and library-related publishing outlets (books, journals, and more) with an online presence. As both of these are comprehensive topical guides, we hope you will make particular use of these resources.

To access the site, you will need an Internet connection and a Web browser. Point your browser to the following address:

http://www.lisjobs.com/careerdev

We hope you enjoy your visit to our site. We would appreciate your e-mailing us with any comments you have, and please also let us know about new or expired Web resources you happen to come across. Contact us at:

Sarah Nesbeitt   Rachel Singer Gordon
snesbeitt@bridgew.edu   rachel@lisjobs.com

Acknowledgments

In the course of writing this book, we have received numerous words of advice, support, and encouragement from a large number of information professionals. We appreciate the willingness of all librarians quoted within the pages of this book to respond to our questions on how they have used the Internet for professional development. We extend particular thanks to the librarians who took the time to expand on their own experiences with online education, as well as the library employers who answered our questions on the employment process at their organizations.

We would especially like to thank the following individuals who went out of their way to assist us. Priscilla Shontz took time out from the writing of her own book to compare notes and to answer our questions on the New Members Round Table. Jack Briody, ALA Web Developer, provided detailed (and fast!) answers to our many questions on the ALA Web site. Blake Carver, Jessamyn West, Susan Scheiberg, and Melanie Duncan responded to our questions on their Internet resources with timely answers as well as great enthusiasm for our project, while Syracuse's David Pimentel described the school's distance education program and helped give insight into online education in general.

Thanks also to those information professionals who gave us permission to use screen shots of their sites to illustrate particular uses of the Internet for career development.

Lastly, we would like to thank our editor, John Bryans, for his unflagging enthusiasm for this project and belief in our ability to pull it off!

Introduction

In August 1999, *American Libraries* published the results of a survey on topics readers would be most interested in reading about in future issues. The highest-ranking answer was "professional development," a topic chosen by fifty-eight percent of the librarians who responded. To a slightly lesser degree, librarians wanted their association magazine to provide more information about the Internet and technology in general. Leonard Kniffel, *American Libraries* editor, wrote in that issue's editorial that he suspected a correlation between these highly ranked topics. He posited that many librarians feel they do not know enough about new technology; consequently, they look to ALA to provide guidance (40).

Clearly, for many information specialists, professional development and the Internet go hand in hand. The Internet can serve not only as a subject of interest for career development, but also as a medium through which to become more involved with the profession.

Many librarians are accustomed to promoting Internet usage among their patrons and honing their own online research skills, yet they may not be aware of the wide-ranging opportunities the Internet offers for their own career development. Likewise, they may not realize the strong positive effect that making themselves known to the Internet audience can have on their career advancement. Internet-literate information professionals will find a variety of career-related online resources at their disposal, from electronic discussion lists and conference information Web pages to educational opportunities and publishers' guidelines. Librarians who are comfortable interacting in an online environment will easily establish a network of associates—and a set of skills—that will be helpful in all stages of their careers.

Our goal in writing this book is to assist information specialists in integrating the Internet into all aspects of their personal career development. Not just for new librarians, this book aims to meet the needs of all types of information professionals, from new graduates out in the job market for the first time to experienced librarians who simply wish to become more involved with the field. The importance of the Internet in our professional lives has never been greater. It enables us to establish connections and conduct research that would not have been possible in the pre-Internet environment. Now more than ever, it is a professional necessity to take advantage of all the career opportunities that the Internet offers.

For the past few years, both authors have maintained Web sites dedicated to helping librarians find employment. The two sites have been used heavily by job-hunting librarians as well as by employers seeking to fill positions in the information field. In the course of running these sites, we have had numerous conversations with information specialists around the world who are interested in discovering the best way to find employment, to send resumes, and to use the Internet to better themselves professionally. Employers, in addition to sending us job ads to post, regularly discuss with us such issues as the best Web sites for finding good candidates, the luck they have had in filling positions posted online, and their overall experiences in the Internet environment.

The authors' very partnership in putting together this book is a reflection of the ease with which the Internet can facilitate communication between information specialists (Rachel Gordon in Illinois and Sarah Nesbeitt in Massachusetts). Although we first learned of each other's presence due to our library employment Web pages, we soon found out that we had much more in common. We have similar responsibilities for both reference and systems work at our places of employment, and we also happened to write "WebWatch" columns for *Library Journal,* which were published one month apart. It therefore seemed natural to join forces to write an article on a topic that interested us both: careers in the library and information field. This article, published as the *Library Journal* cover story on May 15, 1999, contained the results of a survey on librarianship as a career. Responses were collected from postings on library-related electronic mailing lists and from forms posted on our respective employment Web sites (Gordon and Nesbeitt, 36). The article itself was written, researched, and compiled entirely online, via frequent e-mail exchange between the authors. Until July 2000, at the ALA annual conference in Chicago, we had never met in person. We mention this not to demonstrate what e-mail addicts we are, but rather to provide a good example of how the Internet makes possible conversations and connections that would otherwise never exist.

The thirteen chapters in this book are organized into four broad topical sections. In Part 1 (Chapters 1, 2, and 3) "Learning and Growing Online," we discuss how the Internet can help you connect with colleagues and keep up with the flow of professional information. Part 2 (Chapters 4 through 7) "Professional Involvement" presents ways to use the Internet to become more involved with the profession, such as participating in associations and conferences, developing an online presence, and getting published. We cover how the Web can help you make education decisions and locate funding opportunities in Part 3 (Chapters 8 through 10) "Education." Finally, Part 4 (Chapters 11 through 13) "Employment" discusses how the Internet has changed the employment process; in this section we mention specific ways to get the most out of your job search by using online resources. Reading the chapters in order will make the most sense for you, particularly within each section, yet each chapter stands equally well on its own if you are looking for information on a specific topic.

The conclusion covers library "meta-sites" that you can use both on and off the job and looks into what the future may hold for librarianship online. Appendix A lists URLs for professional organizations and conferences, and Appendix B lists professional publishing-related URLs. The book's companion Web site (http://www.lisjobs.com/careerdev) presents these links electronically for your convenience.

In this book, we share some of our personal experiences with using the Internet for professional development. We also provide words of wisdom from other information professionals who have had success in using the Internet for professional activities, based on responses to questions that we posted on various electronic discussion lists. Keep in mind, though, that in some instances it is still better to connect with others offline rather than online, and throughout the book we outline some specific cases in which this is true.

In all, we hope to persuade you that becoming an Internet-savvy information specialist can have as many advantages in the career development process as it does in your day-to-day job-related activities. We encourage you to share with us your stories (both successes and failures!) about using the Internet for professional activities. Please feel free to contact us by e-mail with your comments and suggestions.

| Sarah L. Nesbeitt | Rachel Singer Gordon |
| snesbeitt@bridgew.edu | rachel@lisjobs.com |

Works Cited

Gordon, Rachel Singer, and Sarah Nesbeitt. "Who We Are, Where We're Going: A Report From the Front." *Library Journal*, May 15, 1999: 36-40.

Kniffel, Leonard. "Editorial: Reader Survey Is a Vote for Moderation." *American Libraries*, Aug. 1999: 40.

Part 1

Learning and Growing Online

Chapter 1

Getting Connected

Most information professionals have found that their day-to-day activities in the workplace have changed drastically with the advent of the Internet, especially as the use of the Web has become ubiquitous. The Internet has become such a fixture in the library setting that you may not realize how dependent you are on its presence until you encounter times (hopefully few) when your access is temporarily cut off.

Think back to the last time that you had to get along without the Internet on the job. When your library or organization lost its Internet connection for a short period of time, how did it affect you, your colleagues, and your patrons? Reference librarians may have been forced to turn to their collection of print journal indexes or CD-ROM indexes (perhaps now a few years out of date) because access to the library's Web-based electronic databases was not available. Both reference and systems librarians may have had to deal with a higher number of complaints at these times because library patrons were unable to check their e-mail or surf the Web. Catalogers' and interlibrary loan departments' work may have stopped completely because their access to OCLC or RLIN was down. Acquisitions librarians who place orders via Internet-accessible book vendors may have had to turn instead to other activities. Librarians accustomed to Web-based online catalogs may have found themselves unable even to look up the locations of any library materials.

Librarianship Transformed

At times such as these, librarians and other information professionals realize how much the Internet has truly transformed their profession. Despite the Internet's prevalence in our regular job-related duties, though, not all information professionals take advantage of its tremendous benefits for developing themselves professionally, not realizing its potential use in professional development activities or using it only as a secondary source. Sometimes, of course, it will be most appropriate to approach others (such as employers and publishers) face-to-face or by telephone rather than via e-mail or the Web. At other times, using the Internet for professional development is clearly impractical—when attending a library conference in person, for instance. But in many professional activities, such as job-hunting, investigating training opportunities, and learning about organizations, using the Internet can be less time consuming and more convenient. It also makes some activities possible at all, such as networking with remote colleagues and researching faraway employers. Consider, for example, the following scenarios:

- A librarian who has recently received her degree from the graduate program at Simmons College in Boston wishes to find a professional position in central Ohio, in order to be closer to her family. Instead of accruing expensive long-distance charges to access telephone-based job hotlines, or waiting to see if a job in the location she wants just happens to be listed in a trade journal, she can go online and connect directly to Web-based job sources such as the Ohio Library Council Jobline (http://www.olc.org/jobline.html) or the employment pages of the Central Ohio Chapter of the Special Libraries Association (http://www.sla.org/chapter/ccno/employment.htm). (Find more on job hunting in Chapter 12.)

- An academic librarian in a tenure-track position has written a research article and is curious to see if the publication he is interested in—*College and Research Libraries News*—has made its writers' guidelines available on the Web. He locates first the home page for ACRL, the publisher of *C&RL News*, and by choosing appropriate links, he finds the guidelines that he is looking for. (Read more about publishing in Chapter 7.)
- A new bachelor's degree recipient is interested in attending a graduate program in information science. However, she lives in Alaska—a great distance from any ALA-accredited program—and would prefer to keep expenses down by working a full-time job locally while obtaining her degree. Since she has a connection to the Internet from her home, she can easily find information on MLS degree programs offered via the Internet. (Find more specifics on distance education in Chapter 9.)

In these and many other situations, the Internet can provide valuable assistance to librarians looking to expand their professional horizons. In addition, information professionals' use of and presence on the Internet indicate technological ability to colleagues and potential employers—always important in today's job market. More specifics on the best ways to conduct career development activities online and make yourself known to an Internet audience are provided in greater detail in the rest of the book.

Connecting to the Internet

Chances are that most information professionals reading this guide already have a certain comfort level with the Internet and are familiar with its use either at work or at home. If that is your situation, you may prefer to lightly skim this section in case we've described a method of access with which you are unfamiliar, and proceed to the next section on Learning More About the Internet. For those readers, however, who may not be familiar with the different options for obtaining Internet access, we briefly outline here some commonly used avenues. The route you choose will depend on factors such as a particular service's availability in your area and local rules and regulations, not to mention your financial situation.

Access from Your Library School

If you are still in library school, we recommend that you take full advantage of the computer services offered to you as a student, because it will not get much better (or cheaper) than this. Normally, your tuition and fee payments will include a "technology fee" (either clearly stated or hidden amidst all of your other payments), which will entitle you to computer use on campus, an e-mail account, and perhaps a certain amount of space for a personal Web page. Check with your campus computer center regarding available computers and software programs as well as school policies. As a student about to head out into the job market, you are likely to face few restrictions on your using campus computers for career exploration, job hunting, or other professional development activities. After you graduate, you may be eligible for free dial-up Internet service (and/or an e-mail account) as an alumna/alumnus, and the time to set this up is while you are still on campus.

Access in the Workplace

If you are already working as an information professional, the chances are excellent that your place of employment is hooked up to the Internet. Most businesses, institutions of higher education, and governmental institutions have dedicated, high-speed Internet connections; getting online couldn't be easier or more convenient. Heed this word of caution, however: While it may be permissible for you to use the Internet (and your e-mail account) for on-the-job career training and networking, as this can benefit the institution you work for, employers may have specific rules against surfing the Internet for personal reasons. If so, not surprisingly, they are likely to frown on the use of their computers and e-mail system for your own personal job hunt. Even if your workplace does not have a policy about Web surfing, software products to monitor both e-mail and Web usage are very common and are used by a surprisingly large number of companies in the private sector.

We are not about to tell you what to do in these cases, but with so many fee-based as well as free Internet service providers available, we recommend that you think carefully about this issue. The authors cannot be held responsible for what happens when your supervisor approaches your desk while you have a library employment site prominently displayed on your screen!

Access via Fee-Based Internet Service Providers

A personal computer with a modem (preferably 56K) is the basic requirement to connect to a dial-up Internet Service Provider (ISP). A number of companies offer residential dial-up access to the Internet in return for a monthly subscription fee. The costs for this type of service vary greatly, depending on factors such as the number of hours per month you plan to be online as well as the number of competing companies in your local calling area. If you are not sure what ISPs are available to you, check your local phone book, under the category "Internet Service." If you already have access to the Web, check out The List, "The Definitive ISP Buyer's Guide," at http://www.thelist.com; this site includes details on more than 8,000 ISPs across the U.S. and Canada. Just click on your local area code to pull up a list of Internet providers who do business in your area with links to their Web sites and brief details on their services. Most residential customers will want to concentrate on the information about dial-up services as opposed to dedicated services, which are normally used by businesses that want to

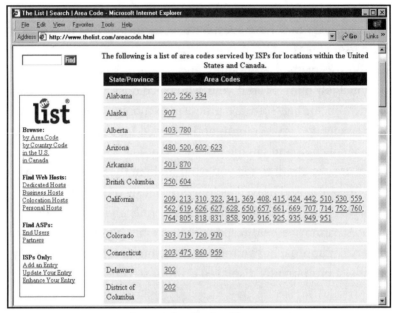

Figure 1.1   "The List" of Internet Service Providers

establish permanent connections to the Internet. Chances are, also, that someone you know is using an ISP; check around with friends and colleagues to see if they have had good (or bad!) experiences with their Internet service.

If you are on staff at a library or other information-related organization, check with your employer (or your institution's computer center) to see if they will subsidize—either partially or completely—access to the Internet from your home as part of a professional development program. Colleges and universities also often make special deals with Internet service providers in their local area to provide at-home access to the institutional community at a reduced cost.

Access via Free Internet Access Providers

Several dozen companies in the U.S. provide Internet access at no charge, usually in exchange for your willingness to put up with annoying animated banner ads. The best known of these is Juno (http://www.juno.com), although it may shortly merge with rival NetZero.net (http://www.netzero.net) to form a larger company, and Address.com (http://address.com). Check with people you know to find the names of recommended free ISPs for your local area. You can also find a list of such providers by doing a search in Yahoo! (http://www.yahoo.com) for the term "free Internet access." (The complete URL for this Yahoo! page is rather lengthy, but is linked on this book's companion Web site at http://www. lisjobs. com/careerdev.)

As with fee-based Internet service providers, you may have to do some searching to find a company with a local dial-up number. Although these companies' services themselves may be free, if you don't find an ISP with a number in your local calling area, you may find yourself paying toll or long-distance charges. Internet4-Free.net (http://www.internet4free.net) and Your Free Sources (http://www.yourfreesources.com) both serve as guides by listing free ISPs offering services to various geographic areas. Users living in densely populated areas will have the best luck finding a provider, but, as a consequence, may also end up dealing with frequent busy signals.

Free ISPs come with a number of caveats. Since you get what you pay for, don't expect much from these companies' technical support departments. Because many free ISPs allow you only a certain number of free hours per month, you may need to keep a log of the time that you have used up. You may wish to sign up with multiple free ISPs in case one disappears or you are unable to get through. As is the case with many free online services, free ISPs come and go, so you may find yourself switching providers on a regular basis. Since signing up with a new provider means a new e-mail address, though, you may wish to sign up with a fee-based provider (or use a Web-based account as a "permanent" address) if you plan to use an e-mail account while job hunting. Also, be aware that some employers may not take you seriously if you use an e-mail address associated with a free ISP. (More advice on this issue is provided in Chapter 2.)

Access at the Library

Most public libraries in the U.S. offer some sort of Internet access for the public. This will likely be your best option for getting connected to the Web if you do not have a computer at home and your employer does not approve of your surfing on company time or company machines. If you are not sure of the location of your nearest public library, check your local phone book. Should you be moving to a different area and need to find the locations and phone numbers of public libraries elsewhere, go to your nearest library and consult the *American Library Directory*. You can also find relevant phone numbers by searching online business directories like Switchboard (http://www.switchboard.com) for the term "libraries-public" or by checking Libweb for individual library home pages (http://sunsite.berkeley.edu/Libweb).

The availability and restrictions on Internet usage at public libraries will depend on each individual library's policies. Most will have sign-up sheets as well as time limits on usage. Some may restrict their services to town, district, or county residents with valid library cards. Others may permit nonresidents to use their Internet computers but will charge them a fee for access. We recommend calling ahead to find out about these policies, rather than showing up unannounced. Internet access at public libraries can be extremely popular, and if you arrive at a busy time, there is a good chance that you will have to wait until a free computer station opens up. Also be prepared to monitor your own time online and to complete important activities early on in your session; when your time is up you do not want to be kicked off in the middle of composing an important e-mail message or pasting your resume into an online job application.

Academic libraries' primary patrons are tuition-paying students as well as their institution's faculty and staff, and are therefore less likely to offer Internet access (free or otherwise) to the general public. Still, some, particularly state institutions and community colleges, may offer Internet access to the local community as a public service. Again, we recommend phoning ahead to see what the policies are regarding Internet access.

Access via Cyber Cafés

Cyber cafés tend to be coffeehouses or sandwich shops in which you can check your e-mail or surf the Web while you relax with a cup of cappuccino. They are not available everywhere, yet they are not limited just to urban areas or college towns, either. You may be surprised to see where they have popped up. The Cybercafes Web

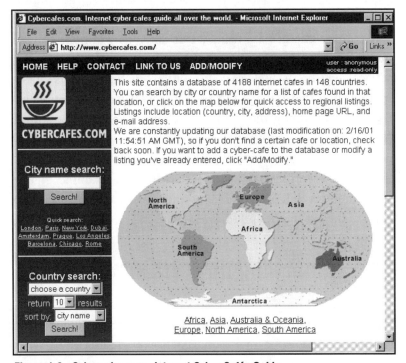

Figure 1.2   Cybercafes.com, Internet Cyber Cafés Guide

site (http://www.cybercafes.com) provides information about more than 3,500 such businesses around the world, including approximately 450 in the U.S. and 120 in Canada. It also lists what you can expect to pay for each hour of computer time. Cyber cafés can be useful if you are visiting an area and just want to briefly check your messages, but the cost of access may be prohibitive if you plan to spend a lot of time online. Costs, of course, vary widely, but usually fall into the $10-$20 per hour range; if you plan to be online regularly it may be more cost-effective to put that money toward the price of your own PC.

Access via Cable

Over the past several years, companies have begun offering high-speed Internet access through the same wires that are used to receive cable TV. This service may not be available in all geographic areas; it requires separate installation and a cable modem, and subscription charges are usually calculated as additions to your monthly cable TV or telephone bill. Your total monthly cost for this service may be as high as $50/month, but heavy users of the Internet find that the benefits of high-speed access far outweigh the costs (including the possible cost of a second phone line). Connection times can become slow, though, when a number of people in your area are connected at once. AT&T Broadband (http://www.attbroadband.com/services) is an example of one such company that offers cable Internet access in various areas in parts of the Northeast and Midwest.

Access via Digital Subscriber Line (DSL) Service

If you are set on getting high-speed access to the Internet, but it is unavailable through (or you do not wish to use) your local cable company, DSL may be an option. DSL uses standard copper wires (your regular phone lines) to transmit digital signals for Internet access, voice, and digital TV all on the same line, and no "dialing up" is required. Special equipment, including a DSL modem, and installation are necessary. Some caveats: The quality of your service (and its availability in your area) depends on many factors, such as your home's physical proximity to the local phone company's central office and the quality of the phone lines in your neighborhood. Check with your local phone company about DSL availability; some phone company Web sites will let you investigate possible DSL access by inputting your home phone number or address into an online form. Cost can also be a factor, as subscription fees are typically $40-$50 per month, plus the price of a DSL modem (about $100). The cost of installation depends on the provider, and some may throw in free installation (and/or a modem) for new customers. Installation of DSL can be a hassle in itself, though.

You can find out more about DSL service on the Web, including reports on providers and their availability in your local area, at http://www.dslreports.com. Some providers may offer free DSL service (check DSL reports for availability) but just as with free ISPs, you will be forced to put up with advertising banners every minute that you are logged on.

Learning More About the Internet

You don't need a thorough understanding of packet-switching and TCP/IP technology in order to use the techniques and tips outlined in the rest of this book. For some chapters, all you will need is a computer with a connection to the Internet and a Web browser. In order to create an electronic resume (Chapter 11), a word processing program will also be necessary. If you do not have your own e-mail account or Web page, Chapters 2 and 6 will give you information on how to obtain them.

Librarians new to the Internet will find a number of books published within the last several years to be useful, as well as some Web-based Internet tutorials, which explain more Internet concepts than we have room to cover here. We recommend these sources for additional information on the Internet.

Books

Benson, Allen C. *Neal-Schuman Complete Internet Companion for Librarians.* 2nd ed. New York: Neal-Schuman, 2001.

A lengthy compendium of useful suggestions and recommendations on the many different ways information specialists can make the Internet work for their organization. If you are a librarian unsure of the difference between a T1 line and a dial-up connection, or if you are curious about the costs (and benefits) of offering Internet access at your library, this is the place to turn.

Levine, John R., Carol Baroudi, and Margaret Levine Young. *The Internet for Dummies.* 7th ed. Indianapolis: Hungry Minds, 2000.

Probably the best-known guide to the Internet, geared toward the general public. One of the advantages of books in the "Dummies" series is that they assume no prior knowledge of the subject.

Murray, Laura K. *Basic Internet for Busy Librarians: A Quick Course for Catching Up.* Chicago: ALA Editions, 1998.

Although a bit dated, this is still a good overall introduction for librarians who are interested in getting hooked up to the Internet. It outlines the basics of logging on, surfing, and Web page creation, as well as signing up for mailing lists and using telnet and FTP.

Poulter, Alan, Debra Hiom, and Gwyneth Tseng. *The Library and Information Professional's Guide to the Internet.* London: Library Association Publishing, 2000.

A brief overview of Internet terminology and connection options, followed by directions on how to contact people and access useful resources. While some of the resources mentioned here are geared toward a U.K. audience, the content can be useful for all librarians.

Web Sites

Internet 101 (http://www2.famvid.com/i101/internet101.html)

A quick introduction to many concepts related to the Internet, including "safe surfing," browsers, and e-mail. According to the author, the point of this site is to convey the basics without including too many details unnecessary for beginners.

LearnTheNet (http://www.learnthenet.com)

A number of free Web-based tutorials for those who wish to become familiar with Internet resources and navigation.

Net for Beginners (http://netforbeginners.about.com)

A complete guide to the Internet for "newbies," which includes subjects such as choosing browsers, joining newsgroups, conferencing, and Web site building. A free online course called "Net 101" is available here.

Chapter 2

Networking Online

Savvy information professionals in the Internet environment look at even informal contacts made through personal e-mail, online forums, and e-mail discussion lists as career development opportunities. The colleague you help on a discussion list today may end up giving you a recommendation or collaborating with you on an article tomorrow; an e-mail message you send to the author of an interesting article or to the Webmaster of a useful site can lead to a long and fruitful relationship. Librarians can also use e-mail to arrange in-person meetings at ALA and other conferences in order to expand on their online working relationship.

Especially in cases where a librarian's institution provides little or no support for formal, in-person professional activities such as workshops and conferences, e-mail discussion lists and similar online venues can provide networking opportunities that would otherwise be unavailable. Such online opportunities also allow geographically remote librarians to support one another in their day-to-day activities without waiting for the chance to attend a yearly meeting. Since much professional development takes place within a community of peers, Internet-facilitated remote discussion allows information professionals to develop their careers by drawing on the support of other librarians. Further, librarians who develop their writing and debating skills through participation in online communities will be better able to participate in other professional activities such as writing articles or composing grant applications.

Information professionals can interact with one another online in a variety of ways. Here we describe some potential uses of each of these methods in your career development.

E-Mail

E-mail has often been described as the "killer application" of the Internet—and for good reason. In the library environment, its convenience and immediacy allow an unprecedented ease of communication between colleagues, whether they are staff members in the same institution or separated by time and distance. A working e-mail address acts as your passport to a virtual community of librarians worldwide and is a prerequisite to almost any kind of online networking.

Technical Considerations

If your only access to e-mail is through your employer, you may wish to open a free Web-based account with one of the major providers such as Hotmail (http://www.hotmail.com) or Yahoo! Mail (http://mail.yahoo.com). You can use these free accounts from any computer with access to the Web, so, even if you do not have a computer at home, you will be able to retrieve and send e-mail over the Web at work, at your local public library, or from a cyber café. Having a nonwork e-mail address is especially important if you intend to subscribe to nonwork or nonlibrary-related e-mail discussion lists, if you wish to make it clear that your opinions differ from those of your employer, or if you are using your e-mail account to search for alternate employment. Keep in mind, though, that such free accounts may have a bad reputation among some recipients of your messages, because Hotmail and others like it often provide a convenient and semi-anonymous home for those seeking to send unsolicited commercial e-mail or other unwanted messages.

Most library employers encourage a reasonable amount of participation on library-related lists as part of your professional development activities. In this case, using your work address will be fine and will allow you to use the more powerful filtering and other tools available in nonWeb-based e-mail software.

If you are not using Web-based e-mail for your main account, carefully review available e-mail software to see what package will meet your needs. Although a full examination of such software is beyond the scope of this book, be sure, at a minimum, that your software allows you to filter incoming messages into different mailboxes and that you will be able to send and receive attachments to messages. Common e-mail software includes Microsoft Outlook Express, which is included with Windows 98/ME, Qualcomm's Eudora Pro (an ad-supported version can be downloaded for free at http://www.eudora.com), and Netscape Messenger, which is included with all versions of Netscape Communicator. E-mail packages are often reviewed in computer magazines, or comparative reviews may be found online at places like PC World at http://www.pcworld.com.

You may be required to use a particular piece of software at work, so be sure to familiarize yourself with its capabilities and eccentricities to help manage your flood of incoming e-mail messages. (More tips for managing e-mail can be found in Chapter 3, in the section on handling information overload.)

Most e-mail packages will also allow you to create a "signature" file that is appended to the end of each outgoing message. In your signature, include such information as contact and institutional information, links to your own or your library's Web site, and a pertinent tag line or quotation. Make sure, however, that your signature file is not unwieldy—try to keep it under five lines of plain text and never indulge in the temptation to draw cute little figures with ASCII characters. You do not want to annoy recipients of your messages and co-participants on e-mail discussion lists by forcing them to view a signature file that may be longer than your actual message. Also, be sure that the material in your signature file is not offensive, political, or otherwise of an unprofessional nature (see examples in the sidebar, Signature Files: Professional and Unprofessional). Some library employers may require you to add a tag line to your signature explaining that your outgoing messages reflect your personal opinions and not the policy of your institution.

Signature Files: Professional and Unprofessional

To keep your signature file professional, especially if it is attached to your work address, try to limit it mainly to contact information. For example:

```
========================================
Jennifer M. Smith
Reference Librarian, Anytown Public Library
phone: (860) 555-2345 | e-mail: jsmith@lisjobs.com
http://www.lisjobs.com/careerdev/demoresume.htm
```

Unprofessional signature files will stand out tremendously on an e-mail list or other professional venue. Avoid signatures such as this one:

```
*+*+*+*+*+*+*+*+*+*+*+*+*+*+*+*+*+*+*+*
Jennifer M. Smith
VOTE DEMOCRATIC! Keep our country liberal and free.
Call me anytime at the Anytown Public Library
(860) 555-2345, unless the phone company changes
area codes again!
"To infinity—and beyond!"—Buzz Lightyear, Toy
Story
```

```
Hire me!! Check out my resume, because I don't
want to work HERE anymore:
http://www.lisjobs.com/careerdev/demoresume.htm
   *+*+*+*+*+*+*+*+*+*+*+*+*+*+*+*+*+*+*+*
```

The second example is, of course, an exaggeration—but think carefully about any element you choose to include in your signature, and how it will reflect on both you and your employer.

Lastly, resist the temptation to "jazz up" your outgoing e-mail messages to discussion lists or library colleagues through the use of stationery or image files. First, such unnecessary information slows the downloading of messages into your recipients' e-mail boxes, and often makes your messages appear less than professional. Secondly, many e-mail software packages do not have the capability to read such stationery, and they may include the background images of your stationery as separate file attachments rather than displaying them with the message. This clutters up the hard drives of recipients unnecessarily, and, if you are in regular contact with them or are a co-participant on a discussion list, they may be annoyed by receiving multiple copies of such image files.

Making Contact with Colleagues

If you read an interesting article, see a useful Web page, or hear a striking quote from a geographically distant colleague, why not drop the author a note via e-mail to share your enthusiasm? E-mail facilitates contact with other librarians, and it is both less intrusive than a phone call and less formal than a mailed letter. Such impromptu contacts can often lead to an interesting discussion or even a useful long-term online relationship. Since few people take the time to respond to articles or Web sites, your e-mail is also likely to be both read and remembered. E-mail can in this way help to expand your network of library colleagues. The more people you get to "know" online, the bigger the pool you have to draw from when it comes to learning from others' experiences, finding a mentor, or collaborating on projects. As Phil Agre notes: "Electronic communication is wasted unless we use it to seek out, cultivate, and nurture relationships with other human beings" (section 2, para. 2).

The co-authors of the book you have in your hand, for example, "met" via e-mail when one contacted the other with a comment on her Web site. Through online conversation, we found that we were interested in working on similar projects. We went on to collaborate via e-mail, first on a survey article and then on the proposal for this book. We worked together for two years in this way before having the opportunity to meet in person at the annual ALA conference in June 2000, and continued to collaborate by exchanging ideas through e-mail and Microsoft Word files as e-mail attachments.

E-Mail Discussion Lists

Library-related e-mail discussion lists provide a space for librarians worldwide to discuss issues in the profession. On such lists, messages posted by any subscriber to the list are disseminated via e-mail to the entire list membership. Any list member can then respond to one of these e-mail messages, or post a new message of his or her own, to participate in the conversation. Often, list archives are maintained and searchable on the Web, so that others can benefit from the collective wisdom of list members. (For an example of this, see the Web4Lib electronic discussion for library Web managers' archives at http://sunsite.berkeley.edu/Web4Lib/archive.html.) Lists that have related Web sites also often provide a way for visitors to sign up on the Web and to read list information and instructions online.

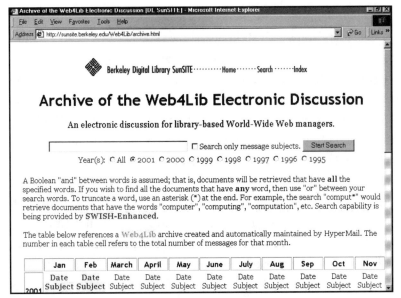

Figure 2.1   Web4Lib E-Mail Discussion List Archives

E-mail lists provide a useful way to meet and network with other librarians. As Lynne Fox, a reference and outreach services librarian who is active on a number of lists, says, "Participation in library related e-mail lists helps me stay aware of best practices, learn about new issues, and ask for assistance in a way that was not possible before the development of electronic discussion lists. I think I perform professionally at a whole new level by having access to a greater variety of ideas and people. I also now have a personal and professional network that exceeds my wildest expectations."

Her experience is far from isolated. List members have used their online networks to broaden their contacts, form professional relationships, and draw on others' experiences in a way that was not possible in the pre-Internet era. Public library branch manager and former NMRT president Priscilla Shontz notes that, "When I've needed a boost for a certain project, input from others in different types of institutions, or just moral support, I've often turned to these lists. Through these discussion list interactions I've developed some e-mail friendships with librarians, some as far away as New Zealand!"

Online discussions also provide a way for librarians to get themselves "out there" and get their views noticed. Those information professionals who have made a name for themselves on lists and who have in this manner established a national network of colleagues often go on to participate in other professional activities. List regulars sometimes seek office in local or national library-related organizations, using their name recognition to help them get elected to ALA Council or other boards. Some go on to publish books or articles outlining on a more formal basis the views they have spent months (or years) refining in online discussion with their peers. Editors also have been known to solicit contributions from mailing list regulars, and lists often attract calls for papers and other publication, scholarship, or speaking opportunities.

This example of one such "call for papers" was posted on an e-mail discussion list in the spring of 2001. It is typical of the calls for papers or for other contributions that may appear on relevant e-mail discussion lists.

```
To: NMRT New Writers List <nmrtwriter@ala.org>
Subject: [NMRTWRITER:116] Call for Papers
   CALL FOR PAPERS
   (Please excuse multiple postings!)

   Serials Reference Services Quarterly
   (SRSQ), a new journal by Haworth Press,
   is looking for articles dealing with all
   aspect of reference work and serials
   librarianship. As the number and format
   of serial information has exploded, the
   challenges and opportunities facing pub-
   lic service professionals has grown expo-
   nentially. SRSQ will publish applied and
   theoretical works aimed at assisting in
   the effective use of serials in both
   print and electronic formats. Possible
   topics include:
```

Tips for managing the public services
journal collections and reading rooms.
Evaluating indexing and abstracting
services for the electronic environment.
Supporting reference services for mul-
tiple electronic journal interfaces.
Promoting Electronic Journals
Collections
Library instruction strategies for
electronic and print journal collec-
tions.
Government Documents Serials.
Web serial resources for the Reference
Librarian.
Effective Public and Technical Services
Collaborations
These are just a few of the topics
SRSQ will cover. The first issue is
scheduled for Spring 2002. SRSQ welcomes
submissions from new writers! Manuscript
instructions may be found at:
http://www2.msstate.edu/~doll/instr.htm

Watch for these if you are interested in contributing to the profession through publication or by presenting a program at a
library-related conference. Exposure to such opportunities is an
additional benefit of being active online. (For more on conferences
and opportunities to present papers, see Chapter 5.)

Mailing List Terminology

Digest format—Some lists can be subscribed to as "digests," where messages are not received one-by-one as sent, but are sent to digest subscribers in large composite messages. These digests compile in one message the body of each e-mail that is sent to a list within a particular time frame or after a certain number of messages have been posted.

E-mail discussion list—An online space set aside for e-mail-based discussion of particular topics or issues. Any message sent to the list is disseminated to each subscriber, and generally each subscriber can respond to any message.

Emoticons—Sometimes referred to as "smileys"; punctuation used to convey emotion online. An example of an emoticon is the sideways smiley face :)—used to indicate that a comment is humorous or intended to be taken less than seriously.

Flame—To personally attack another list member in a message.

LISTSERV®—One of the first software programs for managing e-mail discussion lists.

Lurk—To belong to a list and read its messages without posting any of your own.

Netiquette—Online etiquette.

Post—To write and send a message that will be disseminated to an entire list.

Spam—Unsolicited commercial e-mail. (Although any mass mailing is often referred to as "spam," and is, at the very least, unprofessional.)

Subscribe—To sign up for membership in an e-mail discussion list.

Unsubscribe—To resign your membership in a list and no longer receive its messages.

Before signing up for an e-mail discussion list, it will be helpful to familiarize yourself with some basic principles of list etiquette ("netiquette"). Above all, follow these principles:

- *Keep your posts on topic.* The introductory message you receive when subscribing to a list, and/or its online description, will lay out the scope of that particular discussion. Make sure that your comments are appropriate to the list before posting, or you may receive your share of angry e-mail from subscribers. No matter how interesting a subject may seem to you, there is a time and a place for every discussion—keep your comments relevant.

- *Keep subscription instructions handy.* Nothing annoys longtime members of a mailing list more than some hapless soul trying to unsubscribe by sending repeated requests to the list as a whole. List members are busy information professionals whose tolerance for such requests is low. The introductory message you receive when subscribing to a list will give instructions on how to unsubscribe by sending a message to a special automated e-mail address, so keep this initial message handy in one of your e-mail folders or print it out to refer to later.

- *Avoid flaming others.* On every list, there will be someone with whom you always disagree, or someone who just rubs you the wrong way. Given the seemingly informal nature of e-mail, it is easy to fall prey to the temptation to let this person know exactly what you think. Remember that when you post a "flame" to an e-mail discussion list you are subjecting every other list subscriber to your personal vendetta—and no one else wants to see it. Learn to discuss points based on the issues rather than on the personalities of your fellow list members, and learn that there are times when it is simpler just to let things slide.

- *Keep your comments professional.* Especially if you are participating using your work e-mail address, your comments on e-mail discussion lists are a reflection on both you and your employer. Although such lists are not as formal a method of written communication as articles in professional journals, list participants who are able to balance the informal nature of the medium with a professional attitude will find their comments garner greater respect from other list members. One additional reason to keep comments professional is that archived posts to e-mail lists often show up in search engine results on the topic of the list—or on your name. You do not want a careless comment to show up years later to haunt you when a prospective employer does a search on the Web.

- *Avoid using HTML or attaching files to posts.* Not all e-mail software can read HTML, so save it for recipients you know are using newer software such as Microsoft Outlook that can handle these types of messages. Since you cannot know what programs all members of your lists are using, keep your messages to any list in plain text format. The same holds for e-mail attachments. Not only are some e-mail packages incapable of receiving attachments, but subscribers to a "digest" version of a discussion list may either receive your attachment as gibberish or not receive it at all.

- *Unsubscribe if you will be gone for a long period of time.* Especially on high-traffic lists, you will find that your mailbox will fill up quickly while you are on vacation. Be sure to unsubscribe if you set a "vacation message" in your e-mail software that automatically replies to anyone who writes while you are gone, as this can set up an infinite loop on your discussion lists (not to mention annoy your fellow subscribers).

This being said, e-mail discussion lists provide a place for librarians around the world to share ideas and information with one another, and there is an active list on nearly every library-related topic. Begin your search for such lists with Library-Oriented Lists and Electronic Serials, currently maintained by Wei Wu at http://www.wrlc.org/liblists. While not comprehensive, this directory is searchable by title or browsable by subject, and is a good starting place for finding the major discussion lists in a particular library-related subject area. Library-Oriented Lists also links to a variety of electronic serials and Usenet newsgroups (which are discussed later in this chapter). Also see Library E-Mail Lists and Newsgroups from the Internet Library for Librarians, at http://www.itcompany.com/inforetriever/email.htm.

Figure 2.2   Library-Oriented Lists & Electronic Serials, Subject Listing

Some Major Library-Related Discussion Lists

ACQNET—for acquisitions librarians.
http://acqweb.library.vanderbilt.edu/acqweb/acqnet.html
AUTOCAT—cataloging and authority control.
http://ublib.buffalo.edu/libraries/units/cts/autocat/
BI-L—for librarians interested in bibliographic instruction. http://www.libraries.rutgers.edu/is/bil.html
BUSLIB-L—list for business librarians.
http://listserv.boisestate.edu/archives/buslib-l.html
COLLIB-L—list for college librarians. E-mail listserv@wooster.edu. In the body of the message, type: subscribe COLLIB-L Firstname Lastname
LAWLIB—for law librarians. E-mail listserv@ucdavis.edu. In the body of the message, type: subscribe LAWLIB Firstname Lastname
LIBADMIN—for library administrators. E-mail listproc@list.umaryland.edu. In the body of the message, type: subscribe LIBADMIN Firstname Lastname
LIBREF-L—for reference librarians. E-mail listserv@ listserv.kent.edu. In the body of the message, type: subscribe LIBREF-L Firstname Lastname
LIBSUP-L—list for support staff. E-mail listproc@u.washington.edu. In the body of the message, type: subscribe LIBSUP-L Firstname Lastname
PACS-L—deals with end-user computer systems in libraries. http://info.lib.uh.edu/pacsl.html
PUBLIB—list for public librarians. http://sunsite.berkeley.edu/PubLib
PUBYAC—for children's librarians. E-mail majordomo@nysernet.org. In the body of the message, type: subscribe PUBYAC

SERIALST—serials in libraries.
http://www.uvm.edu/~bmaclenn/serialst.html
    Stumpers-L—list for difficult reference questions.
http://www.cuis.edu/~stumpers
    Web4Lib—list for library Web managers. http://
sunsite.berkeley.edu/Web4Lib

More general directories of e-mail discussion lists include Liszt,
accessible at http://www.liszt.com, and CataList, the official catalog of LISTSERV® lists, at http://www.lsoft.com/lists/listref.html.
(The common practice of referring to all e-mail discussion lists as
"listservs" is incorrect. Although many of these lists use LISTSERV®
software, the term LISTSERV® is a registered trademark of the
L-Soft corporation and does not describe discussion lists that use
other companies' software.)

Individual librarians have also begun creating their own, less
"official" lists at places like Yahoo! Groups (formerly eGroups) at
http://groups.yahoo.com. (For more on creating your own e-mail
list, see Chapter 6.) Subscribers to Yahoo! Groups lists will have to
put up with advertising appended to most messages, but Yahoo!
Groups and similar sites provide an easy method for individual
librarians to start their own discussion lists without having to
invest in their own list management software and without needing
to have access to their own e-mail server.

Yahoo! Groups lists include a diverse range of topics, from
those set up for librarians working in a particular district or who
have graduated from a particular program, to lists set up by
smaller library chapters who cannot afford their own e-mail
server, to more general lists set up by individual librarians interested in discussing a particular topic in librarianship. Lists at
Yahoo! Groups are searchable by keyword from the main page,

http://groups.yahoo.com. Current librarian-created lists at Yahoo! Groups range from reforma-northeast (discussion list for the Northeast chapter of REFORMA) to alms (for library media specialists) to futurelib (to discuss the transformation of librarianship and how it affects library education).

ALA provides its own Web-based directory of ALA discussion lists at http://lp-web.ala.org:8000, where list members can login, manage their own subscriptions, and read discussion archives online. Nonmembers can also gain guest access from this address to see what lists are available before subscribing. ALA-sponsored discussion lists include a range of topics, from YALSA-L (Young Adult Library Services Association List) to PRTALK (focusing on discussions of how libraries can promote themselves and their programs) to CLENERT (a list for ALA's continuing education roundtable). Most ALA roundtables have their own e-mail discussion lists, and lists devoted to specific topics are also available from this site. Similar association lists of lists include those sponsored by SLA, at http://www.sla.org/content/interactive/lists/index.cfm and those from the American Association of Law Libraries (AALL), at http://www.aallnet.org/discuss.

Librarians outside the U.S. should consult their national and regional associations or national libraries to find relevant lists. Canadian librarians, for example, can find selected lists at the National Library of Canada site (http://www.nlc-bnc.ca/services/ecanlist.htm), and Australian librarians will find Australian lists at the Australian Library and Information Association page (http://www.alia.org.au/e-lists).

Stumpers-L: The Making of a Successful List

Founded in 1992, Stumpers-L currently provides a symposium for over 1,000 librarians and other reference experts to pool their collective knowledge in finding answers to difficult reference questions (or "stumpers").

Members are able to post questions and draw upon the collective expertise of the list, allowing access to resources and knowledge that may be unavailable within their own institution. The list's archives are searchable online to facilitate finding answers to questions that pop up on a regular basis, and visitors can also read the Stumpers FAQ (Frequently Asked Questions) on the Web and find links to a variety of online reference resources.

Information about Stumpers-L, subscription instructions, and searchable archives can be found on The Wonderful World of Wombats: The Unofficial Stumpers-L page at http://www.regiments.org/wombats, and at the official Stumpers-L site at http://www.cuis.edu/~stumpers. Why wombats? In May of 1994, several answers to an innocent question about the name of a baby wombat got caught in an e-mail glitch and were sent out to the list multiple times. Librarians being the type of people that they are, this spawned a rash of wombat discussion, jokes, and poetry—leading to the nomination of the wombat as the "mascot" of the list. Wombat t-shirts and other paraphernalia can be viewed at the unofficial Stumpers-L site.

Stumpers members have answered countless questions from their fellow librarians, and the list serves as an example of a truly useful online library community. Stumpers-L also served as the genesis for a 1998 book written by one of the list members, Fred Shapiro's *Stumpers! Answers to Hundreds of Questions That Stumped the Experts* (New York: Random House, 1998).

Smaller lists that focus on specific topics in librarianship may be easier to follow and more relevant to information professionals working in a specific sub-field of librarianship. Such specialized lists also allow librarians to interact with and assist others with similar interests. As EPA reference librarian Beth Roberts notes, "I have found that the smaller, more specialized lists (such as ERMD for environmental libraries) are very good. The people on them are very helpful and we try to help each other solve problems. For example, I recently helped someone in Texas find a document that is not available from any conventional sources, but that I knew how to get because it is a special kind of EPA document." Such specialized lists are also particularly helpful to solo librarians, who can talk online with others in the field in order to help reduce their feelings of isolation from their peers.

Never dismiss the potential usefulness of e-mail discussion lists from related fields. The NETTRAIN discussion list for computer trainers, for example, has a large number of librarians who participate and its issues are often relevant to information professionals who have taken on Internet or other computer training responsibilities as part of their duties. (Subscribe by sending an e-mail message to: listserv@ubvm.cc.buffalo.edu. In the body of the message, type: subscribe NETTRAIN Firstname Lastname.) Cross-fertilization from related fields can help keep your mind fresh, and help librarians bring relevant outside ideas into the library environment. Participation on related lists also allows librarians to promote the profession and clear up stereotypes among list members from other fields.

Once you have joined a list (or two, or twenty), follow the discussion for at least a few days before posting. Familiarizing yourself with the general tone of the list and with perennial questions or comments that may annoy long-established members will save you some grief in the long run. But, once you have become accustomed to the type of conversation on a particular list, do be sure to participate when you have useful information to add or a question to ask. Most of the benefits of being on a list accrue only to those who are willing to jump into the conversation; lurkers miss out on truly being part of the list community.

Employment

E-mail can be an indispensable tool for job seeking. This will be discussed more fully in Chapters 11 and 12, but we would like to emphasize here the importance of keeping all e-mail communications with potential employers professional and to the point. Never send your resume to an employer via e-mail unless specifically requested to do so in an advertisement, and be sure if e-mailing a resume to include it in the specific format requested. Also keep in mind that, in more and more cases, employers are posting position information to applicable discussion lists. Becoming a member of some of the main lists in your subfield of librarianship may expose you to relevant openings before your nonnetworked peers.

Mentoring

Even a relatively informal medium such as electronic mail can be used professionally in more formal activities such as a mentor/mentee relationship. E-mail allows newer librarians to find and communicate with mentors in the field, even if appropriate mentors are unavailable within their local institution or library system. This is especially useful if beginning librarians find themselves in a solo position or if they are looking for mentors in a particular subject specialty or group. The perfect mentor might live across the country, yet e-mail enables the forming of such relationships, regardless of geographic boundaries.

E-mail can also be useful in facilitating regular communication between any mentors and their mentees. Such "telementoring" not only helps both the mentor and mentee grow as professionals, it helps the profession as a whole by introducing newer librarians to the standards and practices of librarianship. More experienced librarians should welcome the chance to serve as mentors; mentorship has been shown to increase retention and also provides an opportunity to give back to the profession. In addition, mentoring can help expand the diversity of the profession by giving potential and new professionals role models with whom they can identify.

Choosing a Mentor

New librarians interested in learning from their more experienced colleagues should take advantage of the less-intrusive nature of e-mail to be proactive in soliciting help and advice. Although much of the available material on mentoring focuses on its importance in a single workplace or company, it is useful within the entire profession, as well. Mentoring gives librarians a network of colleagues to draw upon when in need of another's expertise or experience. Mentors outside your company or institution can also bring clarity and an outside point of view to your situation.

Librarians interested in locating (or serving as) a formal mentor should check first with their own professional association. Many SLA chapters, for example, have established mentorship programs, as has AALL (http://www.aallnet.org/committee/mentoring/index.html). In some cases you can fill out an online form to assist the association in matching you with an appropriate mentor. If you are a student or recent graduate, check with your library school to see if they have a formal mentorship program.

Many librarians also establish informal mentoring relationships with one another via e-mail, meeting on discussion lists or when a mentee contacts a potential mentor directly. Keep in mind that you need not limit yourself to just one mentor—different people may be helpful in differing situations or points in your library career. Choose mentors who possess strengths in different areas than your own or are more advanced in areas of particular interest. Make sure that the mentor(s) you choose is sincerely interested in your career development. If someone is too busy, you should be able to ascertain that fairly quickly—for example, if your e-mail messages go unanswered or elicit consistently curt or unhelpful responses.

Some places to turn to find an informal mentor include e-mail discussion lists, former professors, recommendations of coworkers or colleagues, presenters at workshops or conferences, online forums, and alumni associations. When you contact a potential mentor via e-mail, be polite and professional. Prepare specific questions and identify specific areas in which you would like to grow professionally. Show that you listen to their advice by following up with comments, further questions, or descriptions of how you have used their help in a particular situation. Mentors will be more likely to continue the relationship if they feel that their advice is directly helpful to your career advancement.

Forums

Librarians accustomed to e-mail discussion lists, which "push" conversations directly into their e-mail boxes, may need some practice with the different medium of online forums. Forums (also referred to as "message boards" or "bulletin boards") differ from e-mail lists in that they require participants to return regularly to a Web site or Usenet group to see the messages posted in their absence. Posts are often archived online so that any discussion participant can visit the forum site and read each previous message to follow the thread of a conversation. (Although many e-mail discussion lists are also archived online in a static format, forums differ in that the conversations are still active and participants can read and respond to messages on the Web, even months later.)

In most cases, forum visitors need to register or create an account by filling out some brief information before being allowed to join in a discussion. After a visitor registers and creates a personal user name and password, he or she is then able to participate by posting new messages or responses to existing posts. Some forums are, therefore, semi-anonymous, as the e-mail addresses and real names of subscribers are kept hidden from other members. Members can thus feel more comfortable posting opinions that may not reflect those of their employer on such forums than they may on e-mail discussion lists, where an e-mail address and real name are connected to each of their posts. (In the case of Web-based forums where an e-mail address is attached to your posts, participants may consider using a Hotmail or other nonprimary address, since spammers often troll through such forums to collect addresses.) Many of these online forums will also be moderated, in that one participant has been given the responsibility and tools for keeping discussions on track and for erasing spam messages or flames before they cause problems.

Some of the oldest online forums are those found on Usenet (Usenet "newsgroups"). Formerly, special newsreader software was required to read the newsgroups, and Usenet access had to be provided by one's ISP. Today, however, Usenet groups are accessible and searchable from the Web through services such as Google Groups (formerly Deja.com) at http://groups.google.com. The site NewsOne.Net (http://newsone.net) allows its members to read and post to Usenet groups. (Check with your own ISP for availability if you prefer to access newsgroups through a newsreader rather than over the Web.) Usenet groups for librarians include k12.library and soc.libraries.talk, and librarians may also be interested in forums devoted to discussing and reviewing books, such as rec.arts.books and its subforums rec.arts.books.children and rec.arts.books.hist-fiction. In addition, librarians can branch out and visit other newsgroups and technical support forums that will be helpful in their jobs. Participation in a variety of Usenet forums can also help publicize the profession to nonlibrarians. Usenet users, however, should be aware that the unmoderated nature of most newsgroups often results in visitors having to wade through a large amount of spam (irrelevant mass or commercial postings).

Remember when posting to any online forum that such spam is frowned upon and if you indulge in the temptation to spread it yourself you may find yourself banned from posting again, or your own mailbox might be flooded with angry responses. Remember also the points of etiquette outlined in the previous section on e-mail discussion lists; online etiquette is important no matter the format of the conversation. Although Web-based forums often allow participants to use HTML tags to add emphasis, images, and links to their posts, use such tools sparingly to avoid detracting from the point of your message. Online forums aimed at librarians are often more professional and formal than those aimed at the general public or focused on general topics, so keep the tone and format of your messages accordingly professional.

Although online forums for librarians generally attract fewer participants than do many library-related e-mail discussion lists, there are several sites that contain ongoing discussions. About.com's Librarians and Library Science site, for example, contains a forum that is hosted by About.com guide and librarian Tim Wojcik (http://librarians.about.com/careers/librarians/mpboards.htm). On these boards, Wojcik generally starts a discussion around a contemporary issue facing librarians, and forum visitors respond by providing their own opinions on the issue. The Librarians Chatboard on teachers.net (http://teachers.net/mentors/librarians) is an example of an online forum devoted to issues of interest to school media specialists. (Although unfortunately named, the Librarians Chatboard is an example of a messaging system rather than online chat.)

Forums may be set up temporarily to allow librarians to share their opinions on a topical article or issue. In fall 2000, *The Chronicle of Higher Education*, for example, set up one of these topical forums to discuss a *Chronicle* article by Wayne Wiegand entitled "Librarians Ignore the Value of Stories." Other uses for online forums include

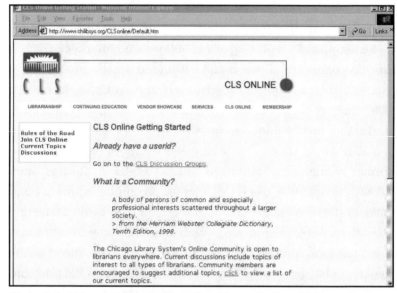

Figure 2.3   Chicago Library System Online Discussion Group Entrance Page

private discussions set up either on the Internet, or an intranet in a large library system or company, to allow employees to converse with one another about work-related issues. One example of this is the Chicago Library System's (CLS) "CLS Online" at http://www. chilibsys.org/CLSOnline/default.html. The CLS forums began as a venue for system members only, and they still retain a CLS focus, but CLS has expanded the topics and now welcomes participation from information professionals worldwide. Current topics include discussions on Internet Access for the Public, Readers Advisory, Outsourcing, and Great Books for Storytime. Their "rules of the road" section at http://www.chilibsys.org/CLSOnline/rules.html may be helpful to librarians who are new to online forums in general.

Systems librarians may find Usenet or other forums that provide user-support groups especially useful when trying to diagnose difficulties with library systems and software. Companies such as Qualcomm (makers of Eudora) and Adobe actually assign staff to monitor forums and answer questions from frustrated users. You may also get assistance from other users who have encountered similar problems. Online forums provide another level of technical support to busy librarians who lack the time to spend on hold or the resources to pay exorbitant support fees. Library vendors also have begun venturing into the forum arena; Dialog is active in this area and provides message boards where its users can discuss ways to improve their experiences with its products at http://www.dialog.com/portals/infopro/dialogue.

Information professionals interested in earning an online degree also might practice their skills in public forums before participating in online class discussions. Distance education programs offered over the Internet generally include a forum component to facilitate class discussions and communication between students. (Forums in the distance education context will be discussed further in Chapter 9.)

Chat

Online chat provides a medium for synchronous, real-time communication between two or more participants. Participants in a chat are said to be in a "chat room," or an online space set aside for people to talk about a particular topic. There are few permanent chat rooms focused on issues in librarianship, but chat is often used as a scheduled adjunct to online forums or classes. Chat also may be less convenient for busy information professionals who appreciate the expedience of asynchronous formats such as mailing lists and online forums. Additionally, librarians whose institutions ban online chat for public Internet users might wish to be careful about participating in chats at visible locations such as the reference desk.

Depending on how a chat room is set up, you may need a special IRC (Internet Relay Chat) software client to connect to and participate in a particular chat. IRC software applications include mIRC for the PC (shareware, $20, available for download at http://www.mirc.com), and Ircle for the Mac (shareware, $15, available for download at http://www.ircle.com). IRC is the most popular chat program, so there are a variety of low-cost clients available. After downloading and installing the IRC client software, you can use it to connect to a variety of IRC servers that maintain lists of the chat rooms available at a given time. The IRC FAQ (available at http://www.mirc.com/ircintro.html) answers a variety of questions about the workings of the software, and books such as Alexander Charalabidis's *The Book of IRC* (San Francisco: No Starch Press, 2000) may also be useful if you intend to spend a good bit of time exploring the medium.

Today, however, many Web sites that have added chat to their offerings have moved away from IRC and are offering Web-based chat rooms that use Java to produce chat functionality inside a Web page. If you have a computer with a newer browser (Netscape Communicator or Internet Explorer 4+) you should have no problem accessing such chat rooms straight from a Web page. (Be sure that you have enabled Java in your browser settings.) If you use America Online as your Internet service provider, however, you may encounter difficulties with Web-based chat, but there are usually workaround instructions available to help you find an alternate means of accessing one of these chat rooms. You may have to use Netscape Communicator or Internet Explorer rather than AOL's built-in browser.

Other chat options include one-on-one formats such as AOL Instant Messenger (AIM), MSN Messenger Service, or Yahoo! Messenger. These "instant messaging" systems can be useful in facilitating collaboration with remote librarians. You can save the cost of a phone call, for example, by using one of these packages to discuss article revisions with a co-author or to talk in real time with someone you have met on a discussion list.

Reference librarians, especially those in larger academic institutions, may wish to familiarize themselves with the chat environment because more and more academic libraries are experimenting with live online reference. Such institutions either add a Web-based chat room to the reference portion of their library Web site or use software such as AIM to enable real-time online conversation between a reference librarian and a patron seeking reference assistance. Examples of libraries using such real-time online reference can be seen at such places as the SUNY University at Plattsburgh's Feinberg Library at http://www2.plattsburgh.edu/acadvp/libinfo/library/iref.html and the NCSU Libraries at http://www.lib.ncsu.edu/risd/libref/chat.html. Chat is also used in many distance-learning environments, so familiarity with its use will be helpful in a variety of professional situations.

Library-related Web sites have begun scheduling chats around specific topics or with dignitaries in the field. The Academic Libraries of the 21st Century Project, for example, held one of these scheduled chats in November 2000 with panelists representing several large digital libraries (http://library.tamu.edu/21stcentury). Chats are archived online, and you may wish to read through some of these transcripts to see how chat can be used to carry on a discussion among a number of simultaneous participants.

Some library associations have also begun experimenting with the possibilities of online chat. SLA, for example, has established online chat rooms in which visitors can log in as a guest or create an account to participate in their real-time discussions (http://www.sla.org/content/interactive/chat/index.cfm). Their chat rooms work with any browser, or visitors can download an optional client program for enhanced functionality. Members can then create chat rooms devoted to specific topics or for individual SLA chapters to discuss issues pertaining to their local group. SLA also schedules chats around particular topics or events. For example, they schedule and promote real-time chats with candidates for SLA office. This

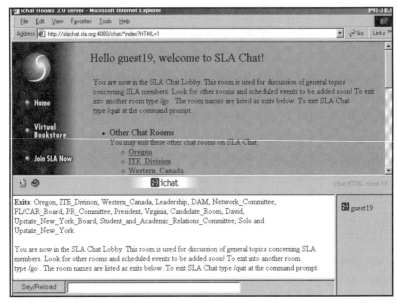

Figure 2.4   SLA Chat Lobby

allows member librarians from around the country to talk with the candidates and find out their views on issues.

ALA also has begun using chat as a tool for ALA committee members to meet in real time between conferences. Chat, in conjunction with Web-based sharing of documents, allows committee members to interact on a year-round basis and to accomplish tasks much more efficiently than a yearly or biennial meeting would allow (Schneider 62). Familiarity with chat and other online discussion formats, therefore, prepares librarians to participate in their associations. (For more on the use of chat in association meetings and other electronic conferences, see Chapter 5.)

Chat rooms are usually much less formal and more spontaneous than e-mail discussion lists or online forums. The synchronous nature of the medium means that participants have less time to put thought into their comments, let alone to spell-check or research their responses. Chat is therefore more analogous to spoken conversation than are the online communication methods discussed previously. Because it is computer-based, however, it is easy to keep "logs" of these conversations as a record of what has been said.

Each of these methods of online communication allows librarians to connect with one another and to share comments, discussion, and stories about their experiences, creating a vast virtual community of interconnected information professionals. Whether librarians lurk on one e-mail discussion list or actively participate in a variety of online forums, this community of colleagues helps all librarians as they develop their own careers. Those who are serious about their own development and learning cannot ignore the opportunities online networking offers.

Works Cited

Agre, Phil. "Networking on the Network." Phil Agre: 1993-2001. Feb. 25, 2001 (http://dlis.gseis.ucla.edu/people/pagre/network.html).

Schneider, Karen. "The Committee Wore Pajamas: ALA Debuts Online Chat." American *Libraries*, Dec. 2000: 62.

Chapter 3

Current Awareness

Librarians and information professionals, by virtue of their career choice, know more about "information overload" than the average person. Although no one can be familiar with all information resources, we have an understanding of the sheer number available, both online and in print. We have also been trained to assist patrons, researchers, and ourselves in weeding through them and evaluating which are the most reliable and useful. When it comes to answering reference questions or conducting research on behalf of others, in many instances it is the most recent information that is of interest. We therefore go out of our way to ensure that the information we provide to our patrons is the most current.

Keeping current with happenings within our own field is a professional necessity, both in terms of our jobs, which require us to keep up to date with changes in the information world, and in terms of our personal career goals. Many of us regularly read the print literature of the information field, both to see what is newsworthy within the profession and to keep up with the latest research. In addition, we regularly discuss new developments in the field with colleagues who may be more in touch with a particular aspect of the profession than we are.

With our busy schedules, why should we spend time keeping current? Paying attention to new developments in the field can provide fresh ideas to incorporate into our career paths, suggest articles or even books we might wish to write, or simply enhance our awareness of the present state and future of our profession. "Feeling like I'm at least familiar with what's going on in the various professional interest areas I have has made me feel more competent and comfortable in my job," writes Pat Ensor, Director of Library Services at University of Houston-Downtown, and developer/maintainer of LITA's Tool Kit for the Expert Web Searcher (http://www.lita.org/committe/toptech/toolkit.htm). She adds, "I believe that staying familiar with what's going on and knowing where to lay my hands on information is my job as a librarian. There are more and more 'automatic' ways of doing this, and whereas before I might have thought of it as 'I don't have time to keep up,' I started to realize I don't have time *not to* keep up!" As a consequence, Ensor developed a systematic plan to keep up with the profession using a wide variety of online current awareness tools.

Staying up to date with new developments within the information field is naturally just a small part of current awareness as a whole. In this chapter, we focus specifically on keeping current *within the information profession*, as opposed to keeping current in other areas, such as world news, business, or the Internet in general.

Because nobody can hope to keep track of every piece of new professional information, a number of companies and individual information specialists have taken it upon themselves to assist the rest of us in keeping current. For the purposes of this chapter, we talk about current awareness as simply the process by which we keep up to date, and about current awareness services as systems or products that notify users about new information of potential use. Patricia F. Stenstrom and Patricia Tegler (725) used similar definitions in their early article on the subject, which presented an overview of current awareness services at that time.

The varieties of ways in which information specialists can keep current are detailed in the following pages. These days, it can be said that keeping up with even current awareness resources in the information profession has become an issue! As such, we have tried to isolate the most useful resources rather than providing a comprehensive list. (The end of this chapter provides a more complete list of current awareness resources in the library and information profession.)

How the Internet Has Changed Current Awareness

Although we are most familiar with online resources, current awareness publications in print form have clearly been around for some time. Those that contain abstracts or tables of contents of the latest research tend to focus exclusively on content published in the print medium, such as traditional journals and books. The publication *Current Awareness—Library Literature* (*CALL*), for example, was published bimonthly between 1972 and 1980. Publications in other disciplines date even earlier; *Current Geographical Publications* from the American Geographical Society published its first monthly issue in 1938. Stenstrom and Tegler's previously mentioned 1988 article on current awareness in the library field, published several years before the Internet began to take hold, describes information professionals' need for knowledge of new developments in the field (726) and outlines a number of newsletter-based current awareness bulletins such as *CALL*, *Library Hotline*, and the Social and Behavioral Sciences section of *Current Contents*, which reprints tables of contents from articles in the professional literature. Specifically in the field of library science, *Current Awareness Abstracts* from Aslib, the Association for Information Management (U.K.), is a print publication that has published abstracts of more than 300 library and information science periodicals since 1992 (subscription information at http://www.aslib.co.uk/caa). An electronic version is available to print subscribers, published ten times annually and relatively current, but its price puts it out of the range of most individual subscribers.

These days there is much more to "library literature" than simply print-based content. As a result, if you rely exclusively on print publications to keep up with the latest research, you may miss hearing about all of the research articles (and other resources) in the library field that are only published online.

Keeping current with all that is newly available on the Web can be difficult, though. Unlike publishing in the print medium, where authors usually submit their materials to an editor or publisher before reaching a wider audience, publishing on the Internet can be essentially unmediated. Just about anyone, given some technical skills, can create a Web page containing whatever information he or she chooses to write about, post it online, and then publicize it by submitting the site to any number of Internet search engines.

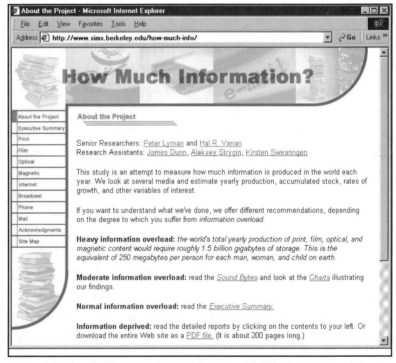

Figure 3.1   How Much Information?, University of California, Berkeley, School of Information Management and Systems

(More about how information professionals can develop such an "online presence" in Chapter 6.) The total number of Web pages in existence grows by the hour, making it impossible for any one individual to keep track of everything. If you are curious about the total amount of information available online, check out How Much Information? from the School of Information Management and Systems at the University of California at Berkeley (http://www.sims.berkeley.edu/how-much-info/).

Jan Davis Tudor, in a 1997 article for *Online* (51), coined the phrase "Internet-Induced Information Overload" (IIIO) to refer to the fact that it is impossible to keep up with all of the content available on the Internet, due to the speed at which new information gets added to the Web. She also mentions that the Web is a good source of "grey literature"—information that is not available in print, and is frequently inaccessible via traditional print indexes or databases. For these reasons, current awareness services, which update users on new online content, are a professional necessity.

Current awareness services available via the Internet offer a number of other advantages over their print counterparts, namely:

- Speed. It is rare for print-based current awareness bulletins in the field, such as *Library Hotline*, to appear more frequently than weekly. Web pages listing current happenings, however, because of the ease in which they can be published online, can be updated as frequently as their creators choose. In addition, services offering "selective dissemination of information" (SDI) permit users to set up profiles listing not only the types of current awareness bulletins they'd like to receive, but also how often they'd like to retrieve them—as frequently as daily, or even hourly in some cases.

- Convenience. In many instances, all you need to do is sign up once for a current awareness service—whether it be in the form of an online newsletter, mailing list, or SDI service—and the results are delivered directly into your e-mail inbox. In other cases, you may be required to visit a particular Web page to view updates.

• Availability. As the Internet is available 24 hours per day (depending on the reliability of your service provider, of course!), you can seek current developments in the information field at your convenience.

Purposes of Current Awareness Services in the Field

What value do current awareness services have for practitioners in the information field? First, we can use current awareness tools and sites on the Internet to keep up with what's happening in the profession. Who was recently appointed to which new position? What new databases are available from which vendors? Why is a particular library's policy on filtering (or outsourcing, or hiring, or just about anything) so controversial? In many cases, these types of news stories can be useful in our day-to-day, work-related activities, but they can also be useful for career development purposes. An information professional who is knowledgeable about current events within the field comes across as interested in the profession as a whole, and interested more specifically in keeping up with new developments, including technological change.

Second, current awareness services can be used to keep up with the latest research in the field. A number of programs—some free, others fee-based—automatically run keyword searches against new entries in a bibliographic database of research articles and e-mail you the results on a regular basis. In addition, online versions of print publications in the field, even if they don't provide the full text of articles, often indicate the content of upcoming issues.

Finally, librarians have created a variety of Web pages and online newsletters to help each other keep current with new Web pages of note as well as new developments on the Internet as a whole. Because new Web site announcements are of interest to more than just information professionals, a number of these services are geared toward a general, nonlibrary audience, and are created by individuals from a variety of fields. Programs that automatically notify users whenever any pre-selected Web site is updated can also serve as current awareness tools. These, too, are geared toward use by a general Internet audience.

Types of Current Awareness Services

Ina Fourie's 1999 article in *The Electronic Library* effectively summarizes the different types of current awareness services available via the Internet (381). While all of the services she mentions are available to Internet users in general, not all apply specifically to the library/information science field. The services most useful for information professionals' career development are these:

- Tables of contents services
- Book and article alerting services, including commercial SDI services
- Electronic newsletters
- Personalized agents
- Bulletin boards and Web-based discussion groups
- Usenet newsgroups and electronic mailing lists

To Fourie's services, we add two more:

- Web pages with newsworthy content
- Web site update notification services

As we describe the types of current awareness services, we revise the definitions slightly for our purposes as well as provide specific examples of programs, services, and sites.

Tables of Contents Services

Services that reprint tables of contents (ToC) of articles from professional journals are not new to the Internet. As mentioned previously, *Current Contents* is perhaps the best-known example in the print world (and has been available electronically for years), having been in existence since the late 1960s. Each weekly issue of a *Current Contents* publication, such as those in the series specific to Social and Behavioral Sciences, serves as an index to a week's worth of journal articles in fields within these disciplines. While there is no doubt that the print versions of ToC services have great use in helping people keep up to date in the field, they have disadvantages as well. First, there is always a certain amount of lag time in any print publication, which means that, depending on the service itself and its frequency of publication, the tables of contents you are now reading may have been taken from journals several months old or older. This may be fine for some research areas, but for others, such as recent important Internet developments, it may not be acceptable. Second, most likely you will not be interested in all of the journals mentioned in the issue.

Fortunately, ToC services available via the Internet have overcome these disadvantages. They are typically more current than their print equivalents, and many also have the ability to notify readers when new issues are available. The best known of these services are Reveal from Ingenta (formerly CARL UnCover; http://www.ingenta.com) and EBSCOAlert from EBSCO Publishing (http://eadmin.epnet.com/ealert). Both are fee-based. EBSCOAlert is currently marketed only to institutions, but it may be available to you if you work in an academic library. Though neither is directed specifically toward information professionals, each

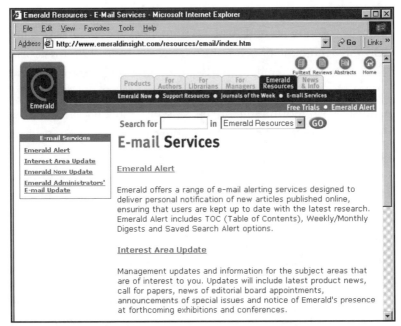

Figure 3.2   Emerald E-Mail Alert Service

indexes a variety of journals in the English language, including a number of publications in library and information science. Both e-mail to subscribers the tables of contents from the most recent issue of specified journals.

In other cases, the contents of a journal's latest issue may be posted on either the publisher's Web site or a public bulletin board. (For a list of Web sites of individual journals in the field, which you can browse for articles of interest, see Appendix B at the end of this book.) One of these journal publishers, Emerald (formerly MCB University Press), from the U.K., offers a separate program called the Emerald E-mail Alert Service (http://wwwemeraldinsight.com/resources/email/index.htm) through which you can sign up for e-mail alerts of tables of contents from journals they publish. Relevant Emerald titles include *Library Management, Library Hi Tech,* and *The Electronic Library.* The Bulletin Board for Libraries

(BUBL), though it does not provide e-mail alerts, has been compiling tables of contents and abstracts from most major journals in the field for a number of years (http://www.bubl.ac.uk/journals/lis). Categories of journals mentioned here range from General Librarianship and Information Management to Library Systems to Acquisitions. Information on back issues remains on the site, though it varies as to how frequently the content for each journal is updated. Both Emerald E-mail Alert and the BUBL journal service are available free of charge. If you find any articles of interest in these sources, you can easily place an interlibrary loan request through your local library if the full text is not available online.

Book and Article Alerting Services

In contrast to ToC services, book and article alerting services notify you of the appearance of new books and journal articles down to the keyword level of description. In other words, with these services you can set up a profile through which you can be notified, usually via e-mail, of newly available books and articles in your field of interest. You can indicate the subject matter of materials you want to keep informed about by telling the program which keywords to search for.

If you would like to be kept informed about new books on a particular subject, try signing up for the free service Amazon.com Alerts (http://www.amazon.com/alerts). You type in keywords that you would like Amazon.com to search for within its database of books in print, and Amazon will send you an e-mail message when new items that are described using those words are released. You won't be notified of pre-publication titles, though. Amazon.com uses Library of Congress subject headings to describe the books it sells, a positive feature for anyone familiar with LCSH.

In a similar fashion, several commercial products offer the opportunity to be notified of new journal articles. Ingenta's Reveal, previously mentioned as a ToC redistribution service, will also e-mail you citations of individual articles if you indicate in your profile which keyword(s) or author(s) you would like it to search for. Reveal will run searches against your chosen keywords every week, for a minimal annual subscription fee. Not limited to the LIS field, Ingenta's database contains articles from more than 18,000 English-language journal titles. Included in the subscription price is a separate book alerting service, with data supplied by Blackwell's Book Services' Academic Book Center (http://www. acbc.com).

Although no free, comprehensive article alerting services based on the latest library and information studies research are available to the general public, Dialog offers a no-cost alert service to its existing customers (http://www.dialog.com/info/support/alerts). In this system, customers are notified by e-mail whenever articles matching a certain profile are added to a database. *Library Literature & Information Science Online* and *LISA* (Library and Information Science Abstracts) are the two Dialog databases likely to be of greatest interest to information professionals.

Electronic Newsletters

Electronic newsletters tend to be more content-rich than the types of alert services mentioned previously. Rather than simply redistributing tables of contents or citations, they can contain news blurbs or even full-length articles. Topics vary. Some inform you of recently published articles, others cover newly available Web sites, and yet others provide updates on what is happening in the profession. Some newsletters require you to subscribe, usually via e-mail, and in return you receive updates of current happenings in the information field in your e-mail inbox. The obvious advantage of e-mail-based newsletters is their convenience. You will not have to make any extra effort to read them, aside from an initial subscription command, and they can be deleted just as easily. On the other hand, they can clutter your mailbox if you are not careful.

Other newsletters are Web-based, which means that you will have to make the effort to check the Web sites of these publications at regular intervals to see if the latest issue has been posted. The best Web-based newsletters also offer an e-mail reminder service for this very reason. If you take the trouble to visit a newsletter posted on the Web, chances are that you will run across other new resources of interest simply by following the links there.

Library Juice, an electronic newsletter published and edited by librarian Rory Litwin since early 1998, serves many of the purposes just mentioned. Distributed primarily by e-mail upon subscription request, it has a companion Web site (http://www.libr.org/Juice), which outlines its purpose—namely, to serve as a news digest for the library field—and makes available the current issue and issue archives. Many news items mentioned in *Library Juice* have a politically and socially liberal focus, but the newsletter also points out new Web sites and presents occasional calls for papers. Similar e-mail newsletters include *Library Journal*'s Academic Newswire (information at http://www.libraryjournal.com/newswire/newswire.asp), which provides news updates for the academic library community in return for a subscription fee, and *The Chronicle of Higher Education* (http://chronicle.com), which e-mails a daily news update to subscribers of the print journal.

When it comes to newsletters that highlight and evaluate new Web sites, perhaps the best-known source is the Internet Scout Project (http://scout.cs.wisc.edu). Published by staff at the Department of Computer Sciences at the University of Wisconsin–Madison since 1994, four different newsletters are available—the original, weekly *Scout Report*, plus three biweekly *Scout Reports* for the sciences, social sciences, and business/economics—and they are all geared toward educators and librarians. While there is no doubt that information specialists can make use of the sites mentioned here in their jobs, they are also good for keeping up to date professionally with new Web sites of interest.

Although there are many more electronic newsletters in the library/information field, we describe only two other major resources here: *Current Cites* (http://sunsite.berkeley.edu/ CurrentCites) and *Technology Electronic Reviews* (*TER*) (http:// www.lita.org/ter). Both are terrific sources for keeping informed on the latest publications and research in the field and are available on the Web and by e-mail. *Current Cites*, truly an Internet veteran after over ten years of continuous publication, is a monthly newsletter containing annotations for current literature (both books and articles) related to information technology. *TER*, published irregularly by ALA's Library and Information Technology Association (LITA), presents reviews of materials in all formats related to networking and information technology, including Internet-related topics.

Personalized Agents

Personalized agents, programs that let you select the subject and types of current awareness resources you would like to receive and tailor the information sent to you, are fairly common when it comes to general news, computer science, and Internet technology. Within the information profession, agents such as these haven't fully caught on. It is likely, however, that they will become more widespread in the near future. One such example is NewsAgent for Libraries (http://www.sbu.ac.uk/litc/ newsagent), a pilot project funded by the Electronic Libraries Programme in the U.K. that ran for two years beginning in April 1996. Within NewsAgent, you can create a free account and then sign up to receive information on particular pre-set topics. The site is still in existence and operating as of the time of this writing, but, because the pilot project has concluded, its activity and output is minimal.

Bulletin Boards and Web-Based Discussion Groups

Electronic bulletin boards (also known as forums), as we saw in Chapter 2, permit fellow information professionals to interact with each other more directly. Discussions on topics of mutual interest can be held online, and the threads of conversation are posted so that others can read them, learn from them, and even join in. Bulletin boards may not be as useful for daily news updates as other avenues, but they are a good way of keeping in touch with the latest issues, ideas, and trends in the profession.

Usenet Newsgroups and Electronic Mailing Lists

Both newsgroups and e-mail lists were described in Chapter 2 as additional ways in which librarians can connect directly with each other to network and share ideas. Mailing lists and newsgroups differ from newsletters in that individuals are allowed to contribute relevant messages to share with other list members. For current awareness purposes, useful Usenet newsgroups to consult include comp.internet.www.announce (announcements of new Web sites) and bit.listserv.net-happenings. Likewise, these mailing lists, Net-Happenings (details at http://listserv.classroom.com/archives/net-happenings.html), which provides announcements of new Internet resources mainly aimed at educators, and New-List (more information at http://listserv.classroom.com/archives/new-list.html), on which you will receive announcements of new e-mail lists, are useful current awareness resources. NewJour is an electronic mailing list that provides periodic announcements of new electronic journals and newsletters. You can find the list archive and subscription directions at http://gort.ucsd.edu/newjour.

Web Pages with Newsworthy Content

Within the last several years, a number of current awareness-based library-oriented Web pages have appeared online. Many, though not all, are sponsored by publications in the information field, familiar library vendors and publishers, or newly formed companies in the information field who make these sites their main focus. For example, the familiar print publications *Library Journal* (http://libraryjournal.reviewsnews.com) and *American Libraries* (http://www.ala.org/alonline) have corresponding Web editions that concentrate on professional news updates. (*American Libraries* also offers an e-mail update of current news for ALA members, with details at http://www.ala.org/alonline/guide/alonews.html.) Recently, a number of Web sites named "Library____.com" have also emerged, and most of these provide news updates and announcements in the field. These sites are known as "library portals," and examples include LibraryHQ.com, Librarycard.com, Libraryplace.com, and Libraryspot.com. Because they also serve as general meta-indexes to professional information, several of these are covered in more detail in this book's conclusion.

In addition to these sites, several self-starting information professionals have taken it upon themselves to create and maintain current awareness Web sites of their own. LISNews.com, which is updated daily by librarian Blake Carver on a volunteer basis, is perhaps the best known and the best maintained of these (see sidebar). His site (http://www.lisnews.com) links to more than a thousand news stories on the Web related to library and information studies. No one interested in keeping up with the profession should miss LISNews.com. The *Librarians' Index to the Internet* (http://www. lii.org) contains a weekly listing of new sites added to an index of useful Web sites for the library profession; you can also sign up to receive an e-mailed version of this listing. Another such "Weblog" (a regularly updated list of links, created by individuals who actively keep track of Internet sites useful to them) is librarian.net, from librarian Jessamyn West. Weblogs are covered in more detail in Chapter 6.

LISNews.com: A Current Awareness Success Story

Blake Carver, the Webmaster, creator, and general idea person behind LISNews.com, brought his site up on November 2, 1999, for a simple reason: "Because it wasn't there." In other words, at that point there was no other single site on the Web dedicated to providing librarians and information specialists with current news on the profession. Maintaining the site currently takes about twenty hours per week, and although Carver currently does the majority of the work, he is assisted at any given time by up to four other librarians who help with story collection and research. LISNews.com receives an average of 750 hits each weekday.

What does LISNews.com consist of? Predominantly short news stories related to librarianship, which can include subtopics such as books, publishing, censorship, filtering, knowledge management, libraries in general,

Figure 3.3   LISNews.com: Library and Information Science News, Web-Based Current Awareness Service (Blake Carver)

and humor, among others. These stories are organized both chronologically (most recent first) and by subject. Normally at least one story, and often several, will be posted every day. Some of these stories are original, while others are simply summaries that link to the full text elsewhere on the Web. While LISNews volunteers write most stories and abstracts, anyone can submit a story for consideration via an online form. You can also sign up to receive headlines of stories posted on LISNews.com via e-mail on a weekly basis.

Web Site Update Notification Services

Services that track changes on Web pages are not geared just toward the library community, but chances are you will find some application for them in your efforts to keep current. As an example, Mind-It, a free service from NetMind (http://mindit. netmind.com), lets you set up an account and select specific Web pages (you type in the URLs) that you would like it to keep track of. After that, you can tell Mind-It to notify you—either via e-mail or on the Web—when the pages you entered either change, move, or disappear. Options include daily, every two days, or weekly notification of these changes. You can also ask Mind-It to differentiate between changes in keywords (words anywhere within the HTML document), text, form results, images/links, or any changes whatsoever. This is particularly useful, because in many cases the only parts of a page that change frequently will be advertisements or images, and these sorts of changes are not terribly useful for current awareness purposes. Spyonit.com (http://www.spyonit. com) searches various Web sites for content that you specify, and then notifies you—via e-mail, pager, instant message, cell phone, Web

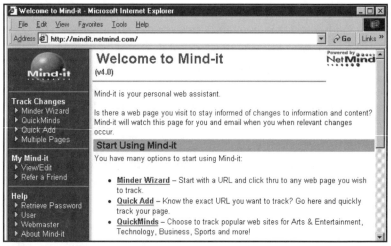

Figure 3.3   Mind-It Web Page Update Notification Service

page, or PalmPilot—when it has found what you specified. Signing up is free.

Three other services are also mentioned as types of current awareness services but are more frequently consulted either outside librarianship or for purposes other than professional development. They are news filtering services, "push" services that require special software and let you decide what information you would like sent to you on a regular basis, and online newspapers/wire services. An example of the latter is CNN.com, whose service entitled myCNN (http://my.cnn.com) lets you create a personal page that searches for recent news stories on any keywords you select (such as "libraries" or "librarianship").

Handling Information Overload

There's no doubt that current awareness resources can play an important role in your career development. However, if you dutifully consult or subscribe to all of the different resources mentioned in this chapter, you risk spending more time keeping up with the latest news than you can really afford. Remember that the purpose of current awareness services is to help you deal with information overload, not create more. Proactively developing a plan for keeping up is a good start. Evaluate the sites mentioned in this chapter, as well as others you find online, and mix and match the various types of resources based on your personal and professional needs.

Librarian Pat Ensor, in her personal current awareness plan, includes sites and newsletters from librarianship, higher education, technology, and the Internet in general, in addition to using a Web site update notification service. What is a good limit for you? This will depend on many factors, such as the amount of free time you have, as well as the particular areas within the field that you're interested in keeping up with. All things considered, though, fifteen to thirty minutes per day is a reasonable amount of time to spend in keeping current. If you are spending much more than that, it may be too much. What can you do to make the most of this time?

- *Organize your time.* Be aware of how much time you are spending just keeping up with the sites, newsletters, and programs mentioned here. If it is more than half an hour per day, you may want to consider what percentage of the information being gained will realistically be of future use to you.

- *Make the most out of bookmark files and e-mail folders.* Bookmark sites that you consult on a regular basis. Use the capabilities of your e-mail system to filter incoming messages into folders. If you don't have time to read them right away, let them wait—and do not be afraid to delete.

- *Be selective.* Take one look at all of the resources we have mentioned, but evaluate them as you go along. Which sites and e-mail lists or newsletters do you find the most valuable? How frequently do you really need to consult each Web site—daily? Or will checking them weekly or monthly suffice? If you are not sure how frequently a particular site is updated, try signing up with a free Web site notification service. And don't feel guilty if you can't keep up with everything.

With a little advance planning in terms of selection, organization, and time spent, you can easily make online current awareness services work well for you.

Additional Sources for Current Awareness Information

The following list provides examples of current awareness services relevant to information professionals; it includes those mentioned in this chapter as well as additional sites, lists, and services. Some of these services can theoretically appear in more than one category, too. For example, LISNews.com, a Web site listing current events in the library/information field, mentioned earlier, also offers readers the opportunity to receive headlines via e-mail in the same way alert services do.

General Meta-Indexes

Steven Bell's Keeping Up Page
http://staff.philau.edu/bells/keepup

Tables of Contents Services

Aslib's Current Awareness Abstracts
http://www.aslib.co.uk/caa

Bulletin Board for Libraries
http://www.bubl.ac.uk/journals/lis

Current Contents: Social and Behavioral Sciences
http://www.isinet.com/isi/products/cc/editions/ccsbs

EBSCO Alert
http://eadmin.epnet.com/ealert/about.htm

Emerald E-Mail Alert Service
http://www.emeraldinsight.com/resources/email/index.htm

Ingenta
http://www.ingenta.com

Book and Article Alerting Services

Amazon.com Alerts
http://www.amazon.com/alerts

Dialog: Customer Alerts
http://www.dialog.com/info/support/alerts

Ingenta
http://www.ingenta.com

Electronic Newsletters

Internet Sites and Information

Internet-On-A-Disk (Richard Seltzer)
http://www.samizdat.com/ioad.html

Internet Resources Newsletter (Heriot-Watt University Library)
http://www.hw.ac.uk/libWWW/irn/irn.html

Librarians' Index to the Internet: LII New This Week Mailing List
http://lii.org/search/file/mailinglist

NetSurfer Digest
http://www.netsurf.com/nsd

Scout Reports (Internet Scout Project)
http://scout.cs.wisc.edu

News of the Field
Academic Newswire (*Library Journal*)
http://www.libraryjournal.com/newswire/newswire.asp

Chronicle of Higher Education
http://chronicle.com

ITI Newslink (Information Today, Inc.)
http://www.infotoday.com/newslink/default.htm

KMWorld NewsLinks (Knowledge Management)
http://www.kmworld.com/newslinks

Library Juice
http://www.libr.org/Juice

Updates on Research
Current Cites
http://sunsite.berkeley.edu/CurrentCites

Technology Electronic Reviews
http://www.lita.org/ter

Personalized Agents
NewsAgent for Libraries
http://www.sbu.ac.uk/litc/newsagent

Usenet Newsgroups and Electronic Mailing Lists

bit.listserv.net-happenings
Companion Web page at http://listserv.classroom.com/
archives/net-happenings.html

comp.info.www.announce
Accessible via http://groups.google.com

New-List
http://listserv.classroom.com/archives/new-list.html

NewJour
http://gort.ucsd.edu/newjour

Web pages with Newsworthy Content (Including Weblogs)

New Internet Sites and Information

Free Pint
http://www.freepint.com

Neat New Stuff I Found This Week (Marylaine Block)
http://marylaine.com/neatnew.html

Net News Today
http://www.netnewstoday.com

Netsurfer Digest
http://www.netsurf.com/nsd

Research Buzz
http://www.researchbuzz.com

Scout Reports
http://wwwscout.cs.wisc.edu

Tool Kit for the Expert Web Searcher (Pat Ensor)
http://www.lita.org/committe/toptech/toolkit.htm

Yahoo! What's New
http://www.yahoo.com/new

News of the Profession

American Libraries Online
http://www.ala.org/alonline

Cites and Insights: Crawford at Large (Walt Crawford)
http://cical.home.att.net

librarian.net (Jessamyn West)
http://www.librarian.net

LibraryHQ.com
http://www.libraryhq.com

Library Journal Digital
http://libraryjournal.reviewsnews.com

Library Planet
http://www.libraryplanet.com

Lis.Oclc.Org
http://lis.oclc.org

NewBreed Librarian
http://www.newbreedlibrarian.org

Web Site Update Notification Services

EoMonitor
http://www.eomonitor.com

Mind-It
http://mindit.netmind.com

SpyOnIt.com
http://www.spyonit.com

Works Cited

Fourie, Ina. "Empowering Users—Current Awareness on the Internet." *The Electronic Library*, 17.6 (1999): 379-388.

Stenstrom, Patricia F., and Patricia Tegler. "Current Awareness in Librarianship." *Library Trends*, Spr. 1988: 725-739.

Tudor, Jan Davis. "The New Alchemy: Using Droids & Agents to Treat Information Overload." *Online*, Nov./Dec. 1997: 51-58.

Part 2

Professional Involvement

Chapter 4

Professional Associations

The influence of associations in the information profession begins early in any librarian's career. The American Library Association has strict requirements for the curricula of graduate programs that it accredits, which means that if you have a degree from such a program, your career has already been shaped in some way by at least one library association. Throughout your career, from student years through retirement, you will have the opportunity to become a member of a number of different associations— from large national groups with tens of thousands of members to local associations or association chapters with several dozen or fewer people.

When it comes to professional development, associations give you the chance to network with peers at conferences, attend continuing education sessions, and transmit ideas to the profession as a whole by publishing books and journal articles. Associations also serve as clearinghouses for employment opportunities and may even provide assistance in the entire job-search process. For guidance in career development, associations should be one of the first places you look.

Chances are that throughout your library or information career, nobody will ever force you to join an association in the field, and membership in any particular group is not likely to be a requirement for any job. Active participation is also voluntary in most cases (unless you have a supervisor who "suggests" that it would be in your best interest to participate), and it is up to you to determine how involved you would like to be with any particular group. All that is strictly required for minimal association involvement will be payment of the annual membership dues. As a way of supporting employees' professional development, your workplace may even pay for membership in one of the major national library associations and in your state organization, or even more; it can't hurt to ask.

As someone interested in expanding your professional horizons, though, you will wish to take a more active role than simply paying your dues and waiting for association publications to arrive in the mail. While large organizations such as the American Library Association (ALA), Special Libraries Association (SLA), or American Society for Information Science and Technology (ASIST) can be overwhelming to the newcomer, they are divided into numerous subgroups that help make them more manageable. These sections within an association go by various names, such as "committees," "subcommittees," "chapters," "special interest groups," or "roundtables." They are usually organized around a geographic area or subject interest, such as the Geography and Map Division of SLA, or the Potomac Valley Chapter of ASIST. Within each organization, the different labels for these subgroups take on different meanings within the hierarchy, so there is no easy way to state the overall differences between them.

Why Join an Association?

There are numerous professional advantages to joining and participating in an association in the library/information field. Many librarians join associations in order to network with their peers. Participation in an organization (both online and offline) is a ready-made way to meet people with similar professional goals. Within the membership, you may find a mentor or at least a group of other professionals sharing your particular interests.

Associations also provide information specialists with opportunities for leadership. On the national, regional, and even local levels, associations offer members the chance to serve as officers on committees. Depending on what type of committee you join within an organization, you may draft bylaws, write or edit publications, participate in continuing education, serve as a liaison to governmental or other organizations, and much more. In particular, there is great potential for leadership within local or statewide organizations, which most people will find easier to navigate than national groups. Participating in this way allows you to serve as an advocate for the profession, both to the association's members as well as to the outside world.

Many organizations provide, as part of your membership, subscriptions to newsletters, journals, or other periodicals of interest to the group. Examples of these include *Information Outlook* (from SLA), the *IFLA Journal*, and, of course, *American Libraries* (ALA). Not all association publications come with membership, though; an example is *CHOICE: Current Reviews for Academic Libraries*, published by the Association of College and Research Libraries (ACRL), which is marketed separately.

Through associations, librarians can also benefit from making presentations at professional conferences. Library associations organize conferences at which members can submit their ideas for consideration by others in the profession and gain speaking experience and professional contacts as a result. (See Chapter 5 for more on conferences and speaking opportunities.)

Association members frequently meet to develop and publish statements of standards and values. Library associations with influence over the profession as a whole, such as ALA or the International Federation of Library Associations and Institutions (IFLA), draft codes of ethics, standards, and "best practices," which serve as guides for professionals in the field.

Many groups offer job-search assistance, from job clearing-houses and hotlines (offered by a growing number of associations in North America) to career counseling and resume help. Some even offer placement services at national conferences.

Major national associations impact the training process for future leaders. As stated earlier, ALA, as an accrediting body, has considerable influence over the curricula offered by graduate programs in the information field. At conferences and other events, associations may also provide training programs, which can benefit both you and the organization that you work for. After a conference is over, many groups offer workshops throughout the year for job-related or personal career development.

Finally, joining an association is a way of demonstrating your commitment to the information field. At the very least, mentioning your association membership on a resume will give some indication to employers that you are interested in participating in and keeping up with the profession.

Professional Associations vs. Library Consortia

Library consortia, systems, and networks, in contrast to professional associations, have the main purpose of serving as points of connection between libraries and information professionals in their *day-to-day, work-related activities*. Membership in these groups will be made up of entire libraries or institutions, rather than individuals. (Although library associations also welcome institutional members, the topic is beyond the scope of this book.) These three terms—consortium, system, and network—have the same basic definition and are frequently used interchangeably. Within one state or region, you may hear a group of libraries referred to as a "library network," while in another, the term used instead may be "library system," "library council," or even "library federation."

Despite the different names, these types of organizations are generally composed of individual libraries within a particular geographic area that band together for the purposes of sharing resources, such as an online catalog or a common interlibrary loan system. Some states, such as Massachusetts, divide the publicly funded libraries within the state into systems for the purposes of budgetary allocation. Libraries within a consortium may also decide to approach vendors of online databases or computer equipment as a group, in order to get a discount on these products or services. A consortium may not have its own headquarters and staff, depending on its size and the role it plays with regard to the libraries involved.

Some of these organizations may be regional in scope, such as NELINET, the New England Library and Information Network (http://www.nelinet.net). Headquartered in Southborough, Massachusetts, NELINET serves as a resource-sharing organization for most public, special, and academic libraries in New

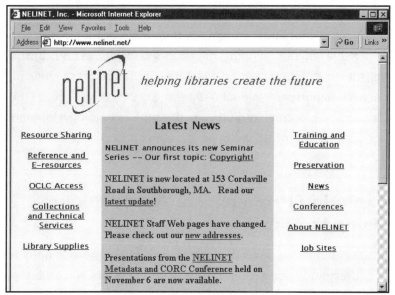

Figure 4.1 Web Page for NELINET, the New England Library and Information Network

England. Libraries belonging to NELINET are frequently offered discounts on database products, as the group as a whole has greater purchasing power than most individual member libraries. In addition, NELINET is an OCLC affiliate, meaning it serves as a contact point for NELINET member libraries who participate in OCLC cataloging, interlibrary loan, and reference services. SOLINET (http://www.solinet.net) and PALINET (http://www.palinet.org) provide similar roles for the Southeast and mid-Atlantic states, respectively.

In addition to serving as points of contact between institutions, library consortia frequently offer opportunities for librarians' career development. NELINET has numerous committees, continuing education workshops, meetings, and conferences in which information professionals can participate. Certification programs in various aspects of library services (interlibrary loan, cataloging, and computer repair, for example) are also offered. These are covered in more detail in Chapters 8 and 9. Professional opportunities offered by groups such as NELINET may be limited to (or significantly more affordable) employees at member institutions.

It is this function of both professional associations and consortia—the providing of career development opportunities to individual information professionals—that we are concerned with in this chapter, with a concentration on the professional development opportunities provided by associations.

Exploring Professional Associations Using the Internet

Considering the several hundred professional associations in the library and information science field, it may take you a while to decide which ones best suit your purposes. In addition to the major national and international professional organizations, each state has at least one library organization, regional association, or consortium. In addition to associations based on geographic location, information professionals have come together to form groups based on particular specialties or subject interests. Because so many associations and groups in the library and information fields have a presence on the Web, if you are interested in learning more about or participating more actively in a particular association, the Internet is a natural place to begin exploring. Association Web sites are in many cases the best places to visit for the most up-to-date, wide-ranging information on the responsibilities, makeup, and purpose of a group. You probably will not find as much information about any association in any other single place.

Locating Association Web Pages

Not all associations in the U.S. and Canada have Web pages to call their own, but most do. If you know the exact name of an association, it should be easy to locate its Web site by using a major search engine such as AltaVista (http://www.altavista.com) or Google (http://www.google.com). Just put the name of the association in quotes so that the terms will be searched as a phrase (in most search engines).

It can be hard to locate associations on the Internet by either geographic location or subject if you are not sure what groups even exist. The *Bowker Annual of Library and Book Trade Information* (Medford, NJ: Information Today, Inc., annual) is a good source for finding the names (and occasionally the Web sites) of relevant associations, but you may not always have a copy of this handy reference book within reach. The National Library of Canada Web site provides a comprehensive online list of library associations in Canada (http://www.nlc-bnc.ca/services/ecanassc.htm), yet there is no up-to-date, comprehensive listing of such organizations throughout the U.S. or in all of North America. We mention the site entitled Professional Organizations in the Information Sciences (http://witloof.sjsu.edu/peo/organizations.html) for its breadth of coverage, but, unfortunately, it has not recently been updated. Himmel and Wilson Library Consultants' page entitled National & International Library & Information Science Associations (http://www.execpc.com/himmel/natassoc.html), in addition to covering large national and international groups, also has lists of links for statewide and regional library associations and for state and regional library media/educational technology associations. This site, though, could use some updating as well.

ALA's Divisions, Units, and Governance page (http://www. ala.org/alaorg) will help you locate Web pages for affiliates of, and subunits within, ALA. Those professionals who are more interested in the "information" (as opposed to the "library") side of the field may also wish to consult Associations and Organizations Related to Information Studies (http://www.fis.utoronto.ca/internet/ assocs.htm), a site maintained by the Faculty of Information Studies at the University of Toronto. This site is also excellent for its links to Canadian regional associations. To locate national library associations worldwide, try searching IFLA's online membership directory (http://www.ifla.org/database/directy.htm) by country name.

Library consortia, due to the sheer number of them as well as their regional nature, are harder to track down via the Internet. However, an online guide to many library consortia within North America can be found via Libweb (http://sunsite.berkeley.edu/ Libweb/usa-consortia.html), and a number of consortia Web pages (mostly for larger regional organizations) can be located via the International Coalition for Library Consortia (http://www. library.yale.edu/consortia/index.html). Other than that, you may wish to phone the consortia to which your institution belongs to find out their Web page addresses.

Appendix A includes a detailed list of association Web sites in the U.S. and Canada, with Web addresses. We also encourage you

to visit this book's companion Web site at http://www.lisjobs.
com/careerdev for direct links to these pages.

Content of Association Web Pages

Information-related organizations have Web pages for the same
reasons that other groups do. At minimum, they can serve as
online "brochures" for a group, including contact information
(street address, phone, and e-mail), basic information on the
group's membership, and its overall objective. However, most
association Web pages offer much more information than a simple
print brochure can provide. For members or potential members,
they provide reports from subgroups or committees within the
organization, conference information and/or proceedings, job
announcements, and activity calendars. These Web pages are also
good sources for member recruitment. To outsiders, such as members of the media, organization Web sites provide contact information on officers or specialists in a particular area, as well as
news and event announcements.

Each organizational Web page will differ slightly. Many, such as
those for ALA, SLA, and other large national or international
organizations, are comprehensive, with detailed lists of activities,
news briefs, publication guidelines, and much more. Because of
the high traffic they receive as well as the many news items and
organizational changes to announce, they are also updated frequently. On the other hand, Web sites for regional or other more
specialized organizations may have only a single page of information to present. In the majority of cases, the size and depth of an
organization's Web page will be directly related to the size of its
membership—or the enthusiasm of its technical staff.

Large organizations in the information field can afford to hire
full-time Webmasters, smaller groups may have a member or
members take on Webmaster responsibilities as a committee
project. Others may find a member to maintain the Web site on a

volunteer basis. Some of these organizations, such as the Virginia Library Association (http://www.vla.org), are good at keeping their site current even with a small staff, while others tend to neglect their Web presence. It is always a good idea to check for the "last updated" date on an association site, located in many cases at the bottom of the home page. If, after browsing the site, you find a date that is more than six months old or no date at all, you should regard the content with suspicion. Officer lists more than a year old or scales of membership fees from two years ago will not be very helpful to you. (If you do see outdated information on one of these Web pages, though, and you happen to be a member and also an amateur Web designer, this could be a great opportunity for you to volunteer your services!) In the case of old information, it is best either to phone or write to the organization for an update. If all else fails, the *Bowker Annual*, mentioned in the previous section, is a good source of contact information for most organizations in the library and information field. Be sure to consult the most current edition.

Association Web Pages: What to Look For

As an example of a well-done association Web site, take a look at the Web page presented by one medium-sized library association, the Michigan Library Association (http//www.mla.lib.mi.us). Although not all associations have the same categories of information listed on their Web sites, many provide the following categories. Some examples and suggestions may be self-explanatory, such as using an organization's e-mail address as a point of contact, but we go into detail to foster idea generation for your career development.

Any well-done association Web page will list contact information. This is the best way to get in touch with the people involved. Web pages should list these basic details at a minimum: name of the association, address, phone number, fax number, and e-mail address.

Figure 4.2   Michigan Library Association Web Page

An association's mission statement should be prominently fea-
tured. What is the purpose of the association? What population
does it serve—individual information professionals, or libraries
and information organizations as a whole? If a Web page has no
link clearly labeled "mission statement," look around for information that seems to define an association's purpose. In the case of
the Michigan Library Association, it is clear that its members are
individual library personnel in Michigan, and that at least part of
its goal is to serve as a source for members' professional development. The site states that the association "provides an opportunity
to meet library peers and associates."

Pages labeled "About..." will generally also tell you more about
an association's history, membership, activities, and goals. What
specific projects is the association currently involved in with

regard to career development opportunities? Do they offer workshops, other continuing education opportunities, programs, or conferences? Do they sponsor speakers for programs (and are they looking for presenters)? Are these programs limited to members only? Are grants, awards, or scholarships available for individuals, for libraries as member institutions, or both?

Most associations provide a "who's who" of the group on their Web pages; these usually include, at a minimum, lists of officers or board members. Although you are not likely to be approaching association officers via e-mail if you are simply considering joining an organization, knowing who is responsible for what and where to find their e-mail addresses can help if you are already a member and are considering signing up for committee work. (See Chapter 2 for more specifics on contacting other professionals via e-mail and on the basics of online networking.)

Many associations are broken down into subunits, and these should be described online. This level is where the majority of association members become involved (if they become involved at all). Check an association's Web page to see what committees operate within an association. This information can be found under "MLA Units" on the Michigan Library Association page. Read the descriptions of each subgroup to find out which one(s) you may be interested in, and contact the committee chair in order to find out how to become involved. Committee chairs and other officer positions usually change annually or biennially, so if you are not sure how recent the information on a Web page is, it is best to phone the main association number to find out current names (and e-mail addresses).

While you are visiting an association's Web page, make note of any e-mail based lists for association members or committee members. Active participation in these lists, as we discussed in Chapter 2, is an excellent way of making yourself known to the membership at large. National associations such as ALA may offer a variety of these lists (see sidebar on the offerings of the ALA Web site).

In many cases, the current issue (and occasionally back issues) of the association's newsletter is online. Depending on the size of the group, you may find online versions of other publications, such as committee reports, position papers, and research reports. Information in these publications can help to determine whether you would be interested in participating in a particular group and can serve as samples of what an association is looking for in terms of contributors—individuals interested in writing for one of these publications.

News and announcement pages on association Web sites are a good way of keeping up with what is going on, both with an organization's internal activities as well as with what is new on the Web site. Of course, these are most useful when they are updated regularly.

Many national and some statewide and regional associations provide an online membership form. The Michigan Library Association offers such a service at http://orders.mlc.lib.mi. us/mla/Individual.html. In most cases, the association will use a secure Web server to handle these activities, so that members can be assured of security when typing in credit card numbers for online payment. For individuals uncomfortable with this, though, alternatives (such as a form that can simply be printed out and mailed) may be available. Even if an association does not provide you with a way to join the group over the Web, it will probably list, at minimum, the current membership rates as well as a snail-mail address to which payment can be sent. (And again, if you are not sure how current the information is, it is best to phone an association directly.)

Last but not least, many association Web pages list career opportunities that reflect the geographic or subject-specific nature of the group. The Michigan Library Association Web site, for example, has a Jobline that is linked from the home page. It lists positions open in Michigan libraries. (More detailed information on job hunting online is presented in Chapters 11 through 13.)

Web Pages of Specific Organizations

Now that we have seen the basic information that most association Web pages can offer, let's take a closer look at the special features of the Web sites for some of the major national and international organizations of interest to information professionals. Because it is not really practical for us to provide comprehensive information on each site, we encourage you to visit these sites individually to see what they offer. We present the highlights likely to be most useful for information professionals' career development. Just like the organizations they represent, many of these sites can be overwhelming, and you might find yourself getting lost in lists of links. It may also not be apparent during your surfing, unless you are watching the location box on your Web browser carefully, whether you have actually exited an association's site and moved elsewhere. "Site maps" (look for links labeled as such; they may not always be available) can be useful tools, serving as menus listing all or most of the individual Web pages within large Web sites.

National Organizations in the U.S.

American Library Association (ALA)

http://www.ala.org

As befits an organization that boasts over 55,000 members, the American Library Association Web site is correspondingly complex. Information professionals can easily spend an hour or two simply browsing through all of the pages at this site, including the subsites belonging to suborganizations and affiliates of ALA. There are groups within ALA for just about everyone in the library field: school library media specialists, reference librarians, catalogers, public librarians, systems librarians, and more. Those new to ALA should first consult

the page describing ALA Divisions, Units, and Governance, at
http://www.ala.org/alaorg. In addition to a staff directory and hierar-
chical organizational charts, it links to personal pages maintained by
ALA officers, pages listing committees and their descriptions (including an online volunteer form), and pages maintained by ALA offices,
chapters, roundtables, and affiliates. If you are not sure of the difference between all of these subgroups, click on the page labeled "ALA
Overview" (direct address http://www.ala.org/alaorg/mission.html)
for an explanation. This page also boasts the ALA mission statement
and details on its history and membership.

Librarians interested in either supporting others' research in the
field or publishing their own should check out the ALA Editions
page (http://www.ala.org/editions). Here, you can purchase

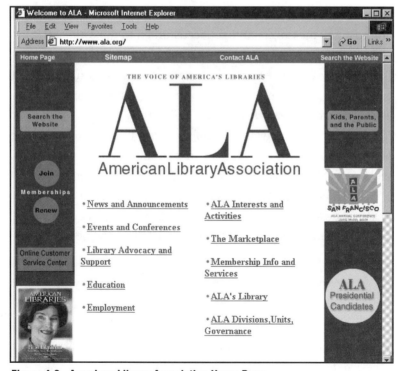

Figure 4.3   American Library Association Home Page

professional books through the online store or read the writers' guidelines. (More information on locating and using publishers' guidelines via the Internet is covered in Chapter 7.)

Individuals interested in networking online with others in various groups within ALA should consider signing up and participating in one of the sponsored electronic discussion groups, a Web interface to which is available at http://lp-web.ala.org:8000. There are many to choose from—more than 100 in total—with many of interest mainly to ALA members belonging to a particular task force, section, or other subgroup. Topics range from the receipt of news bulletins from various ALA sections to information literacy to intellectual freedom. Active participation in most is restricted to subscribers. While the "do's" and "don'ts" of online networking have been discussed more thoroughly in Chapter 2, we repeat the important concept that new subscribers should "lurk" (read, but not post any messages) and get accustomed to the tone of the list before taking an active role.

Other areas of the ALA Web site dedicated to assisting librarians in the career development process include options for browsing job listings (from *American Libraries, College and Research Libraries News,* and more) as well as simply signing up or renewing your membership online. Librarians can also add membership in any section, roundtable, or division to their current ALA membership.

A final area in which the ALA Web site assists librarians in the professional development process is through the page labeled Events and Conferences, which is described more fully in the next chapter.

The ALA Web Site:
A Team Effort Years in the Making

ALA's Internet presence debuted in 1994 as a Gopher site, hosted at the University of Illinois at Chicago ("ALA Gopher Debuts" 588). Its current Web presence is the most comprehensive and most frequently visited library association site; in April 2001, over three million hits were recorded for the ala.org domain, for an average of 103,000 requests per day. (For current site statistics, see http://www.ala.org/stats/.) The most popular sections include book reviews from *Booklist, American Libraries'* online job ads, Internet Resources columns from *C&RL NewsNet*, conference information, and resources for parents and children. The ALA site typically receives between fifteen and thirty e-mail questions per day, many of which are handled by ALA's own library staff.

A variety of individuals are responsible for the development and design of the site, including ALA employees, members, and professional Web designers. Each ALA unit takes responsibility for its own pages. In June 2000, just before the ALA annual conference, the site hosted approximately 13,000 distinct Web pages. "My best guess at the number of ALA employees who have Web-related activities as a decent portion of their job would be around 40, but the number of people who actually edit or change a page would be much more," reported Jack Briody, ALA Web Developer, in July 2000.

The American Society for Information Science and Technology (ASIST)

http://www.asis.org

The ASIST Web site is maintained by a cooperative agreement between ASIST and the School of Library and Information Science at Indiana University. Membership is open to all individuals and institutions interested in using technology for information access and retrieval. Recent ASIST publications (books and journals) are highlighted, as are publications and PowerPoint presentations (which have been converted to HTML) from its annual meetings.

Members and potential members should consider reading the page entitled "How to Get Involved in ASIST," which links to the portions of the Web site relevant to professional development. For involvement at the local rather than the national level, the Web site lists professional and student chapters located throughout the U.S. as well as in Taipei (where both a professional and student chapter of ASIST are located). It also lists details on the subject-specific, special-interest groups (SIGs) within ASIST, covering topics such as digital libraries, knowledge management, information architecture, and medical informatics. Many of these SIGs have their own Web pages, which are hosted on external servers, as well as their own e-mail discussion lists in which members and interested parties can participate. (The name of this organization changed from ASIS, the American Society for Information Science, in late 2000.)

The Association of Independent Information Professionals (AIIP)
http://www.aiip.org

AIIP is an organization formed to unite entrepreneurial members of the information profession: those who work as independent information brokers, researchers, consultants, writers, and publishers. Its Web site describes the evolution of this profession from the 1960s until today, including the roles that these individuals can play in the current "information revolution." Those considering developing a career along these lines—and wondering in which areas employment opportunities might lie—would do well to read the online document entitled "What Is an Independent Information Professional?" Also online is the AIIP code of ethics, as well as recent news releases.

New Members' Round Table (NMRT; part of ALA)
http://www.ala.org/nmrt

NMRT is the subgroup of ALA aimed at easing librarians into the role ALA can play in the development of their careers. As such, the NMRT Web site goes out of its way to introduce newcomers to its many services and to librarianship as a profession. Membership is open to any librarian who has been a member of ALA for ten years or less. Librarians interested in becoming involved with NMRT have many choices, all of which are described online: serving on committees, starting a new committee, having your resume reviewed, becoming a mentor/mentee, volunteering at the ALA National Conference, and much more. You can also become more involved with the profession and gain public speaking experience

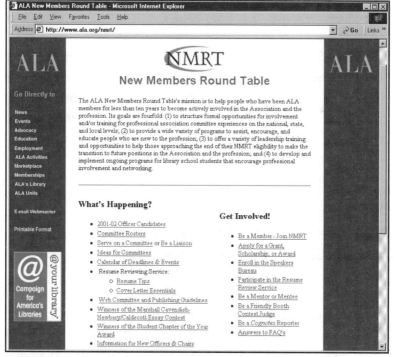

Figure 4.4   New Members Round Table (Part of the American Library
Association)

through the NMRT Speakers' Bureau (http://www.ala.org/nmrt/speakers/speakersbureau.html). Another page we especially recommend is the FAQ ("Frequently Asked Questions") about NMRT involvement, at http://www.ala.org/nmrt/faq.html.

Society of American Archivists (SAA)

http://www.archivists.org

Called "North America's oldest and largest national archival professional association," with more than 3,400 members, SAA has a Web site with current, comprehensive information about its purpose, programs, publications, and more—including a search engine and site map. In addition to all of the details typically found on an association Web site, it provides nomination forms for awards and Fellows. SAA's Council Handbook is completely online, and this includes detailed descriptions of standing committees, task forces, sections, and roundtables with which members can become involved. Even some individual SAA roundtables have Web pages and electronic discussion lists. The organization as a whole sponsors a number of discussion lists on topics ranging from archives in general to archives for the new professional (restricted to students and those in the profession three years or less) to electronic records and Native American archives. Also, SAA's continuing education page highlights "So You Want To Be an Archivist," an introduction to the archival profession.

Non-U.S. and International Organizations

Australian Library and Information Association (ALIA)

http://www.alia.org.au

For information specialists in Australia, the ALIA Web site has a good deal to offer. In addition to a careers section (with the results of a nationwide salary survey and useful advice on employment contracts), the site includes details on ALIA publications, online PowerPoint presentations given at conferences, names and e-mail addresses of association contacts, and the group's organizational structure. People interested in applying for membership can submit an information request online and receive an application packet in the mail. For ALIA, continuing professional development (CPD) is a priority, and members can formalize their career development activities through the association. To this end, a career development kit, containing a workbook and record-keeping sheets, is free upon request by members (http://www.alia.org.au/education/cpd/career.kit.html). Formal mentoring programs are available for both new and experienced librarians, and ALIA produces a Mentoring Manual to assist in the process.

Canadian Library Association (CLA)
http://www.cla.ca

CLA is to Canadian librarians what ALA is to librarians in the U.S. Just as its membership isn't nearly as large as that of ALA (roughly 3,000 members, including personal, institutional, and associate members), its Web site is not nearly as complex. Still, there is plenty of information here for the career-minded Canadian librarian.

Those new to CLA or to the profession in general—not just Canadians—should first visit CLA's Career Information page (http://www.cla.ca/careers/careerinfo.htm), which contains links to a variety of career sites. The link labeled "Connections: Linking People with Information, Your Career in Library or Information Science" is required reading for anyone considering obtaining a library degree in Canada. It explains the responsibilities traditionally associated with the title of librarian, library technician, and teacher librarian, among others. A listing of degree and diploma programs offered by Canadian universities follows.

The International Federation of Library Associations and Institutions (IFLA)
http://www.ifla.org

IFLA is the organization dedicated to serving the professional needs of information specialists worldwide; it also serves as a means for international cooperation among librarians and library agencies. While IFLA's only voting members are other library associations and institutions (including individual libraries and information centers), information professionals may join as "personal affiliates." In total, more than 1,600 members of all types belong. Since a large number of countries have national library associations that focus on professional issues specific to each country's librarians, looking through this membership list can help you identify library associations outside of the U.S. or Canada. The headquarters of IFLA is The Hague, Netherlands.

Those interested in joining as an IFLA affiliate should consult the Membership section of its Web page, which also lists available divisions, sections, and roundtables. (Online registration is not currently available; you must fill out the form online, print it out, and mail it in.) Another highlight of this Web site is an archive for, and directions for subscribing to, the LIBJOBS electronic mailing list—a recommended place for finding out about open library positions. A warning: Be prepared to receive a large number of messages per day.

Library Association

http://www.la-hq.org.uk

Subtitled "The Association for Librarians and Information Managers," the Library Association (LA) aims to meet the needs of information specialists in the U.K. As expected, the site includes typical association details (regional branches, annual reports, interest groups, and publication information). Some unique contributions, however, include Professional Issues, LA's official responses to a number of professional issues, such as copyright, lifelong learning, and access to information. Online Discussion describes discussion lists hosted by LA, and Careers and

Qualifications includes the LISjobnet (an online job board), tips and guidelines for working overseas, and job exchange possibilities. For British information specialists interested in continuing their professional education, a catalog of training and development courses is available online (http://www.la-hq.org.uk/directory/training/train.html).

Special Libraries Association (SLA)

http://www.sla.org

Information professionals unsure about what SLA members have in common should first read the association's statement on special librarianship at http://www.sla.org/content/professional/meaning/what/index.cfm. Special librarians can be found working for corporate libraries or information centers, government agencies, law firms, museums, or consulting firms, among others. Information specialists within subject-specific departments of public or academic libraries, such as map libraries, life science libraries, etc., can also fall into the "special librarian" category. Like other large associations, SLA is organized into subject-based divisions, descriptions of which are online. Members may also join one of the geographically based SLA chapters, many of which have their own Web sites (or at least their own electronic mailing lists). Special librarians outside the U.S. have several chapters to call their own; examples include the Arabian Gulf, Asian, Eastern Canada, and European Chapters. Links to information on both divisions and chapters are available from SLA's Membership page.

In order to get the word out on their services, SLA members who do consulting work may list themselves in CONSULT Online (http://www.sla.org/consultonline). A search in this database reveals a detailed profile of each consultant's area of expertise. Other information unique to the SLA Web site includes upcoming distance learning courses, a chat room that facilitates online contact with other professionals, and a career services section that lets employers and applicants connect via job ads and online resumes. The "members only" section provides access to current and back issues of the journal *Information Outlook* as well as a "who's who" of special librarians. After logging in, SLA members can also update their own profiles, which list addresses, affiliations, and committee memberships.

Other Specialized Library Associations

Aside from large, national associations (and branches or subunits of these organizations), U.S. states and Canadian provinces have numerous professional associations for information specialists. Many additional associations bring librarians together based on subject-specific interests held in common. Examples of associations in these two categories include the Michigan Library Association, mentioned earlier, the American Association of Law Libraries (http://www.aallnet.org), and the California School Library Association (http://www.schoolibrary.org). It is easy to get a start in the profession by joining and participating in smaller organizations, such as groups on the statewide or local level.

Getting Involved in Person

The Internet offers a tremendous amount of information on associations in the information field, including ways to join online, participate in discussion lists, view committee descriptions, and peruse job listings. It can also serve as a good point of first contact with leaders within professional groups you are interested in joining. However, continuing these relationships in an offline environment is equally important for those librarians interested in developing their careers. It *is* possible to participate in an organization only through electronic discussion groups—but activities that put you in face-to-face contact with other professionals in your chosen subfield will make your name more widely known and will demonstrate your commitment to the profession. An excellent way of connecting with other information professionals is through conferences; and, not surprisingly, the Web offers a plethora of information on when and where these conferences are held, the programs they offer, and the organizations that sponsor them. Your employer may even help subsidize your attendance at conferences as part of a professional development program. Our discussions on ways you can use the Internet to learn about and participate in conferences in the field continue in the next chapter.

Works Cited

"ALA Gopher debuts." *American Libraries*, Jun. 1994: 588.

Nielsen, Brian. "Library Resources in Cyberspace: The ALA Gopher and Beyond." *American Libraries*, Mar. 1995: 278–279.

Chapter 5

Learning About and Participating in Conferences

There is no doubt that conference attendance can be a hectic experience. Picture, if you can, more than 20,000 librarians converging on a city for a period of three to five days. Then add the confusion of determining travel and hotel arrangements; planning meals; deciding which conference presentations, meetings, vendor breakfasts, and parties to attend; and navigating the huge exhibit hall. Anyone who has attended ALA Annual has experienced this craziness firsthand.

The broader the focus of the conference, the greater the number of attendees. This means that conferences dealing with specialized topics—such as academic libraries (ACRL), library technology (LITA), or public libraries (PLA)—attract smaller numbers of information professionals, namely those with interests in one particular subset of the profession. Those sponsored by statewide or other organizations can be smaller still, and if you are not a current participant in these organizations, you may have to be proactive in seeking out conference information in order to keep up with what is happening.

How can you find out about conferences if you are not familiar with the groups offering them and when they are offered? Conferences and meetings can be sponsored by a variety of different organizations: professional associations, consortia, publishers, corporations, and vendors, to name just a few. If you are not familiar with the names, types, locations, and sponsors of conferences in the library and information world, the Web is a great place to begin looking. While it is true that conference announcements appear regularly in the professional literature, receipt of publications can be delayed, particularly if you are not first on a routing list within your institution. Also, while many librarians receive meeting flyers in the mail, their timing is not always the best; we have found advertisements for a professional meeting waiting in the mailbox after returning from the very same conference! Information professionals who browse the Web for conference information can save a great deal of time in the planning process. Online conference listings, in addition to providing dates and locations, often list agendas and speakers—which can help you decide in advance which events you would like to attend. Finally, after a conference is over, check the Web page of the sponsoring organization or corporation to find reports and summaries of what went on. These may help you decide whether a topic you are interested in presenting is appropriate or whether you might want to attend this conference next year.

Conferences Sponsored by Organizations

The majority of professional organizations in the library/information field sponsor, at minimum, annual meetings to which the membership at large is invited. (Nonmembers may typically attend for an additional charge.) In addition, subunits within organizations often have meetings that are held more frequently throughout the year. Because these smaller meetings may be strictly limited to officers, they may not be announced publicly on the Internet. However, organizations with a well-established Web presence are likely to announce conferences geared toward the entire membership.

Naturally, the best place on the Web to start for finding out about association-related conference information is via the Web pages listed in Appendix A. If these sites do not have prominent links labeled "Conferences," try reading through online newsletters or news pages to see if upcoming conferences are mentioned. Back issues of newsletters may contain reports of what happened at past conferences. You may also find this information hidden within the "What's New" section of the association's Web site.

For large organizations such as ALA, check out their Web pages to find more information about subgroups within organizations, such as committees and roundtables. Many of these units sponsor programs at the group's national conference, and sometimes you can get ideas on which presentations to attend by reading about the topics each group deals with regularly. Some organizations only provide brief conference information online, while others go all out. For an example of the latter, see the Web page of Library Research Seminar II (http://www.dpo.uab.edu/~folive/LRSII), a conference on LIS research organized by the Library Research Seminar Planning Committee, with help from the Library Research Round Table and the Library History Round Table of the American Library Association.

Conferences Sponsored by Publishers

In addition to professional associations, a few publishers in the library/information field sponsor conferences. These conferences tend to be technology-based. For example, Information Today, Inc., this book's publisher, currently offers five national and international conferences each year, the best known of which are InfoToday (formerly known as the National Online Meeting), Computers in Libraries, and Internet Librarian conferences. These meetings are all geared toward the technology-savvy information professional. Agendas, preliminary programs, registration forms,

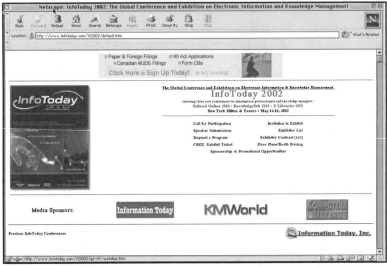

Figure 5.1   Information Today, Inc. Conference Page Describing the InfoToday Conference

and information on previously held conferences are available at Information Today's Web page (http://www.infotoday.com/ conferences.htm). Online, Inc. is another publisher/corporation that sponsors annual conferences, such as eContent (http://www. onlineinc.com).

Connecting with Vendors at Conferences

Companies and vendors operating within, or selling products to, the information field can sponsor conferences of their own. In the case of companies producing integrated library systems such as Data Research Associates (DRA), Endeavor Information Systems, or Innovative Interfaces, Inc., these conferences are often referred to as "user's group meetings." Annual conferences occur at the national level and are often supplemented with smaller get-togethers held at the regional or statewide level. The formal parts of these meetings consist of a combination of vendor demonstrations/product updates and presentations by users on how they made a particular system work well for them.

Most online catalog vendors sponsor such meetings, although information professionals who are not part of a library's systems or technical services staff might not always be aware of them. Library staff can easily keep current with user's group meetings held by a vendor by going online. Start at your library system vendor's Web site. If you are not sure of the address, ask your systems librarian/system administrator, or check Marshall Breeding's comprehensive list of system vendor Web pages at, http://staffweb. library.vanderbilt.edu/Breeding/librarycompanies.html. Most of these corporation Web sites provide information on conferences they sponsor themselves and on the library association conferences (such as ALA) at which they will be present either as exhibitors or as presenters. Joining an electronic mailing list for users of a particular system or product is also a good idea, because you will receive regular notices of future conferences.

After the conference is over, vendor Web sites are good places to look for PowerPoint presentations that were used at the conference, as well as the texts of papers that were presented. In many cases, vendors may have separate Web sites for the public and for their users. They do not want proprietary information, such as documentation and presentations, out on the Internet for their competitors to see. In the case of Endeavor Information Systems' Internet presence (http://www.endinfosys.com), for example, their SupportWeb site (which includes the text of conference presentations) is password protected, and only people belonging to Endeavor libraries are permitted to join the electronic mailing list (VOYAGER-L) and to search the online mailing list archive.

If you know that you will be attending a conference and you are interested in speaking with a particular vendor, it is a good idea to check that vendor's Web site to see whether its representatives will also be attending. In addition, you can check the Web site of the conference's sponsor to find out what vendors will be exhibiting—many provide a list. If you are in regular communication with any individual vendor via e-mail, conferences are a good opportunity to make face-to-face contact. These types of meetings are easy to arrange in advance via e-mail.

Conference Presentations and Poster Sessions

Information professionals looking to advance their careers will consider being a conference speaker. Presenting at a conference not only enhances your resume, but also gets you and your research known to a large audience of your peers—and provides you with valuable public speaking experience. Conference presentations can also be the first step along the path to publication. Many articles appearing in the library literature originally started out as presentations. Authors frequently use audience feedback as a way of focusing their topics.

The subjects of conference presentations need not be limited to formal research; many librarians use such opportunities to share ideas about which specific tools and techniques worked well for them and their libraries. Naturally, the best way to determine whether your idea is appropriate for a conference presentation is to view the names and descriptions of presentations that were held at conferences in the past (or ones that will take place in the near future). Visit the Web sites of professional organizations and publishers, as described earlier, to locate links to conference information. Electronic discussion lists are good sources for locating information on upcoming conference topics. Calls for presenters frequently appear on mailing lists as well. (Note that "calls for papers" can refer either to conference papers or to journal articles; read carefully to determine which is being referred to in a particular post.)

If you feel overwhelmed by the thought of presenting your ideas in front of a large national audience, begin at the local or regional level and work your way up. Also, while you need not be an expert in order to be a conference speaker, librarians who are new to conference attendance may chose to get their foot in the door by participating first in a poster session. For these sessions, librarians present their ideas in the form of an exhibit, with displays (usually posted on easels) and handouts. Poster sessions are good outlets for librarians whose topics, while valuable to the profession, may be too narrow for a formal presentation.

In addition, consider serving as a presenter at a regional—or national—user's group meeting. Presenting your library's success story to a specialized audience will give you instant recognition as an expert in a particular area of library technology. Librarians interested in the professional opportunities that conference presentations offer should consider registering themselves and their preferred topics in LibraryHQ's Speaker Source (http://www.libraryhq.com/speakers) or the NMRT Speakers' Bureau (http://www.ala.org/nmrt/speakers/speakersbureau. html).

Electronic discussion lists are good places to find calls for presenters and poster sessions, such as the following, which appeared on the Web4Lib discussion list in January 2001. (The complete message is available online at http://sunsite.berkeley.edu/Web4Lib/archive/0101/0098.html.)

```
The Virtual Reference Desk
3rd Annual Digital Reference Conference
November 12-13, 2001, Orlando, Florida,
USA
Call for Proposals
```

Proposals are invited for breakout session presentations and poster sessions at
the VRD 2001 Annual Digital Reference
Conference. The third annual VRD conference will highlight digital reference
service in a variety of contexts:
libraries and information centers, government, business, education, etc. This conference will explore the nature of
Internet-based question-and-answer service
as well as the specific issues involved
in providing all types of digital reference service.
DEADLINES:
Proposals will be accepted until April 2,
2001 (see proposal submission instructions below). Selected presenters will be
notified by May 15, 2001. Presenters will
receive free admission to the conference.
Final papers or materials are due August
1, 2001 for inclusion in the conference
proceedings.
    Proposals should address issues of dig-
ital reference from the following perspectives: libraries and information
centers, professional associations and
organizations, government agencies, business, K-12 education, higher education,
and other contexts involved in providing
or receiving digital reference service.

If such a call for presenters is posted on a list, pay attention to the list discussion that follows. If you are looking for a co-presenter, you may be able to find someone interested in helping out.

In addition to bringing together conference organizers and presenters via Web page announcements or mailing lists, the Internet can assist in the organization of conferences themselves. For example, ASIST (the American Association of Information Science and Technology) now uses Web-based software to automate the planning and organization of their meetings. The software, from

Community of Science (http://ams.cos.com/cgi-bin/login?institutionId =2039&meetingId=54), allows interested parties to submit and review their conference proposals online. This procedure was used first in preparation for the 2001 ASIST Annual Meeting in Washington, D.C.

Best Online Conference Listings

Rather than visiting individual association or publisher sites to look for conference information, you may prefer to get an overall listing of upcoming conferences. Information Today, Inc.'s Calendar (http://www.infotoday.com/calendar.htm) is a good source for this, listing events occurring within the next twelve months. ALA's Events and Conferences page (http://www. ala.org/events) is an excellent pointer to ALA-related meetings, including division and chapter conferences and institutes. Information about additional conferences in the information field can also be found on this site, via American Libraries Online's Datebook (http://www.ala.org/alonline/datebook/ datebook.html), which is updated frequently. *Library Journal*'s news calendar (available via http://libraryjournal.reviewsnews. com) is one additional meta-listing of conferences for information professionals.

Faxon, a library subscription vendor, offers information on ALA programs of interest to serials and collection development librarians via its Web site (http://www.faxon.com). You will also typically find listings of recommended restaurants and hotels in conference cities here; these are worth noting, as they are compiled by librarians from the local area.

Your local library consortium's Web page may also list conferences in your local area. NELINET's Library Conferences and Meetings Page (http://www.nelinet.net/conf.htm), listing upcoming events in New England, is a good example, as is Amigos'

Conference Calendar (http://www.amigos.org/conferences/calendar. html), which lists conferences in the U.S. Southwest.

In addition to the sites just mentioned, conference announcements are regularly posted to electronic mailing lists. Chapter 2 provides information on where to find, and how best to participate in, mailing lists within subfields of librarianship and information science.

Electronic Meetings and Conferences

While this chapter has so far concerned itself with using the Internet and the Web to discover information on and plan for conferences to attend in person, electronic conferences—"meetings" that happen purely in cyberspace—are becoming more and more frequent. Electronic conferences save participants the time, inconvenience, and expense that accompanies any kind of travel. Of course, there are disadvantages to this method, such as missing out on in-person contact with your colleagues, the fun of exploring a strange city, and all the social events and exhibits that accompany most conferences.

ALA's New Members Round Table (NMRT) organizes what they call "eMeetings" in both the fall and spring, and posts guidelines for participation on the Web site (see sidebar). Unlike NMRT's electronic conferences, which are held through e-mail, SLA offers members the chance to conference online through chat rooms (http://www.sla.org/content/interactive/chat/index.cfm).

Although, in theory, any librarian can use this site, the guidelines restrict its use to legitimate SLA business and mention that the content of chat sessions may be used and reproduced by SLA. With SLA's chat room, any Web browser that supports Java will work, and plug-ins are available for added functionality. ALA has begun to investigate the possibilities that electronic meetings offer for the organization as a whole; the final report of the ALA Electronic Meeting Participation Task Force (EMPTF) for 2001 can be found online at

Figure 5.2   ISIS2000 (Information Services in Schools) Online Conference Page

http://www.ala.org/alaorg/council/documents/emptffinal.pdf. In a survey completed by participants in chat sessions sponsored by the EMPTF, the general reaction to electronic conferencing was favorable.

In July 2000, the Centre for Studies in Teacher-Librarianship of New South Wales, Australia, organized their Information Services in Schools (ISIS2000) conference, which was held entirely online. Just as at a traditional conference, papers were presented, workshops organized, and issues explored. This ten-day event brought together 256 teacher-librarians from around the world via real-time online workshops (held via a Multi-User Dimension [MUD], Object Oriented [MOO] environment) and asynchronous e-mail discussion. Papers were posted to a password-protected Web site. For those who had not participated in a MOO, training sessions were available. While some participants found time management to be a problem, the conference as a whole was judged to be successful. More information on ISIS2000 can be found online at http://www.csu.edu.au/cstl/isis.

NMRT's eMeetings

In October 1999, ALA's New Members Round Table began holding eMeetings, official board meetings at which business is conducted entirely through e-mail. Priscilla Shontz, President of NMRT during 1999-2000, created this method of communication for NMRT. The eMeetings serve the dual purpose of supplementing regularly scheduled meetings at ALA Midwinter and Annual conferences and helping to cut down on the time spent in meetings at these two events. In her opinion, the eMeetings successfully meet these goals. Furthermore, she reports, they allow for greater participation among the membership and increase awareness of issues discussed by NMRT. An additional benefit is that they create a handy written record for the secretary to use in recording minutes.

eMeetings are scheduled for the fall and spring, halfway points between the ALA national conferences. Before an eMeeting begins, officers and committee chairs subscribe to an electronic mailing list created for this purpose. The list owner also invites other NMRT members to attend (via an invitation posted on NMRT-L), because ALA requires that board meetings be open. The typical meeting lasts from one to two weeks, in order to allow enough time for everyone to respond. Participants indicate their presence by replying to an e-mail with the subject line "ATTENDANCE." If a quorum is reached, official NMRT business can begin.

Business at these mini-conferences is conducted in the same fashion as it would be at in-person meetings, with guidelines, agendas (posted online at http://www.ala.org/nmrt/nmrtbd.html), votes, and official reports. The eMeeting takes the form of an electronic discussion group to which members can post messages, and standard subject lines are used to distinguish various types of motions. Because parliamentary procedure is followed as strictly as it is in person, at times the officers must prompt the group for motions to be made and seconded. Overall, though, eMeetings run smoothly. Topics not requiring a vote can easily be discussed, and issues requiring more time may be outlined in advance, setting the stage for further discussion at ALA Midwinter and Annual conferences.

In theory, any two members of an association (or any two parties on the Internet in general) can schedule a time to "meet" electronically in a chat room to discuss topics of mutual interest. These ad-hoc meetings won't be considered official association business, though, if the association in question has not previously sanctioned them. Chat rooms, as well as the technological requirements for participation, are covered in more detail in Chapter 2.

Registering for Conferences and Housing Online

If you are allergic to paperwork, or if you constantly find yourself getting lost amidst the piles of papers scattered on your desk, online conference registration is an excellent option. At approximately the same time that conference registration announcements begin appearing in the print literature (February or March for the ALA Annual Conference, for example), large library associations such as ALA begin to offer online registration forms that serve the same purpose. All you will need to do to sign up is select your membership category, choose which events you would like to attend, type your contact information and credit card number, and click on Submit—you will be all set. Your payment will be processed online via a secure Web server, and you will receive a confirmation receipt via e-mail.

For the Midwinter and Summer ALA conferences, travel and housing applications can also be processed online via ALA's Web page. You will be prompted for your choice of hotels and rooms, including alternates, and the program will tell you immediately which hotels have rooms available on the nights you select. (Be prepared to accept your fifth or sixth choice of location—hotels tend to fill up very quickly.) As with conference registration, a receipt with a confirmation number will be forwarded to your e-mail account.

In order to keep all of this information organized, we suggest that you create a folder or mailbox within your e-mail software specifically for conference e-mail receipts. This will ensure that you don't misplace your confirmation information (or will at least make it more difficult to delete it by accident). This folder would also be a good place to store any other e-mail messages you receive regarding conference presentations, meetings, or other events you would like to attend. (Each e-mail program handles "folder creation" differently; we recommend that you use the Help function of your e-mail package in order to find out how to do this.) If you are worried about keeping information as important as this in your e-mail, by all means print out a copy—in fact, it's a good idea to bring a print-out of your e-mail receipt to the hotel as proof in case there are any problems at check-in. Registering for housing online (or through the ALA Travel Desk in general, via telephone or fax) is not for those who are overly particular about the type and location of the room they get; those who have specific needs will want to phone individual hotels directly.

Practicalities: Conference Travel

If you have ever attended a large conference such as ALA Annual, you know that a great deal of your time will be taken up by travel, both to your final destination and within the city you are visiting. Sites such as Travelocity (http://www.travelocity.com) can help you find the best route and compare airline fares, while Mapquest (http://www.mapquest.com) will give you maps of a local area down to the street level.

Should you find yourself driving to a conference or within the conference city, Tripquest (http://www.tripquest.com), which is part of Mapquest, will give you door-to-door directions if you include a street address at both ends of your destination, or city-to-city directions otherwise. One caveat: occasionally, you may find that Tripquest plots a route that looks short either distance-wise or time-wise but that may not be very practical or convenient. For example, it may suggest you use local roads rather than going a little out of your way along a highway. It is always a good idea to compare the route that Tripquest suggests with a local map of the area.

Business directories such as Switchboard (http://www.switchboard.com) or Bigbook (http://www.bigbook.com) can provide lists of businesses such as banks, restaurants, or used bookstores within a city or within a particular distance from a street address. Also, don't forget Excite Travel (http://travel.excite.com), formerly CityNet, or Yahoo! Local (http://local.yahoo.com) for directories of Web sites of local areas, including public transportation maps. Try Zagat.com (http://www.zagat.com) for restaurant reviews.

Print Journals and Journal Web Pages

Although you are likely to be able to do the majority of your conference planning online, particularly for larger conferences, don't neglect the print literature. Trade publications such as *American Libraries, Library Journal,* and *College & Research Libraries News* are particularly useful. *Library Journal,* for example, usually publishes detailed conference agendas for major events like ALA Annual several months before the conference, and some of this information may not be available online. *Library Journal* frequently highlights and describes individual conference sessions and presentations (and parties!) that will be happening at ALA, as a way of suggesting how you will want to spend your time. You may find it worth your while, though, to peruse the Web pages of trade publishers in the field for pre-conference information as well as post-conference synopses. These journals often publish conference reports in the issue just following an event. Chapter 7, Professional Literature, provides information on locating the Web pages of publishers within the field of librarianship and information science.

Conference attendance and participation can be a valuable part of any information professional's career. While there is still no real substitute for attending a conference in person, take full advantage of the Internet to help you plan, prepare for, and even participate in conferences in the information field.

Chapter 6

Your Online Presence

Beyond realizing the importance of networking with others online, savvy information professionals who are serious both about promoting themselves and advancing their careers will want to establish their own online presence. It is often said that the Web makes everyone a potential publisher. Librarians can use their professional skills to participate in this grand publishing experiment by creating a personal home page, Weblog, or other library-related resource such as an e-mail discussion list or newsletter (sometimes referred to as an e-zine).

This chapter focuses on how librarians can use (and are using) the Internet to personally publish material related to libraries and librarianship—although information professionals use similar tools to create resources of personal interest and sites for patron use also. Using Internet tools to establish a professional online presence can only help your career. Creating your own presence online gives you an easily accessible body of work to which you can refer potential employers, editors, and/or clients, and also helps show your Internet and content creation savvy. In an Internet environment, information professionals who take advantage of the opportunity to establish their own online presence are being proactive in promoting themselves and their careers.

Librarians using Web sites and other online creations to promote themselves professionally, however, should be careful to maintain a professional image throughout. If you wish to create a personal page showing pictures of your pets, family, and friends, for example, be sure to keep it separate from your professional presence. Just as this sort of information is inappropriate on a resume, it is also irrelevant to a Web site intended to promote your professional qualifications or to provide a service for other librarians. And remember, anything you put up on the Internet is broadcast publicly, so do not include anything you would not want your current or potential employer to see!

Web Sites

Librarian-created Web sites range from the humorous (such as the Laughing Librarian at http://internettrash.com/users/lafnlibn) to the radical (such as the Street Librarian at http://www.geocities.com/SoHo/Cafe/7423) to the serious (such as Roy Tennant's home page at http://escholarship.cdlib.org/rtennant). Many of these sites focus on issues in librarianship, and, taken as a group, they provide a wide variety of resources and support to other librarians.

Information professionals' organizational and evaluative skills put them at a distinct advantage when it comes to creating and arranging Web content, and librarians have established a formidable presence online.

Why Create Your Own Site?

Librarians create their own sites for a number of reasons, including these:

- Simple bookmark management

- The need to create an online resume or professional portfolio

- A place to post and link to professional writing, papers, and speeches

- Advertising for their business or freelance services

- The wish to provide a resource for other librarians or the general public

- The need to improve their Web design skills in order to take on a work-related Web project

Often these purposes are combined within a single site, which can grow to encompass a variety of related resources.

Before beginning work on your own site, be sure that you have a clear picture of its purpose. You should have something you want to say to the library community, a service you wish to provide, or a product you wish to promote. (This product can simply be yourself and your skills!) You may have multiple reasons for creating your site. Former NMRT president Priscilla Shontz says: "I enjoy creating Web pages, so I do it partially just to learn more about it—to practice and develop my skills. Also, when creating your own personal Web page, you can be more creative than you can when creating something for work or a committee. I also created pages, such as my resume page, to prove to potential employers that I can create Web pages."

A simple Web site can serve as a useful bookmark manager. (For an example of one of these librarian-created, library-related "lists of links," see Donna Reed's faves page at http://www.spiretech.com/~dreed/favorites.html.) Rather than scrolling through lists of bookmarks or searching through favorites folders, a links site allows you to see all related resources on one page, which you can then set as your personal home page, if you desire. Links that are useful to you may also prove to be useful to your fellow librarians, and such sites can develop into extensive lists of resources.

Other simple sites include an online resume to which librarians can refer potential employers. (Electronic resumes are discussed at length in Chapter 11.) From their resume, information professionals can also link to a fuller online portfolio that displays their strengths in particular areas. Such a portfolio can incorporate

PowerPoint presentations that have been converted to Web format, images or downloadable files of brochures and handouts, letters of recommendation, and any other displayable material that shows your skills. This gives potential employers a concrete demonstration of your skills and achievements. Even as an MLS student, you might consider creating an online portfolio that highlights the work you have done in your classes.

A natural extension of the online portfolio or resume is the use of the Web to post and/or link to your articles, speeches, or other writing. Since many library-related journals post all or part of their content online, if you are published in one of these outlets, you may be able to link directly to your article (or at least an abstract) at the journal's own Web site. Be sure, however, to check the links to your work periodically—publishers often rearrange their online content. If your article is not online and you retain the copyright, you may be able to post it yourself. (Check with your editor.) You may also choose to mix in previously published articles with original content, or to post on your site articles for which you have been unable to find a publisher or which you wish to post unedited and in full. Be aware, however, that most journal publishers will not publish previously posted material. Posting an article online is a type of publication, and editors generally prefer to publish original content.

Hints for a Successful Web Site

- Include useful, unique, and substantive content
- Keep navigation and themes simple and consistent
- Describe your credentials and qualifications
- Answer all inquiries promptly and professionally
- Promote your site tactfully and graciously
- Find out what visitors are looking for and try to provide it

---

An example of a librarian-created site providing links to articles, papers, and speeches is Walt Crawford's Web page at http://walt. crawford.home.att.net. To back up his availability for speaking engagements and writing assignments, Crawford also provides site visitors with a biographical statement, publicity photos, information on his professional interests, his vita, and contact information.

Entrepreneurial Librarians

The "information revolution" has created a market for librarians who have established themselves as consultants, writers, researchers, and speakers. Many information professionals have been able to strike out on their own, creating businesses that supply such services either to other librarians or to the larger business community.

Any such consulting business today requires a Web site to advertise its services. The most successful librarian-created business Web sites provide more than just a simple brochure describing their services. Content is what keeps visitors coming back to your Web site, and content is what will make customers keep you in mind when it comes time to hire someone to speak, research, provide training, or produce other projects. Independent librarians may consider tactics such as creating an e-zine, providing relevant directories of links, posting columns and presentations, or creating other content to draw visitors and make their site memorable. Each column, presentation, and resource should link to a resume or a page describing available services.

One example of a great site by a librarian-turned-entrepreneur is Marylaine Block's Web page, at http://marylaine.com. Block uses her site to promote her services as an Internet trainer, speaker, and writer. Yet Marylaine.com is much more than an online brochure advertising her services. Site visitors will find a good deal of useful information, such as *Ex Libris*, a weekly e-zine

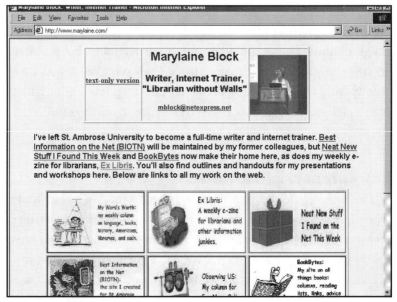

Figure 6.1   Marylaine.com

for "librarians and information junkies" that discusses library, information, and Internet-related issues. The site also includes the archives of "Neat New Stuff I Found This Week," which is available both online and via e-mail. Each week, Neat New Stuff lists and annotates a number of Web sites that may be useful for librarians.

When browsing through Marylaine.com, note that each section of the site also links back to her resume, which is arranged by skill set rather than in the more traditional chronological format. Since she is selling her skills as an Internet trainer, speaker, and Webmaster, she describes her abilities in each of these areas and adds links to examples of her accomplishments. Although Marylaine.com provides a great deal of free content, all of it relates back to her skills as a speaker, writer, Webmaster, and trainer. Entrepreneurial librarians should take note of how she has integrated free content throughout her site that supports her reputation in these areas and encourages potential clients to take advantage of her services.

Before creating a page of your own, take a look at those created by other librarians to see what has been done and what can be done in the area of library-related Web design. Use lists such as *Library Juice's* Home Pages of the Week at http://www.libr.org/Juice/homepages. html to find Web sites run by individual librarians. Also watch librarians' signature files on e-mail discussion lists; many link to a personal home page.

Tools and Resources

New tools and WYSIWYG ("What You See Is What You Get") Web editors have made it less necessary for information professionals to become Web design experts before posting a decent-looking Web page. Such editors include Microsoft FrontPage ($149, http://www.microsoft.com/frontpage), Trellix Web (free if you use their hosting partners, $69 otherwise, http://www.trellix.com), Softquad's HoTMetaL ($129, http://www.hotmetalpro.com), and Macromedia Dreamweaver ($299, http://www.dreamweaver. com). Many of these products offer free 30-day trial versions so that you can experiment with their features before purchasing a copy. Beginning Web authors can also use products such as Microsoft Word to create a document and convert it to a Web page. The tools included in Word and other products that are not specifically designed to be Web editors are much more limited, however, and they produce HTML that is less standard and more troublesome for anyone needing to go into the code and modify it at a later date.

Even if you purchase one of these Web editors, a basic knowledge of HTML is useful. WYSIWYG editors have a way of forcing you to use their formats, and you sometimes need to manually correct their assumptions. You will also need to delve into the HTML code if you want to add more interactive or advanced features to your site, such as those utilizing Java, JavaScript, or CGI scripting. If you do not wish to invest in editor software, you can compose an HTML document in any text editor, such as Windows Notepad.

There are a plethora of resources available for librarians wishing to learn HTML. Especially if you work in a public library, you should be able to find a wide number of general guides on your own institution's shelves. Good titles include Elizabeth Castro's *HTML 4 For the World Wide Web* (Berkeley: Peachpit Press, 2000) and Peter Kent's more general *Poor Richard's Web Site: Geek-Free, Commonsense Advice on Building a Low-Cost Web Site* (Lakewood, CO: Top Floor Pub., 2000).

Other HTML guides can be found on the Web, including the Web Developer's Virtual Library at http://www.stars.com (which includes information on all aspects of site development in addition to basic HTML), the Bare Bones Guide to HTML at http://werbach.com/barebones, and NCSA's A Beginner's Guide to HTML at http://www.ncsa.uiuc.edu/General/Internet/WWW/HTMLPrimer.html. Librarians also may be interested in Eric Schnell's Writing for the Web: A Primer for Librarians at http://bones.med.ohio-state.edu/eric/papers/primer/webdocs.html. His is a more general guide to Web content creation, covering topics from accessibility issues to adding multimedia content to Web pages. One more general resource for librarian-created sites is Web Design for Librarians (http://scc01.rutgers.edu/SCCHome/policies/web.htm). Note, however, that these sites on Web design for librarians generally work from the assumption that you will be creating a Web page for your library rather than a page for professional purposes.

If you want to post graphics on your site (and you probably will), you should invest in a piece of graphics software such as Paint Shop Pro ($99, free 30-day trial from http://www.jasc.com). Such software enables you to draw and modify your own images, resize and retouch photos, and create animated graphics for your page. Web editors such as Microsoft FrontPage also come with a variety of freely distributable clip art, and there are a number of free clip art Web sites from which you can copy graphics. (See sidebar. Right-click an image on the Web and pick "save as" to copy to your own hard drive; be sure not to link directly to images on another person's Web server.) When locating images for your own Web site, respect others' copyrights. If images are not explicitly labeled as being freely available for distribution, they are most likely copyrighted, and you will need to get permission from their creator to use them.

Clip Art Sites

Library-Related

ALA Symbols (Olson's Library Clip Art)—http://www.libraryclipart.com/alasymbols.html

Books and Reading—http://webclipart.about.com/internet/webclipart/msub56.htm

Library Media and PR—http://www.ssdesign.com/librarypr/toolbox.html

General

Clip Art Searcher—http://www.webplaces.com/search/

Google Image Search—http://images.google.com

Icon Bazaar—http://www.iconbazaar.com

Whole Internet Clipart Guide—http://www.clipartguide.com

Here are some other useful design-related sites:

- ANYBrowser Web site viewer (http://www.anybrowser.com/siteviewer.html)—See how your site looks in multiple browsers and multiple versions.

- Atomz.com (http://www.atomz.com)—Add free search to your Web site.
- Bobby (http://www.cast.org/bobby)—Identify accessibility issues with your site.
- Doctor HTML (http://www2.imagiware.com/RxHTML)—Analyze problems with your site.
- Hexadecimal Colour Numbers (http://houseof3d.com/pete/applets/tools/colors/index.html)—Calculate the hexadecimal value of colors.
- HTML Tidy (http://www.w3.org/People/Raggett/tidy)—Clean up your HTML code.
- JavaScript Source (http://javascript.internet.com)—Free Java-Scripts and tutorials.
- Perl Archive (http://www.perlarchive.com/guide)—Free CGI and Perl scripts.
- Top Ten Mistakes in Web Design (http://www.useit.com/alertbox/9605.html)—From Web usability expert Jakob Nielsen.
- WDG HTML Validator (http://www.htmlhelp.com/tools/validator)—Validate your HTML.
- Writing for the Web (http://www.useit.com/papers/webwriting)—Summarizes research on how people read online and how authors should write for the medium.

These sites are just a few examples of the wide variety of online resources available to any Web author. Use them as a starting point to help make your site both usable and interesting.

Finding a Home for Your Site

After you have decided on the tools you will use to build your site and on its content, the next step is finding a space to house your creation. Many commercial ISPs include a set amount of server space with each personal account; check with your own provider to find out its policies. This may be the easiest and most cost-effective option for librarians who already have personal Internet accounts at home. In this case, your Web address will most likely be in the form: http://www.internetprovider.com/users/~yourname. Note that the "~" in an address generally denotes a personal site on a larger provider's Web presence, and that visitors will thus be able to identify your site as a personal page.

Some large ISPs may also provide built-in Web page creation tools for their customers, but keep in mind that using these tools can result in "cookie cutter" sites that all look very similar. Free Web hosting services such as Yahoo! GeoCities (http://www.geocities.com) and Lycos' Tripod (http://www.tripod.com) use "wizards" or "site builders" that also contribute to the cookie-cutter look. Such free services generally slow down the time it takes to access your Web site, due to the large load on their servers, and also subject your visitors to intrusive advertising. We suggest using these general free services only as a last resort. If your intended site has a social orientation, you may be able to house it on the Libr.org Web server (home of *Library Juice* and the Progressive Librarians Guild). See http://www.libr.org.

Students and faculty librarians are generally allotted space on the campus Web server, but may be constrained as to the opinions they can express and format they must use while using their school's resources. Many universities have posted specific guidelines as to what may and may not be included on pages hosted on their servers. These guidelines generally state that university Web pages may not contain advertising and that authors must post a disclaimer noting that views stated on the site are those of the author, among similar restrictions. (For an example of a typical set of Web publishing guidelines, see Bridgewater State College's instructions at http://www.bridgew.edu/website/webguide.htm.) Employers are unlikely to want to host a page with the main purpose, for example, of helping you find a new job.

Figure 6.2   Web Publishing Guidelines from Bridgewater State College, Mass.

Some ISPs and Web hosting services let you purchase your own domain, in the form: www.yoursite.com (or .org or .net), and will host your domain on their servers for an additional fee. Pricing varies depending on whether you also use the company for Internet access, whether you also want e-mail addresses @yourdomain, and the amount of space you require for your site. Budgetweb at http://budgetweb.com/budgetweb/index.html lists a large number of low-cost Web hosting services.

You can check the availability of your desired domain name at a number of online domain registration services; if a name has been taken, the service can also tell you who has registered it. The most well-known of these is Network Solutions, at http://www.netsol.com. Domain registration fees from Network Solutions are generally $35 (for a one-year registration). Before you register, however, you need to contract with a Web hosting service so that you can provide their hosting information to Network Solutions. Another option is to host your site at Network Solutions' own servers, for an

additional charge. Domain name registration services are also provided by several other companies, including Register.com
(http://www.register.com).

Weblogs

At first glance, a Weblog may appear to be quite similar to a personal Web site. Weblogs, however, differ in format, purpose, and
frequency from other Web pages. They allow their author to make
frequent (usually daily) updates in short posts, which can be brief
thoughts, journal entries, or links to other Web sites or articles.
These posts appear on the Weblog in reverse chronological order,
so visitors can rapidly browse new material by date. Although
Weblogs sometimes include the capability to allow multiple users
(or all site visitors) to post, many are limited solely to contributions
from the log's creator/owner.

The first Weblog is generally credited as being the first Web site,
Tim Berners-Lee's creation at CERN, the European Organization for
Nuclear Research, that provided links to every other new Web site as
it came online. "What's New" pages have persisted since that time,
but Weblogs have become more creative and more focused, usually
concentrating on one broadly defined topic and including links to
new and pertinent sites or articles and (often irreverent) comments
on the contents of those sites. For more information about the
Weblog phenomenon and links to lists of logs, see the Weblog FAQ at
http://www.robotwisdom.com/weblogs.

Librarian-Maintained Weblogs

LibLog
(http://www.redwoodcity.org/library/news/liblog/index.
html) from the staff of the Redwood City Public Library.

Weblog of current sites and stories dealing with technology and librarianship.

librarian.net (http://www.librarian.net) maintained by Jessamyn West. Librarian culture with a progressive focus.

Library_geek (http://www.freespeech.org/librarygeek) maintained by library school student TJ Sondermann. Collects and comments on a wide range of library-related stories.

Library News Daily (http://www.lights.com/scott/) maintained by Peter Scott. Somewhat more commercial effort linked from Libdex that includes daily links to library-related news articles.

Library Stuff (http://www.librarystuff.net) maintained by Stephen M. Cohen. Any and all library-related "stuff."

LISNews (http://www.lisnews.com) maintained by Blake Carver. Wide range of events and news—with a tangential library focus.

NewBreed Librarian (http://www.newbreedlibrarian.org) maintained by Juanita Benedicto and Colleen Bell. A combination e-zine and Weblog; the owners post daily library- and book-related news/links/comments.

The Virtual Acquisition Shelf & News Desk (http://resourceshelf.blogspot.com) maintained by librarian Gary Price. Resources and news for information professionals and researchers.

Chapter 3 discusses Weblogs in more detail as a good way to keep up with library-related news and issues. Librarian-created Weblogs

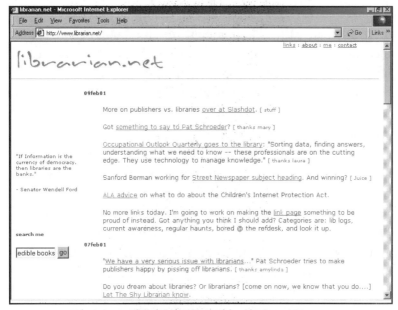

Figure 6.3   librarian.net Weblog, Maintained by Jessamyn West

provide a valuable filtering service for other librarians who appreciate the selection of links and views of the Weblog's creator.

Why Create Your Own Weblog?

Information professionals have a variety of reasons for creating
their own Weblogs. One of the first library-related Weblogs was
Jessamyn West's popular and radical creation, librarian.net
(http://www.librarian.net), which she has been running since the
spring of 1999. Her original goal in starting her Weblog was to create
an online library-related resource that would be both fun and interesting. As she says, "I wanted to amuse people and show them a different side of librarianship and poke fun at the ALA." Maintaining
the Weblog also helps her network with other librarians. She notes
that "keeping up on it—even some days when I am less-than-
inspired—also encourages me to keep up with the worlds of my colleagues, plus many of them write in with link suggestions."

Blake Carver's LISNews.com is an example of a Weblog that is more interactive than librarian.net. The site allows visitors to post their own comments on stories, and is constantly searching for new authors who will commit to adding story summaries or writing their own stories. Its interactivity makes it a good example for librarians who are interested in forming a community around their own Weblogs. (Read more about LISNews.com in Chapter 3.)

Creating a Weblog will not only provide you with your own impetus for keeping up with news, articles, and sites relating to the profession, but will also give you the opportunity to express your point of view on professional issues. Weblogs are interesting partially because of the commentary provided by their creators. Site visitors are likely to respond to your comments either via e-mail or online, creating a forum for professional dialogue.

Tools and Resources

The growing popularity of Weblogs has spawned a number of companies that provide free tools for their creation. Weblog companies include Blogger (http://www.blogger.com), Weblogs.Com (http://www.weblogs.com), Pitas.com (http://www.pitas.com), and GrokSoup (http://www.groksoup.com). Some allow you to host your Weblog on their servers, while others merely provide updating tools and require you to have your own Web server space in order to use their service. The latter may be more useful if you are adding a Weblog to your existing Web site. Services such as NewsBlogger also allow you to add and comment on news stories on your own site (http://newsblogger.com).

E-Mail Discussion Lists and Newsletters

The basics of participating in e-mail discussion groups were covered in Chapter 2. Although most of these groups are sponsored by associations or by universities, there is a growing trend of individual librarians starting their own discussions on topics that have not been covered by other, more "official," groups. Library-related discussion lists also often have moderators whose responsibility it is to keep the discussion moving smoothly and to deal with problems that may arise; the moderator may or may not be the same person who originally created the list.

E-mail newsletters differ from discussions only in that they serve as a broadcast list rather than as an interactive discussion. The only person who has the power to post a message to an e-mail newsletter is the list's owner, who in this way can use an e-mail list to distribute the electronic newsletter as a large message to all list members. The list then functions much like a subscription to a print newsletter—users subscribe and then receive a copy of each newsletter issue in their e-mailbox until they choose to unsubscribe from the publication. Some e-mail newsletters approach the formality of print serials, and, as electronic serials, they are also eligible for ISSNs. (Publishers of newsletters based in the U.S. can apply online for an ISSN at http://lcweb.loc.gov/issn/ISSN.html.)

Why Create a Discussion List or Newsletter?

Your own discussion list or newsletter can be a great way to form a professional network and to get your views on the profession out to a larger audience, and a wide range of topics are there for discussion. Those who have created such resources reap both personal and professional benefits. Librarian Rory Litwin, for example, publishes the e-mail newsletter *Library Juice* (http://libr.org/Juice), a weekly news digest focusing mainly on progressive and intellectual freedom issues. Since he began disseminating the newsletter in January 1998, it has grown to more than 1,500 subscribers. *Library Juice* is archived on the Web, so that back issues are also accessible to nonsubscribers. Although Litwin started *Library Juice* as a forum for items of personal and political interest after exhausting the patience of fellow students on a library school's discussion list, the professional possibilities have outgrown his original expectations. As he notes: "This investment of time and energy has paid off. *Library Juice* has become a great tool for professional networking, both for myself and my contributors. It is also good to know that I have a voice when I find that I have something to say to the library community (although having a voice can also be dangerous)" (Litwin para. 6).

Another example of a librarian-created e-mail newsletter is Lisjobs.com's *Info Career Trends*, a bi-monthly publication focusing on career development issues for information professionals (http://www.lisjobs.com/newsletter). This newsletter was created to fill a niche in the professional literature, which tends to focus more on libraries than on librarians. If you are considering creating your own newsletter, try to find a topic that receives insufficient attention in the existing literature. Refrain from duplicating others' efforts—your newsletter will find greater success if you carve out your own niche and define your own voice.

Reference librarian Melanie Duncan maintains the e-mail newsletter/e-zine and Web site *The Bookdragon Review* (http://www.bookdragonreview.com), which focuses on reviewing genre fiction and announcing forthcoming titles by popular genre authors. Her e-zine combines personal and professional interests; like most librarians, Duncan is herself an avid reader and has taken on reader's advisory duties within her own library. *The Bookdragon Review* allows her to provide better service to her patrons, as she explains, "Reader's advisory service is much easier when I'm exposed to a large number of titles and reviews. I may not get a chance to read a particular book, but if I trust the reviewer's judgment because I find our views on other books have meshed, then I won't hesitate to recommend it. ... The forthcoming titles list also helps me keep up with the library patrons who can't wait for the

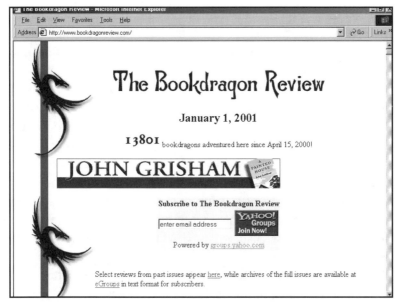

Figure 6.4   The Bookdragon Review, Maintained by Melanie C. Duncan

next John Grisham/Danielle Steel/Nora Roberts/etc." *The Book-dragon Review* is maintained at Yahoo! Groups, so the newsletter costs nothing but time.

If you do decide to create an electronic newsletter that includes reviews of books or online products, consider e-mailing publishers to request review copies or database trials. Be sure to give the publisher information on the number of subscribers your newsletter attracts and the niche audience it represents. And, as a bonus, you get to keep the books! Publishers appreciate the free publicity offered by your reviews, but be sure to request only titles that are relevant and suitable for review in your newsletter.

E-mail discussion lists provide another venue for information professionals to create useful online resources. Librarian Susan Scheiberg owns and maintains NEWLIB-L, an e-mail discussion list for newer librarians (http://www.lahacal.org/newlib). As a newer librarian herself, she started the list to provide a forum both for new librarians to share their questions and concerns with one another and for more experienced information professionals to mentor their newer colleagues. The list is maintained on servers at Scheiberg's former employer, the University of Southern California, using LISTPROC software.

NEWLIB-L has brought unexpected professional and personal benefits. Scheiberg notes: "First, faculty promotion at the University of Southern California is based, in part, on how you enhance the reputation of USC—that is, how much you are 'out there' spreading USC's name through your professional and scholarly work. Therefore, this discussion list was met with much praise, as USC's name is going out internationally daily. I got a good amount of credit for it in my annual review the year I started it, much to my surprise! Also, when NEWLIB-L gets press, it benefits my professional reviews." These professional benefits are more likely to accrue to academic librarians; electronic newsletters and mailing lists are akin to professional publication in that they promote the university where their creator is employed.

Creating an e-mail list also provides a built-in forum for networking and professional communication. Scheiberg continues: "It has also benefited me in that I think that NEWLIB-L has engendered a network of people, and I have met (virtually and in person) a number of very nice people ... who are working on great projects, and [this] may eventually lead to collaborations, ideas for publications, presentations, papers, or just lunch at a meeting! I have had a number of people come up to me to introduce themselves, and vice versa when I recognize their names. It's been a wonderful networking experience."

This view of the electronic mailing list or newsletter as a combination of a contribution to the profession and a venue for personal enrichment is echoed by other librarians who have chosen to donate their time and expertise as list creators and moderators. As Karen Begg Borei wrote in a 1999 article, "the professional contribution that the existence of such lists makes within librarianship is significant, as is the personal satisfaction for the list manager(s) in making that contribution. Without question or doubt, electronic mailing lists have significantly enriched the lives of library professionals" (697).

Melanie Duncan concurs, saying, "You should create an e-zine or newsletter because it will fulfill a creative need in you, not because you expect to make money."

Keep in mind, though, that the market for library-related e-mail lists is much more crowded than that for newsletters. Use the tools mentioned in Chapter 2 to find out what topics are covered by existing lists before starting your own.

Tools and Resources

Yahoo! Groups (formerly eGroups) at http://groups.yahoo. com, Topica at http://www.topica.com/create, and similar ad-supported products have made it easy for anyone to create an e-mail discussion list or newsletter. Such tools allow users to create both open and restricted lists (which are limited to invitees only). Creating a group at most of these sites just requires you to fill out a Web-based form, as shown in Figure 6.5, and later administration is nearly as simple. These sites also allow registered users to subscribe to lists and read archived messages and list descriptions online.

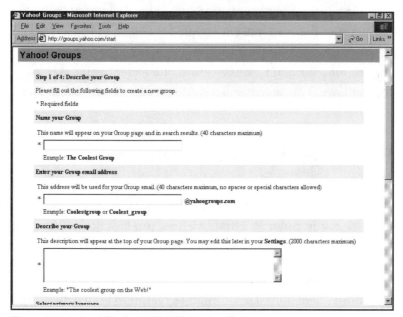

Figure 6.5   Yahoo! Groups E-Mail List Setup Screen

Librarians wishing to avoid using ad-sponsored or commercial sites, however, will need access both to mailing list software and an e-mail server to house the list. The software automates most list tasks, allowing users to subscribe and unsubscribe by sending special commands and broadcasting messages to all list subscribers. The cost of such software and server access exceeds the price range of most individual librarians, and is more appropriate for companies and larger institutions. Companies such as L-Soft (makers of the LISTSERV® e-mail list software), however, have begun expanding into the "personal" market with lower-priced outsourcing options for low-traffic lists. See http://www.lsoft.com/products/default.asp?item=ease_home.

Many academic institutions maintain their own e-mail server and may be willing to allow faculty space and access to create and manage their own lists. Keep in mind, however, that problems may arise should you decide at some point to leave the institution; you will probably need to find another person within the university to take over list management responsibilities. Whatever tools you use, be sure that you make it simple for people to subscribe and unsubscribe to your e-mail list or newsletter. Provide an online subscription form, if possible, and create a companion Web page that outlines the resource and provides instructions to subscribers.

Promoting Your Online Resource

Although you do not want to inundate other librarians with advertisements for your online creation, you will need to promote its presence in order to attract visitors or subscribers. Here are some nonintrusive promotional methods:

- Add a link to your Web site or other online resource to your e-mail signature. This is another reason to keep active on relevant discussion lists.

- Ask for others' contributions. If you have an e-mail newsletter or post librarian-written articles on your Web site, post a call for contributors on NMRTWriter and other discussion lists.

- Create reciprocal links. Have other librarians created related resources? E-mail them and ask if they would be interested in establishing a reciprocal link with your site.

- Contact your library school and see if they have a list of alumni-created sites to which you can add yours.

- Submit your Web site or Weblog to search engines. Get yourself listed in the major search engines and directories so that others can find you online. Use a META tag builder to add keywords to your site so it is more effectively indexed (http://vancouver-webpages.com/META/mk-metas.html). You may wish to use a service such as Submit It (http://www.submit-it.com) to add your page to many search engines at once.

- Submit your e-mail newsletter to directories such as Newsletter Access (http://www.newsletteraccess.com) and Electronic Journal Miner (http://ejournal.coalliance.org/suggest.cfm).

- Add your list or newsletter to Library-Oriented Lists and Electronic Serials (http://www.wrlc.org/liblists).

- See if your newsletter can be indexed by sites such as Index Morganagus (http://sunsite.berkeley.edu/~emorgan/morganagus)

- Announce your site in newsgroups such as comp.info.www.announce.

- Get your site listed on library portals such as the Internet Library for Librarians (http://www.itcompany.com/inforetriever).

- Write articles and books. Most journals and publishers include brief biographical information in which you can post your Web site or list information.

- Speak at conferences. Mention your online resource in your speech, include it on handouts, and make sure it is listed in conference materials.

Get yourself out there and known!

Whatever method you choose for establishing your own online presence, your Web site, Weblog, discussion list, or e-mail newsletter will serve as an important professional development tool and will increase your recognition within the profession as a whole. If you have something you wish to say to the profession, the Internet is your forum—all it takes is time and dedication.

Works Cited

Borei, Karen Begg. "The Rewards of Managing an Electronic Mailing List." *Library Trends*, 47.4 (1999): 686–698.

Litwin, Rory. "Creating Library Juice." *Info Career Trends*, Nov. 1, 2000. Dec. 29, 2000 (http://www.lisjobs.com/newsletter/archives/nov00rlitwin.htm).

Chapter 7

Professional Literature: Reading and Contributing Online

Beyond posting your ideas and articles online, you may also wish to use the Internet to help you contribute to the professional literature. Publishing opportunities abound, both at professional journals and library trade publishing houses, and at more general magazines and publishers that publish library-related material. Those interested in contributing to librarianship through publication will find a variety of applicable online resources, from author guidelines to research tools. The Internet exposes information professionals to a wider variety of publishing opportunities and publications than was previously available. Librarians are no longer limited to submitting their work to familiar journals received by their institutions; they can familiarize themselves with many additional journals' contents and guidelines online. Many library-related publishing houses also maintain an online presence, and savvy librarians can locate a large variety of Internet resources to help them research their chosen topic. Information professionals who are serious about publishing their work cannot afford to ignore the opportunity that the Internet affords.

Writing for publication also helps librarians hone their writing skills in general, which is helpful in many aspects of a career. An information professional who has submitted a successful book proposal, for example, will be less likely to be stymied by the need to complete a detailed grant application. One who has written a research article will more easily be able to pen a press release or write a compelling job description to advertise an open position.

Peer Review

Academic librarians, especially those at larger or more research-oriented institutions, are often required to publish in peer-reviewed journals in order to be considered for tenure and/or promotion. Academic libraries that do not specifically require peer-reviewed publication of their faculty librarians can be favorably impressed by refereed publication as a sign that your work is more academic or research-oriented in nature. The Internet can serve as a useful tool for locating such refereed outlets and is expanding information professionals' options with access to electronic-only journals and online guidelines for both print and Web-based publications. Those interested in scholarly publication have a variety of electronic peer-reviewed journals to choose from, as the backlash against outrageous journal prices in academic libraries has spawned a movement toward lower-cost publishing on the Web.

High subscription prices notwithstanding, reviewers on editorial boards of peer-reviewed journals are almost never compensated monetarily for their work. Writers for such journals should also note that the assistance of peer-reviewed publication toward achieving tenure or promotion is generally seen as compensation in itself, so if you are writing primarily as a means of supplementing a librarian's salary, you may wish to choose a different path.

When submitting your work to an academic journal, be sure that the section you choose is indeed peer-reviewed; some publications combine refereed with nonrefereed sections in the same journal. Also note that the presence of an editorial board often, but not always, indicates that a journal is peer-reviewed. Look for a more specific statement of its status under the "About" or "Editorial" section of a Web site.

Appendix B lists Web addresses for a large number of library-related publishing outlets, and notes journals that identify themselves as refereed. Among the resources that provide more information about the peer-review process in scholarly publishing is a book from the American Society for Information Science and Technology (ASIST) by Ann C. Weller, *Editorial Peer Review* (Information Today, Inc., 2001).

The information presented in this chapter will assist publication-minded information professionals in locating appropriate outlets for their work, navigating the Web sites of publishers and journals, formatting and submitting queries, and researching their chosen topic online. As a first step, especially if you are fairly new to the library publishing process, you should consider joining the NMRTWriter e-mail discussion list. (See Chapter 2 for more on participating in e-mail discussion lists.) Sponsored by ALA's New Members Round Table, NMRTWriter allows librarians to support one another in the process of writing and publishing everything from articles to books to grant proposals. It often includes calls for contributors from editors of library-related journals as well as advice on the publishing process. To subscribe to NMRTWriter, send an e-mail message to listproc@ala.org. In the body of your message, type "subscribe NMRTWriter." View a fuller list description and archives at http://lp-web.ala.org:8000/guest/listutil/NMRTWRITER. (You will need to register with the site to search the list's archives or to subscribe/unsubscribe online.)

All information professionals also need to be aware of the usefulness of the Internet in helping them keep up with their professional reading. While current awareness services such as online tables of contents and newsletters are described in Chapter 3, here we discuss how to locate and make use of the Web sites of journals in your field of interest. Depending on the policies of the individual journal, librarians are often able to read online either the full text of articles or abstracts that will let you know what types of material it publishes. If an abstracted article seems compelling, you can then locate the article itself in a full-text database or request it through interlibrary loan. As you read the sections on locating publishing opportunities online, also keep in mind that you can use material from the journals you locate to keep up with your professional reading and supplement the professional print journals available through your institution.

Locating Publishing Opportunities

Finding the right place to submit your idea can be daunting. Many journals and publishers, however, provide online guidelines to help you ascertain whether they will be appropriate outlets for your work. Information on the Web can save a great deal of time and effort as you begin to locate such outlets, and using the Internet to peruse both the contents of online journals and the catalogs of relevant publishers can also help give you ideas for additional topics and show you what the current "hot" issues are.

Academic librarians may also want to investigate Alice Bahr's e-book *InPrint: Publishing Opportunities for College Librarians* (Chicago: ACRL, 2001). This publication is available at http://acrl.telusys.net/epubs/inprint.html, and visitors can purchase two years of access to the *InPrint* database of publishing outlets for $25 (ACRL members) or $35 (nonmembers). Each record includes information on the publication's needs,

Figure 7.1   *InPrint: Publishing Opportunities for College Librarians* E-Book

contact information, average response time, brief article guidelines and length, as well as a link to the publication's Web site if available—and new information will continually be added to keep the e-book current.

Library Journals

If you are just starting your library publishing career, there are a variety of serials for information professionals that are welcoming to new writers. State library journals, for example, are often actively seeking contributions from local information specialists (although you should note that there is generally no monetary compensation involved in writing for such publications and that their audience will of necessity be somewhat self-limiting). State journals or newsletters are usually published by your state library or library association. Check their respective Web sites for a "Publications" link. (A list of state library Web sites is provided by the Library of Congress at http://lcweb.loc.gov/global/library/statelib.html, and Syracuse's list

of links to state associations is accessible at http://web.syr.edu/
~jryan/infopro/sassoc.html. See also Appendix A for a list of Web
addresses for all types of library associations.)

If you are seeking a broader audience for your work, or if you
have a more specialized topic, a huge variety of library-related
journals with a national or international scope is published both
on- and offline. (See Appendix B for brief descriptions and Web
addresses of many of these journals.) Most such journals have a
Web presence where they provide either the full text of or selected
content from the print edition, subscription and editorial information, and guidelines for contributors. Begin your search for the
Web sites of relevant periodicals with online lists such as the
University of Michigan's Finding Professional Literature on the Net
at http://www.lib.umich.edu/libhome/ILSL.lib/Literature.html,
and then move on to individual larger library publishers, such as
ALA, that keep lists of links to the Web presence of each of their
journals online.

While you are browsing publishers' sites, check the ALA
Periodicals list at http://www.ala.org/library/alaperiodicals.html,
Emerald's list of its library and information services-related journals at http://www.emeraldinsight.com/librarylink/journals.htm,
and BUBL's searchable list of library and information science journals at http://bubl.ac.uk/journals/lis. The Librarian's Online
Warehouse also has an online alphabetical list of relevant publications at http://www.libsonline.com/publish.asp, but oddly (and
unfortunately) lists only postal addresses for most publications
and omits Web site links.

If author guidelines are available on a journal's Web site, study
them carefully (look for a link to "Instructions to Authors," "Writers
Guidelines," "Notes to Contributors," or similar verbiage). These
generally describe the scope of the publication, the types of articles the editors are interested in receiving, manuscript length, the
format in which they wish to receive submissions, and contact

information for the appropriate editors of different sections of the journal. Following such guidelines increases the chances of your material being accepted for publication.

Some journals also allow you to request a sample issue from their Web site. Especially if articles are not available online, reading a sample copy can be a helpful way to find out whether your work will be appropriate for a specific publication. The Haworth Press is one example of a publisher that will provide journal samples by mail. Visit their Web site at http://www.haworthpressinc. com and click "Journal Sample" at the top of the screen for information on requesting sample copies. You can then search for individual journal titles, or click on the browse button and choose Library and Information Science from the list of subjects. Haworth publishes a variety of library-related journals.

If no sample copies are available from the journal publisher, be sure at least to read any articles that are freely accessible online. A common complaint of editors is that they receive material that is

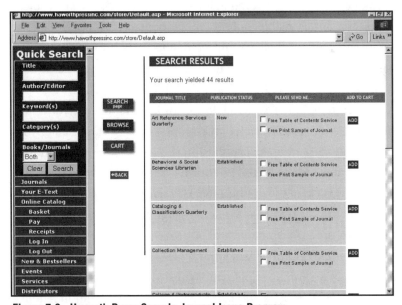

Figure 7.2   Haworth Press Sample Journal Issue Program

inappropriate for their publication. Familiarizing yourself with the type of articles a journal publishes will help you tailor your work to their expectations.

Book Publishers

Most library trade publishers (and those publishing books of interest to information professionals) maintain a strong Web presence. On publishers' sites you will often find information on submitting proposals, editors' specialties, catalogs of recent publications, and descriptions of the types of material the company is interested in publishing. A list of publishers and their Web sites can be found in Appendix B. LibraryHQ's list of library and information science publishers, online at http://www.LibraryHQ.com/publishers.html, is also a good starting point for finding presses that specialize in information science topics.

When submitting a book proposal or query to a publishing company, be sure to follow the guidelines stated on its Web page. If guidelines are not available online, either contact the publisher and request a copy of their current guidelines or limit yourself to first sending a brief query letter rather than an entire proposal. Even if you have already written a proposal for one publisher, resist the temptation to simply re-send it to a second library press in the unfortunate event that it is rejected by your first choice. Always tailor your presentation to the specific publishing house, and be sure to address it to the appropriate editor. Editors' names are usually listed online, and if not, pick up the phone and verify names and spelling.

If you are seeking brand-name recognition for your book idea, look into the publishing arm of your national library association. The American Library Association's ALA Editions (http://www.ala.org/editions), for example, publishes around thirty-five manuscripts a year, most written by library and information science practitioners. ALA markets its books through exhibits and sales at

Figure 7.3   ALA Editions Writers Only Section

ALA conferences, direct mail flyers and catalogs to association members, and press releases and review copies.

The "Writers Only" section of the ALA Editions Web site, at http://www.ala.org/editions/writers.html, describes the publishing process from the proposal stage through marketing of the finished product. ALA Editions' proposal guidelines are fairly typical of library publishers; they request that prospective authors send a description of their project, a detailed outline, the anticipated market for the work, a list of competing works, author information, anticipated date of completion, form of submission, special considerations, and representative samples of the work (if applicable). Any library publisher will need to look at a proposal prior to approving your project so they can evaluate whether your book idea is appropriate for their press.

Compare ALA's guidelines to those from other library and information science publishers such as The Haworth Press. Haworth's book proposal guidelines can be viewed online at http://www. haworthpressinc.com/AuthorInfo/bookpropguide.htm. Unlike ALA, The Haworth Press requires potential authors to submit one to three sample chapters with their proposal, although the rest of its guidelines are similar to ALA's. These variations show the importance of explicitly following the guidelines provided—a publisher such as Haworth, which requests sample chapters, will probably not be satisfied with the same two or three page proposal you might send to ALA.

A publishing house such as Libraries Unlimited (LU), which focuses largely on reference materials, manuals, and textbooks, asks potential authors to describe their methodology and presentation as part of any proposal. (See LU's guidelines at http://www.lu.com/ lu/manu.html.) Academic publishers may also require you to describe your research methodology, and will not be an appropriate outlet for more practical titles or for "how-to" manuals. You can use online guidelines in conjunction with publishers' online catalogs and descriptions of their focus to help you determine whether a house will be an appropriate outlet for your work. If a publisher fails to list guidelines online, either send just a query letter or mail or e-mail a polite note requesting that guidelines be sent to you.

Electronic Journals

With the explosive growth of the World Wide Web, electronic journals have become major publication outlets in their own right, rather than existing as a mere afterthought to print publications. The several types of online journals include those that exist independently of any printed serial, those that duplicate or provide selected content from a printed journal, and those that expand on what is available in print with online-only articles. Electronic journals are published either on their own Web sites or as e-mail newsletters that are delivered directly to subscribers' inboxes on a regular basis. Academic librarians in particular should be aware that some institutions and tenure committees do not regard electronic-only publication as highly as more traditional print publication.

To locate electronic journals in your field of interest, start with *Information Research*'s subject guide to digital resources at http://www.shef.ac.uk/~is/publications/infres/subguide.html. The site's international guide includes only journals that make part or all of their content freely available online, so note that some subscription publications will not be listed. While reading journals online for your own edification, also keep an eye out for those that are actively soliciting content.

Although many electronic journals tend to focus on digital libraries and new media issues, enterprising information professionals can find online outlets for nearly any article topic. A typical example of a professional electronic journal is *LIBRES*, a semi-annual, scholarly electronic publication focused on publishing new research in the field of library and information science. The journal is accessible on the Web at http://aztec.lib.utk.edu/libres, where site visitors can also subscribe to receive a table of contents via e-mail each time a new issue is published. *LIBRES* includes both refereed and nonrefereed sections, and seeks both peer-reviewed scholarly articles and essays or opinion pieces. As with many electronic journals, the full text of each issue is freely available online. E-mail addresses of authors are listed online so that readers can contact them with questions or comments about their research. Other information on the *LIBRES* Web site includes contributor guidelines, information about the editorial board, and journal archives.

Since electronic journals can be produced and distributed much more cheaply than can print serials, you also may be able to find titles online that focus on narrower topics or more specific disciplines. This expands the number of potential outlets for your work. A second advantage of electronic journals includes the speed of publication; often there will be less of a lag time between submission of an article and its publication than in more traditional print publications.

Related Magazines

Librarians can often find publishing opportunities in nonlibrary journals that occasionally publish articles related to libraries, research, or other relevant topics. If your subject is relevant to librarians, yet of interest to a broader audience, consider submitting it to a publication outside the library field. Information professionals who publish library-related work in the popular press can help raise the image of the profession and explain its philosophy to a much larger group of readers. Writing for general magazines can often also be more lucrative, as library trade publications are not generally known for their high pay rates. Yet keep in mind that writing for more "popular" journals, although perhaps more immediately profitable, may seem less prestigious in the eyes of your colleagues—or of a tenure committee.

The information revolution means that, lately, popular magazines have been publishing more library and information-related articles than ever before. Recent articles have appeared in mainstream publications from *U.S. News & World Report* to *The New Yorker*. As a beginning information professional-turned-author, you are not likely to publish your first popular article in a magazine with as wide a reach as these national magazines. Think of local opportunities. Could your local paper use an Internet columnist to review Web sites? Does it need book reviewers? What about a bi-weekly feature about programs and services available at the public library where you work? While publishing in such venues may not help an academic librarian achieve tenure, writing for a more general audience can help raise the profile of the profession. It can also give you writing practice and credits that you can then use to move on to writing for either general publications with a higher circulation or for library trade publications.

If publishing in a peer-reviewed forum is important to your career, or if you have a more academic topic in mind, you can also turn outside the field of library journals to other refereed outlets. Opening yourself up to these nonlibrary publications gives you a plethora of outlets where you can submit your research. The electronic journal *First Monday* (http://www.firstmonday.dk), for example, is a peer-reviewed, often-cited Internet journal that has published several articles on topics such as librarianship, digital libraries, and Internet research.

Search for both library- and nonlibrary-related magazines, journals, and newsletters at Publist.com (http://www.publist.com). Publist.com lists publisher information for and links to the Web sites of more than 150,000 print and electronic serials. The site is searchable by title, publisher, subject, and descriptive keyword.

Reviewing Opportunities

Writing reviews of books, software, videos, or Web sites can be a useful way of easing into the publishing process while also having the opportunity to contribute to the profession. Since the collection development process is such an integral part of librarianship, reviews provide the tools information specialists need for selecting materials. A variety of on- and offline publications are actively searching for reviewers and/or provide reviewer guidelines online. Note that reviewers are not usually compensated for their work, but they nearly always get to keep a copy of the book or product reviewed.

When contemplating becoming a reviewer, begin by checking the Web sites of publications that you use in the collection development process for guidelines and application forms. Usually the best qualification for a reviewer is serving as a practitioner in the field. The first question on the reviewer guideline Web site for prospective *VOYA* (*Voice Of Youth Advocates*) book reviewers, for example, is: "Are you a librarian, library or teacher educator,

English teacher, or other youth-serving professional?" (Access their guidelines at http://www.voya.com/voyarevwr.html.) Some previous familiarity with the genre being reviewed is also helpful.

The format and length of reviews vary greatly depending on the publication. *Library Journal*, for example, publishes short reviews (around 150 words), while outlets such as *Book Magazine* often include much longer review articles, running to a full printed page or more. The word count feature in your word processor is useful when writing to strict limits.

Aspiring reviewers should also examine some of the online information available on improving one's reviewing skills. Start with veteran book reviewer and librarian GraceAnne DeCandido's brief introduction to "How to Write a Decent Book Review," available on her Web site at http://www.well.com/user/ladyhawk/bookrevs.html.

Calls for Papers

Also keep your eye out for "calls for papers" through which conference organizers solicit program presenters. Often such calls for papers are disseminated on e-mail discussion lists or posted on organizational and/or conference Web sites. (See Chapter 5 for an example of one of these posts as well as discussion on how to locate conference information online.)

Presenting a paper at a local, national, or international conference is a great way of getting your ideas in front of a broader audience and getting immediate feedback from your peers. Conference proceedings are sometimes later compiled and published as books or posted online, or your paper can later be turned into a professional article on the same topic. When perusing the Web site of a conference you are interested in attending, look for a link to a "call for papers" or for proposals. Keep in mind, however, that conferences start looking for presenters well in advance of the conference date so they can plan for needed space and advertise the programs to be made available.

Query Submission

Carefully peruse the Web site of the magazine, journal, or publishing house you are considering for your article or manuscript. While some will accept queries via e-mail, many prefer the more traditional use of regular mail for both queries and manuscript submissions. The publisher's guidelines usually spell out the way and format in which they prefer to receive queries from aspiring authors. Although some journals may accept unsolicited completed manuscripts, most prefer first to receive a query outlining the substance of a proposed article. Publishing houses always require you to first submit a query or proposal.

Successful Manuscript Queries

The following letter is an example of a successful query—one that resulted in the eventual publication of the book you are now holding. Although the query itself was not submitted online, we used the Internet to research potential publishers and to locate contact information. Whether you submit your query online or by postal mail, include the same types of information and hold yourself to the same level of formality. If submitting by postal mail, make your single spaced query less than two typewritten pages; if submitting by e-mail, try to make it a bit shorter than that for easy on-screen reading.

April 28, 2000

Mr. John Bryans
Editor-in-Chief
Information Today Books
143 Old Marlton Pike
Medford, New Jersey 08055-8750

Dear Mr. Bryans:

An August 1999 *American Libraries* survey found
that 58% of respondents wanted the journal to include
more coverage of "professional development" issues.
Clearly, there is a desire among information specialists
to develop themselves further on their chosen career
path and become more involved with the profession,
as well as a wish for more guidance and advice along
the way.

This need for professional development information
can in large part be met online. A huge variety of
career-related resources awaits the Internet-savvy
librarian, from library-related e-mail discussion lists
and job ads to organizational information and publishers' guidelines. An information specialist with an
established online presence is well on the way to
forming a network of associates that will be helpful in
all stages of a career.

Unfortunately, while librarians spend considerable
time marketing the Internet to others and honing their
online research skills, they tend to neglect the Internet
as a resource for their own career development. Many
librarians are unaware of either the wide range of professional development resources available online or

the professional advantages inherent in making them-selves known to the Internet audience.

To fill this need, we propose a book entitled: *Professional Development Online: A Handbook for Information Professionals.* This title will meet the needs of all types of librarians and information spe-cialists, from the new graduate seeking his first posi-tion to the veteran librarian interested in advancing her career through publication or through participation in library and information science organizations.

More than just an annotated list of relevant Internet resources, *Professional Development Online* will dis-cuss ways to integrate the Internet into all aspects of a career in the information field, including:

- Networking via e-mail discussion lists and per-sonal home pages
- Composing and sending an electronic resume
- Choosing the most appropriate online job sites
- Identifying and communicating with library organizations
- Finding publication opportunities and writer's guidelines
- Staying current with content-awareness resources
- Locating opportunities for continuing education and professional training

The book will take information professionals step-by-step through the ways in which the Internet can assist in all stages of their career. It will address online career development as a whole, stressing that the establishment of an online presence and network of professional contacts is as essential—if not more so—online as it was in the pre-Internet environment.

Our experience as practicing librarians who have written on career issues in the library/information field gives us insight into the need for librarians to look online for professional development resources. We each host long-running, heavily trafficked library employment Web sites, which can be found at http://webhost.bridgew.edu/snesbeitt/libraryjobs.htm and at http://www.lisjobs.com. Our sites will be used to market the book to a self-selected audience of job-seeking librarians.

Information Today is a publisher known in the information marketplace for producing timely, practical books on Internet-related topics for librarians and other information professionals. We believe that our proposal would fit well with your current publishing program.

Please find several clips and an SASE enclosed for your convenience. If you are interested in this project, we will be delighted to send a more detailed proposal or discuss it with you further. Thank you for your consideration, and we look forward to hearing from you soon.

Sincerely,
Sarah Nesbeitt
Rachel Singer Gordon

Note that the above query letter lists: the need for the title, how the title will meet this need, the contents of the proposed book, the authors' qualifications to write it, and why the project is appropriate for this particular publisher. Always include this basic information in any query. If submitting your query by postal mail, include a

self-addressed stamped envelope for the publisher's convenience, as well as several examples of your previous
work. If submitting by e-mail, include links to online
examples of your work, if available, and offer to send
clips by postal mail, if not.

When preparing an article query or submission, be sure to read back issues of the journals you are interested in. Familiarizing yourself with their format and focus allows you to target your query directly to a specific publication. Consider submitting your idea to journals you regularly read or that your institution receives, since you will already be aware of their usual content and focus. Do not limit yourself merely to these publications, however, as the sheer variety of library-related periodicals ensures that few institutions subscribe to even the majority of library-related journals available.

Following Guidelines

Once you are familiar with the publication's features and style, check its site for submission guidelines and other information:

- Author guidelines. Format and submit your query exactly as laid out on the site, if guidelines are available. Do not submit your query through e-mail unless the guidelines specifically request that you do so.

- Catalog of books or tables of contents from previous journal issues. See if the press or journal has previously published items on related topics.

- Editor and contact information. Spell names properly, and be sure to send your idea to the appropriate editor.

Use common sense to get your idea in front of the appropriate editor in an appropriate format. Adherence to guidelines increases the chances that your idea will be accepted. There is often a link directly from the main page to these guidelines, or check under the "About" link on some sites.

If editors and/or e-mail addresses are not listed online, use the old-fashioned method of phoning the magazine or publisher to find the appropriate editor. Some publications do not list e-mail addresses for editors precisely because they prefer not to be contacted in that manner. Contact information in hand, you can then submit your query to the editor of the section you are interested in writing for, or contact the publisher to request guidelines.

Publishers may also request that you include in either your query or your book proposal information on books that will compete with or complement your work. Such information is often easily located online. Check large online library catalogs and request related titles through interlibrary loan, and use huge online bookstore databases such as Amazon.com (http://www.amazon.com) to identify relevant titles.

E-Mailed Queries

Publications that list e-mail addresses of editors are often more open to being queried online, and some editors may even prefer to receive queries and/or submissions via e-mail. Microforms coordinator Shelly Burns notes that "editors seem to appreciate the efficiency (and easy editability) of e-mail attachment submissions." Submitting your article or other project via e-mail saves the publisher the time of keying your text into the computer, and cuts down on errors that can creep in during that process.

E-mail can also speed up the process of communication. Shelly Burns continues describing her first foray into professional publishing: "I heard of the journal from the NMRT-Writers Listserv [sic] and went to the Web site for more information. I found that e-mailing the editor was comfortable to do. I heard back from him within a couple days and I submitted my article to him online." One caveat: Although many publishers will respond more promptly via e-mail, some will not. Do not expect an immediate response, and never badger the editor for an answer. If you have not received a response after four weeks, send a polite note to verify the receipt of your initial query.

When querying an editor by e-mail, keep in mind the online etiquette tips discussed in Chapter 2. Although e-mail may appear to be more informal, you are engaging in professional communication and should treat your correspondence as formally as if you had typed, printed out, and mailed a letter. Also note that text formatting such as bullets and italics will most likely be lost, and format your submission to look professional even if it is received as plain text. To help editors get the gist of your e-mailed query as quickly as possible, be sure to follow these tips:

- Use a descriptive subject line. Make it clear that this is a query and try to catch the editor's attention by succinctly stating your proposed topic.

- Be liberal with white space. It is no easier for an editor than for anyone else to read long chunks of text on-screen. Use asterisks or dashes as bullet points when making a list.

- Avoid "cute" backgrounds or images. Again, you need to be professional.

- Avoid sending attachments (unless specifically invited or instructed to do so). If instructed to send an attachment, be sure to send it in the format requested.

- Use spell check.

- Give the editor several ways to contact you. Include a phone number, e-mail address, and postal address.

Check your e-mail frequently, and if an editor does respond, get back to him or her promptly. One advantage to the online medium is that many journal editors—especially those responsible for electronic journals or who serve as editor on a part-time or volunteer basis—work flexible hours, so you may receive an e-mailed response more quickly and may hear from them on evenings and weekends. Try not to depend solely on your e-mail address at work for this reason, or find out if you are able to check your work e-mail from other locations (at home, on vacation).

Some journals now even allow prospective authors to submit queries online. If a journal includes an online query form on its Web site, consider using the form rather than e-mailing a query letter. This will ensure that you provide all required information in your query. For an example of an online query form, see *Computers in Libraries*' at http://www.infotoday.com/cilmag/query.htm.

Researching Your Topic Online

Enough has been written on the finer points of doing online research that we merely mention here a couple of the major ways to use the Internet to research article topics by doing research in online journals and databases and collecting feedback from fellow librarians. Use online periodical databases, search engines, Web sites, and interaction with your peers to help research related material and find ideas for your own writing.

Librarians involved in lengthy research projects may also wish to register their research in Emerald's Internet Research Register so that others can see what they are working on and find contact information if they wish to contribute or collaborate (http://www.literaticlub.co.uk/research/registers.html#lm). The register is searchable, so you can use it to find out if others are investigating similar topics and to see what types of projects particular financial bodies are funding.

Journal Research

Online research is essential to any foray into the world of library publishing. As one academic instructional librarian states, "I wouldn't even contemplate writing a paper unless I did a full search in *Library Lit* and the Web first. We used to search just the literature but now so many of us have published papers on the Web, and so many conference papers are there, that the Web is essential when beginning research." When conducting research on your article or book topic, be sure to search both the open Web and the library literature—and note that there are useful ways of searching the "official" library literature online.

Free Web-based periodical indexes such as EBSCO's Library Reference Center (LRC) at http://www.epnet.com/lrc.html, which indexes and abstracts over thirty of the most popular library trade journals, can let you see which journals have published articles on related topics. (LRC's complete list of journals indexed can be viewed once you click to login.) Journals that have previously printed related articles may be more open to your idea, and seeing the format and length of previous articles can also help you tailor your presentation to that publication. You can also use LRC and other indexes to note where there may be gaps in the professional literature.

While researching your topic, also check Eric Morgan's full-text Index Morganagus (IM) at http://sunsite.berkeley.edu/~emorgan/morganagus for similar articles in "library-related electronic serials." In addition, IM provides an alphabetical list of indexed titles with links to the Web sites, which you can use in your search for an appropriate outlet for your work. Note that IM provides tips for searching right on its main page, and keep specific search instructions in mind while using these databases. These indexes will be

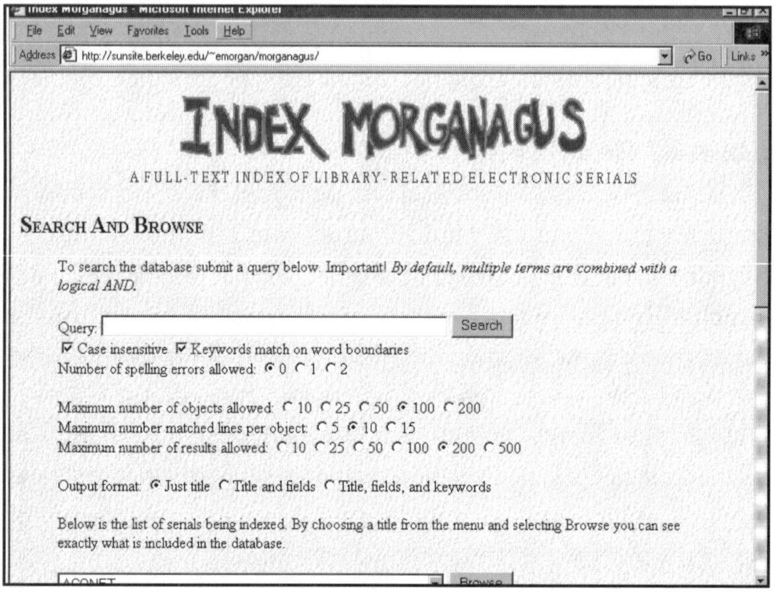

Figure 7.4   Index Morganagus: Library-Related Electronic Serials Full-Text Index

useful as you are researching your topic, and you can also use them to see if someone has already published an article exactly duplicating your idea.

Another site that is helpful in doing article or book research is The Researching Librarian, at http://www2.msstate.edu/~kerjsmit/trl. If your library has access to *Library Literature and Information Science* online through OCLC's FirstSearch, this can also be a good place to begin your research and to see what else has been published on your topic. Lastly, check Documents in Information Science, at http://dois.mimas.ac.uk, which is a database of articles and conference proceedings in the area of information science. Many are full text, but some include only abstracts.

Working information professionals have a built-in advantage over most aspiring authors in that their places of employment generally provide electronic access to subscription periodical databases. If you are using full-text online databases such as those from EBSCO or Gale's InfoTrac to research your topic at work, how-ever, remember that many institutions have policies prohibiting personal use of the Internet and related electronic resources dur-ing working hours. You may be required to conduct your research with these databases on your break time or during your lunch hour, or by accessing them from home. Academic librarians may be more fortunate in this respect, as the requirement to publish is often a requirement for tenure and such research is seen as a legit-imate, work-related, professional development activity.

Information professionals who are between positions or other-wise lack access to pertinent databases can research more general topics online through sites such as MagPortal.com (http://www.magportal.com) and LookSmart's FindArticles.com (http://www.findarticles.com/PI/index.jhtml), which each index a variety of full-text magazine articles. Also check to see what databases may be available from your local public library.

Collecting Feedback

The online medium is a wonderful way to gain input from fellow information professionals. E-mail discussion lists such as NMRTWriter encourage members to talk about their article ideas, and you may also find a receptive audience on lists or forums that are focused on the discussion of issues related to your topic. (For information on locating discussion lists and forums in your area(s) of interest, see Chapter 2.) Use online networking to find out if there may be an audience for your topic, to elicit suggestions on material that could be included, or to request assistance in track-ing down facts or statistics. As with any post, however, be sure to keep your comments succinct, professional, and on topic. Your list membership gives you a built-in network of both direct and indi-rect contacts, as members may also forward your request to other lists they belong to or to their coworkers or colleagues.

Past NMRT president Priscilla Shontz explains the impact of e-mail on the writing process: "When writing my book, I relied extensively on discussion lists and e-mail messages to and from colleagues/contacts/friends. Since the book was intended to be a compilation of advice gathered from professionals in various type of LIS careers, I e-mailed lists and just about every contact I knew. I encouraged those contacts to pass the message on to others, which some of them did. It was great to get responses from people I've never met! I could never have written this book without e-mail collaboration. I did interview some people in person, and I did get some information from books, articles, and presentations, but e-mail was a huge, huge part of the information gathering process."

If you are interested in collecting more formal input, consider creating an online survey and compiling the responses for use in your work. Librarians are often willing to contribute their opinions in this way, and the Internet provides you the means to reach a large number of potential respondents with minimum effort. You can direct respondents to a survey posted on your Web site as an interactive form, or send them questions as text within an e-mail message. Survey results or quotes from the participants can then easily be copied and pasted from your e-mail software into other applications such as your word processor. E-mail can also be useful in conducting interviews with prominent people in the field, who might be too busy to talk to you by phone but will appreciate the convenience of being able to answer questions via e-mail at their leisure.

Information professionals conducting a large survey or poll (or those who wish to post a survey on the Web but who lack Web design experience), may wish to make use of free online tools such as Zoomerang (http://www.zoomerang.com). Zoomerang offers the advantages of tabulating results for you and giving you graphical charts to use.

Additional Online Advantages

Several additional advantages accrue to librarians who are proactive about using the Internet to help their publishing prospects.

Locating Grants and Awards

Most grants and awards from ALA and related organizations apply to libraries and individuals who wish to improve (or have improved) some aspect of service in their institution. A variety of personal grant offerings and awards, however, are relevant to information professionals interested in the publishing process or who have made an outstanding contribution to the profession by publishing innovative research or a thought-provoking article. The following list mentions only a few such opportunities. Information professionals interested in nominating themselves or others for such awards or grants should, however, start their online search for applicable opportunities with ALA's Grants and Awards Index at http://www.ala.org/work/awards/grtscidx.html. Applicable grants and awards include:

- WNBA—Ann Heidbreder Eastman Grant. For librarians interested in taking a course or institute devoted to the study of publishing as a profession; it yearly awards $500-$1,000. http://www.ala.org/work/pubs/eastman.html

- Best of LRTS Award. This award goes to the author of the best paper published each year in Library Resources and Technical Services. (See Appendix B for journal Web site information.) http://www.ala.org/alcts/awards/bestoflrts.html

- Frederick G. Kilgour Award for Research in Library and Information Technology. Winners receive $2,000 and an expense-paid trip to the annual ALA conference for

research relevant to the development of information technologies. http://www.lita.org/a&s/awards.htm#kilgour

- Highsmith Library Literature Award. This award consists of
  $500 and a 24k gold-framed citation given to an author or
  co-authors who publish a book that is an outstanding contribution to the professional literature. http://www.ala.
  org/work/awards/appls/highappl.html

For more information on locating professional development
grants online, see Chapter 10. If you are considering a book-length
project, also look into applying for a research grant that will give
you the time and resources to develop your topic fully.

Practicing your professional writing skills can help you secure
other grant opportunities, as well. The EBSCO ALA conference
sponsorship grant, for example, requires applicants to submit an
essay explaining how conference attendance will contribute to
their professional development (http://www.ala.org/work/
awards/appls/ebscappl.html). The writing practice you gain as
you contribute to the professional literature will help you create a
coherent argument as to why you deserve funding.

Online Collaboration

You may wish to recruit a co-author for your project if you are
used to bouncing ideas off others, if you feel somewhat unsure of
your ability to complete a large project such as a book, or if you
simply feel that your topic would benefit from another perspective. Basic tools such as e-mail and word processors now allow
librarians to collaborate easily, regardless of their geographic locations. Be sure to keep one another up-to-date by e-mailing sections as they are completed and by sharing input and advice every
step of the way.

When collaborating on a book or article via e-mail, keep in
mind that you will lack some of the visual clues that help with

offline collaboration efforts. You will need to rely on text to convey your respective ideas, so be sure always to answer your collaborator promptly and thoroughly. Divide the workload equitably and be sure to choose (and be!) a co-author who will keep up his or her end of the work. If you are actively seeking a co-author, look at your peers' posts on e-mail discussion lists, their articles that are accessible online, and their Web pages (if applicable) to see whether their philosophy seems compatible with yours and whether they present themselves professionally. E-mail them and feel them out about your project.

Working with a co-author via e-mail can also help you establish strong professional contacts and friendships. You already know you share some similar professional interests, and your e-mail collaboration will inevitably bring you closer to your geographically distant colleague.

Editing an anthology or other multi-contributor work offers a similar opportunity for information professionals to collaborate with distant colleagues. Electronic mail facilitates the process of receiving, editing, and compiling chapters from contributors in any location. As written communication, e-mail can also help create an atmosphere of mutual respect and concentration that is not subject to the stresses of a face-to-face working relationship.

Julie Still, editor of *Creating Web-Accessible Databases*, notes: "Editing work with contributors in different geographic areas is in some ways easier than working with people nearby. For one thing, they only know you on paper. I'm not very tall or physically imposing, but I look very impressive on paper. So people at a remote location often take me more seriously than people who see me every day and know I can't tell left from right and have a terminally messy office." If your skills lie in editing others' work and fashioning multiple contributions into a coherent whole, you will find online communication invaluable.

Style Guides

Each journal and publishing house has its own rules as to which of the many style guides you will need to use. Few are available entirely online or for free, but you can often use the Internet to locate summaries, FAQs, example citations, and/or information on citing electronic resources. Try these resources:

- *The Chicago Manual of Style* FAQ. Style questions that puzzle you have probably previously puzzled others. Read answers from the editors. http://www.press.uchicago.edu/Misc/Chicago/cmosfaq.html

- The Modern Language Association's guide to documenting sources from the World Wide Web. http://www.mla.org/style/sources.htm

- FAQ for *The Publication Manual of the American Psychological Association.* http://www.apa.org/journals/faq.html

- The American Psychological Association's recommended formats for citing electronic resources. http://www.apa.org/journals/webref.html

- *The Elements of Style*: The full text of William Strunk, Jr.'s 1918 classic. http://www.bartleby.com/141/

- *The MLA (Medical Library Association)* Style Manual includes guidelines for all MLA publications. http://www.mla.org; click on "MLA style"

Do a Web search for the style guide that is recommended by your publisher to see what information its publisher may make available online. Links to other style guides are also available online at NASIG's (North American Serials Interest Group) Publications Committee's Resources for Authors at http://www.nasig.org/publications/pub_resources.html.

Writing Advice

When planning your contributions to the world of library publishing, do not overlook the plethora of general online resources dedicated to writers of every kind. Because the Web is still largely a text-based medium, it has become a natural gathering place for writers, who have created a large number of virtual writing communities. At such sites, you can find advice on all aspects of the publishing process, from writing query letters to formatting manuscripts to researching your project. One good meta-site in this area is Writing World (http://www.writing-world.com), which includes writing advice, market listings, and a free e-mail newsletter for writers. Writing World itself links to a variety of other writing-related sites that may be worth exploring if you intend to make publishing a major part of your professional life.

A judicious use of Internet tools will enable you to launch or expand your career in library publication. The Web should be a natural starting point for any information professional who is serious about contributing to the profession in this way.

Reading Professional Literature Online

Many of the indexes listed previously are useful in locating places online to keep up with your professional reading. Use the list of journals in Appendix B and the online tools discussed above to locate professional journals that publish articles in your area of interest. Some publications with an online presence let you sign up to be notified via e-mail when a new issue is posted online, or issues may even be available in their entirety through an e-mail subscription. Take advantage of such offers to avoid having to remember to visit a journal's site on a regular basis. If e-mailed notices are not available, bookmark individual journals' sites and set aside time each month or so to go through the list and see what new articles have been posted.

Use the wide variety of resources available online to supplement the print library-related journals your institution receives. The explosion of journals and niche interest of many publications means that no library can subscribe to them all—yet the Internet presence of many of these journals allows you to keep up with new developments in the field and read otherwise unavailable articles in your area(s) of interest.

Book publishers generally have less free material available on their sites, but may post sample chapters or tables of contents from their authors' books, so that you can get a better idea of whether a title will meet your needs before purchasing or inter-loaning it from another library. ALA Editions, for example, maintains an Open Stacks section at http://www.ala.org/editions/ openstacks/index.html that contains interviews with authors, companion Web sites, .pdf and HTML editions and excerpts, and peeks at upcoming titles. Many journals also include reviews of forthcoming professional titles, and you will be able to locate a number of these reviews online.

Overall, the Internet provides an invaluable resource for librarians who wish to keep up with—and contribute to—the professional literature and developments in the profession.

Part 3

Education

Chapter 8

Education Decisions

The days of writing to schools for catalogs and waiting anxiously for packets of information to appear in the mail are long gone. Most institutions granting the MLS[1] degree and those offering Ph.D. programs or continuing education opportunities now also offer a wealth of online information about their programs and courses. Many allow students to apply, register, and even complete some or all of their coursework over the Internet. Such distance learning opportunities are discussed in the next chapter. In addition, articles on and information about many library schools' programs can be found on a variety of independent and organizational Web sites.

Even if you choose to complete your degree in the traditional manner by physically attending classes at the library school's geographic location, the Internet can smooth the process of finding information about and applying to the program by allowing you to conduct the following activities:

- Identify admission requirements and download application forms

- Research financial aid and scholarship opportunities

- Request information packets

- Read course descriptions and view syllabi

- Locate information about professors' areas of academic interest

- Learn about the strength and availability of programs in your area of interest

- Find information on student life and post-graduate support

Using the Internet can help ease the decision-making process, not to mention save on long-distance phone bills and postage.

Beyond using Internet resources to locate information on library schools, you can also use the Web to identify continuing education courses and find information on certification opportunities and requirements. A variety of classes and workshops are available from state libraries, associations, consortiums, independent training institutes, library schools, and local colleges—and the Web is the best single source of information on all of these educational opportunities. The following sections discuss how information professionals can use the Internet to locate and evaluate MLS, certification, continuing education, and Ph.D. opportunities.

Locating LIS Programs

The MLS is the basic degree for most information science professionals. Many practitioners, however, work in the field for years before going back to school to complete their classes. If you are among this group, or if you are just beginning your career in librarianship by seeking the degree, spend some time online investigating your options.

Your research should begin with the American Library Association's Directory of Accredited LIS Masters Programs, accessible online at http://www.ala.org/alaorg/oa/lisdir.html. ALA's directory includes contact information, Web links, and accreditation status for master's programs in the U.S. and Canada that are accredited by ALA, as well as a list of related degrees offered by each school (such as educational media certification programs or the Ph.D.). Each listing also contains a brief note indicating whether the school offers distance learning opportunities—online, via videoconferencing, and/or at satellite campuses in neighboring cities and states. In addition, the ALA site provides basic guidelines for choosing a program (which are, of course, strongly biased toward the selection of an ALA-accredited institution[2]).

How Important Is Accreditation?

Some schools have made the decision to no longer seek accreditation from ALA. The University of California at Berkeley's School of Information Management and Systems (SIMS) is the most famous example of an information science program that has foregone the accreditation process. They argue that ALA accreditation has become irrelevant for programs focusing on the management of information in a digital environment—and report that their graduates have had little trouble finding employment. SIMS graduates pursue a variety of largely nontraditional information-related careers, finding jobs as, for example, information analysts, consultants, and usability engineers. The average starting salary of a SIMS graduate, as reported on the school's Web site at http://www.sims. berkeley.edu/academics/applying/faq/career_stats.html, is $73,400 —much higher than that of most entry-level traditional librarians.

Other newer programs, such as that at the University of Denver, failed to receive accreditation on the first try. As of mid-2001, Denver is still appealing ALA's decision while continuing to offer the MLS degree as well as several certificate programs.

To locate information on the program at Berkeley and other nonaccredited LIS programs, start your search at San Jose State University's Library Schools in the United States and Canada (http://witloof.sjsu.edu/peo/library.schools.html). Their guide includes links to the Web sites of both accredited and nonaccredited schools. Unfortunately, the San Jose site contains a number of outdated links, but it remains the most comprehensive list of North

American library schools. You may also wish to visit general college sites such as Peterson's Guide (http://www.petersons.com), which allows you to browse graduate programs by major. Pick "Library Science" from their list to bring up LIS programs. Peterson's is also useful because it allows you to see a snapshot profile of each school, providing statistics on, for example, the number of full-time and part-time students, the number of male and female students, the percentage of applications that are accepted, the number of students enrolled in the program, the percentage of minority students, the number of degrees awarded in the last year, accreditation status, and application fees/due dates.

If you choose to complete your degree at a nonaccredited institution, be aware that many libraries and other organizations employing information professionals do specify an ALA-accredited degree as part of their requirements for professional positions. Before enrolling in such a program, peruse the job ads in your area to see how willing employers are to accept a nonaccredited degree. This will be less of an issue if you intend to pursue a career in special or nontraditional librarianship, however, in which the programs not accredited by ALA generally specialize.

Lisjobs.com Education Survey

You are being contacted to fill out a short survey because you recently placed a job advertisement on Lisjobs.com.

Please be assured that your e-mail address has not been given to any other party, and that your job ad has already been placed and is not contingent upon your answering this survey. The results of this survey will be used in the education section of a forthcoming book on librarian professional development.

Thank you for your time and help!

Survey Follows:

- Do positions within your organization generally require an MLS or equivalent degree?
- Would you be more or less likely to consider a candidate for employment if he or she had a degree from a non-ALA-accredited institution?
- Would you be more or less likely to consider a candidate for employment if she or he had received a distance learning MLS degree over the Internet?
- When considering a candidate for employment, do you take into consideration his or her commitment to ongoing continuing education? Do you ask that candidates demonstrate such commitment by describing classes, workshops, or conferences they have attended?
- Do you have comments on these questions or on related issues not addressed above?
- May we quote you in the book? If yes, please indicate if you would prefer to remain anonymous.

Thank you for your assistance! Please return completed survey to: survey@lisjobs.com

This survey was e-mailed to 177 employers who placed job advertisements on Lisjobs.com during May, June, and July of 2000. Sixty-eight employers responded to the questions, representing answers from a variety of institutions that employ information professionals.

An unscientific survey of employers who placed advertisements for information professionals on Lisjobs.com during May and June of 2000 (see sidebar) found that fifty-nine of the sixty-eight respondents (eighty-seven percent) would be less likely to consider employing a job applicant if he or she had earned an MLS degree from a nonaccredited institution. Many respondents, especially those at academic libraries, mentioned that their institutions specifically require an ALA-accredited degree for a full-time professional position. Some states also require that either the directorship or all professional positions at public libraries be filled by ALA-accredited graduates as a prerequisite for state grants or funding. Candidates from a nonaccredited program could never be considered for these types of posts; as one survey respondent from an academic institution states, "A candidate without an ALA-accredited MLS would not even be considered. They might as well have no degree at all."

Some respondents from academic libraries did note that an ALA-accredited degree was not a requirement for an adjunct or temporary (nontenure-track) faculty position. Candidates lacking such a degree may be able to get their foot in the door this way, and those without an MLS at all can consider completing their coursework while employed as an information professional. Many institutions, academic, private, and public, also have some sort of tuition-reimbursement program that pay for you to take coursework toward an MLS. Most, though, require a one- or two-year commitment to remain at that institution after the completion of the degree.

The requirement for an ALA-accredited degree may lessen in time if more schools choose not to seek accreditation and as librarianship evolves into a variety of information-related professions. As one survey respondent notes, "Accreditation is important. ALA-specific accreditation is not as important, but they are the 'only game in town.'" Schools such as Berkeley's SIMS note that they may choose to seek some kind of accreditation in the future, should appropriate accrediting organizations and standards emerge for a new type of graduate education.

International Degrees

If you are interested in earning a degree outside of North America, a few online directories have pulled together links to Web sites of LIS programs around the world. Reflecting the confusing proliferation of library-related degrees, such directories include the University of Sheffield's World List of Departments and Schools of Information Studies, Information Management, Information Systems, Etc. at http://www.shef.ac.uk/~is/publications/worldlist/ wlist1.html and the Danish Royal School of Library and Information Science Library's Library Schools, Universities, and Departments at http://www.db.dk/dbi/internet/schools.htm.

Also check the Web site of your country's national library organization, if available, or contact them for information on local programs. U.S. employers who do not consider applicants with a nonaccredited MLS degree from a U.S. school do generally accept an MLS-equivalent international degree.

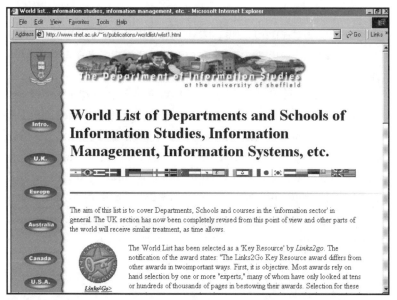

Figure 8.1   World List of Departments and Schools of Information Studies, Information Management, Information Systems, Etc.

The MLS Decision Process

Once you have used these online directories to locate potential programs, spend some time perusing the Web site of each of the library schools you are considering. In addition to seeking information on the school's programs, services, and fees, also look at how the site itself is constructed. Note whether the presentation is professional, see how the school's material is laid out and organized, and how often the information is updated. A library school's Web site often contains important clues as to whether the institution has kept up with changing technology. If a school's site lists only a catalog of courses or provides only a brief brochure, you may wonder about the currency of its program.

In all fairness, however, the design and content of a school's Web site may in truth have more to do with the institution's IT department or outside contractor than with the library department. Yet, if the design and maintenance of a school's Web site are outsourced, ask yourself why, given that Web design and development is becoming such an integral part of many librarians' jobs. You may be able to get a better sense of a school at which the Web design is kept in-house.

Schools such as the University of Wisconsin, Madison's School of Library and Information Studies (SLIS) at http://polyglot.lss.wisc.edu/slis use current students to design and maintain their sites. Such maintenance becomes part of a real-world effort in classes on Web design or as an independent effort by students, and the Web site reflects what is taught in the curriculum. This also shows that the school promotes the importance of technology and the use of the Internet as an information resource.

Faculty Information

Clues about the atmosphere of a school and the technological comfort level of its professors can often be found on the faculty section of the school's site (look under "People" or "Faculty"). Many schools also post online information about faculty research interests and activities, which can assist you in choosing a school where there is a professor working in an area of interest. If faculty members have personal Web pages, note whether the pages are designed and maintained by the individual faculty member or by the school.

The University of Buffalo's (UB) Department of Library & Information Studies promotes its faculty by highlighting faculty activities, publications, and awards right on its front page (http://www.sils.buffalo.edu/lis/index.htm) and links to a staff directory that includes faculty interests, bios, photographs, home page links, and syllabi. If a school does not overtly promote its faculty, dig deeper. Is it merely failing to list accomplishments on a main page, or has its faculty lately produced little work of note?

For examples of well-maintained and informational faculty pages, see those at the University of Illinois at Urbana-Champaign Graduate School of Library and Information Science, at http://www.lis.uiuc.edu/gslis/people/faculty/index.html. Click on a faculty member's name to see his or her personal page, which generally includes a description of research interests, links to articles and other projects, and courses taught. (Figure 8.2 shows an example of the type of information that can be found on such faculty pages.) Also examine those at Indiana University's School of Library and Information Science, at http://www.slis.indiana.edu/Faculty. Although not all faculty at these institutions take advantage of their Web presence to provide a great deal of information, many do.

Look to see if the program's site links to a faculty e-mail directory. Do faculty members encourage e-mail interaction? When was the faculty information last updated? Did several professors have publications "forthcoming" several years ago, or does the "last updated" note at the bottom of the faculty pages proudly proclaim

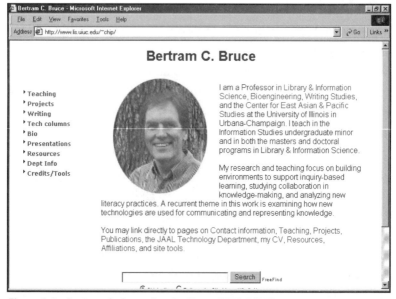

Figure 8.2   Bertram C. Bruce Faculty Page, UIUC GSLIS

1996? Some schools provide little information on professors' interests, activities, and abilities, but you should at least be able to locate a list of faculty e-mail addresses, such as that at Dominican University, at http://www.dom.edu/gslis/faculty.html.

Student Life and Support

While examining a school's Web site for information about programs, services, and faculty, also look at whether it provides space for students to post personal Web pages or resumes. Madison's SLIS (http://slisweb.lis.wisc.edu) is one academic program that allows free server space for students to practice Web design techniques and to promote their interests online. Indiana University's SLIS site has a thorough "Students" section (http://www.slis.indiana.edu/Students) that provides links to student resumes, campus organizations and associations, and student projects.

You can decide how important it is to you whether a school gives an online voice to its students. Examining student projects and resumes online can also help you see what is expected of that school's graduates, what students have a chance to accomplish while attending, and whether the program promotes technology in its courses and outlook. A great example of a student project that shows how a school can integrate research, Web design, and current issues into a curriculum is Librarians in the 21st Century (http://istweb.syr.edu/21stcenlib/index.html), created and maintained by students at Syracuse University's School of Information Studies.

Student pages and information can usually be found in a "People" or "Student Resources" section of a school's site, which often include information on topics such as scholarships, student organizations, employment opportunities, and student handbooks. Buffalo's Resources page for current students (http://www.sils.buffalo.edu/lis/studentresources/resources.htm) includes links to student organizations, library-related e-mail lists, computer lab schedules, calendar of events, university forms, and other useful on- and off-campus information.

You also may wish to solicit feedback from some current students or recent graduates of the program(s) you are considering. This is where e-mail discussion lists such as NEWLIB-L (http://lahacal.org/newlib) can serve as an invaluable resource. Even if list members are unwilling to provide their opinions on an open discussion forum, they may be willing to e-mail you privately to discuss their experiences in a particular school's program. Discussion list contacts will be especially useful if you are considering attending a school outside of your local area, as local librarians are less likely to have graduated from a particular distant institution.

Some programs, such as the University of Michigan's School of Information, allow prospective students to fill out an online form in order to have a current student contact them to answer questions about the program. (The form is available at:

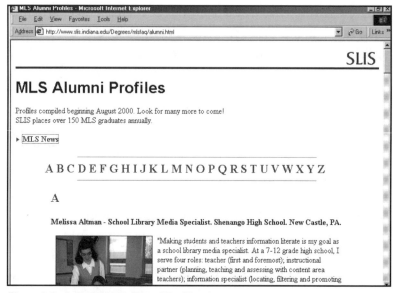

Figure 8.3   Indiana SLIS Alumni Profiles

http://www.si.umich.edu/admission/student-contact.htm.) Although the students representing the school through this service are obviously chosen by the administration, talking with current students can help you get an idea of the school's environment before applying.

Lastly, investigate the support a school provides to recent graduates. Does the program have its own placement office? Does it provide online job listings, resume space, mentoring programs, networking opportunities, and/or mailing lists? Examine the school's Web page for links to sites such as the UB's Put a Buffalo in Your Library directory of recent graduates and their interests at http://www.sis.buffalo.edu/dlis/studentresources/pab and its Job Postings page at http://wings.buffalo.edu/sils/alas/job.htm. Indiana's SLIS has a nice Alumni Happenings page at http://www.slis.indiana.edu/Alumni/index.html that includes alumni profiles, job success stories, and an alumni newsletter. Whether alumni appear to be active and still attached to the school can be one sign of the quality of a program.

Applying to MLS Programs

Most MLS programs now allow prospective students to download an application packet in Adobe Acrobat (.pdf) format rather than waiting for one to be sent through the mail. (If you do not have the free Adobe Acrobat Reader installed on your computer, you can download it from Adobe's Web site at http://www.adobe.com.) Check under the "Admissions" portion of most library school sites for application forms and information. Some schools, such as Berkeley's SIMS, even allows prospective students to apply online (http://gradadm.berkeley.edu:7200).

Any graduate program's site should also include detailed admission requirements and procedures. Examine these before applying to help you predict whether there will be any difficulty with your application. Under "Admissions" you will generally find information on related topics, such as whether previously earned credits will transfer, requirements for matriculation, fee schedules, and information on requirements for special programs such as school library media.

Researching with Other Sources

In addition to examining the Web sites of the particular schools you are considering, spend some time online looking at articles and other information about their programs. *U.S. News Online (USNO)*, for example, provides a yearly ranking of graduate programs in library science, available on the Web at http://www.usnews.com/usnews/edu/beyond/bcinfos.htm. Its site ranks the top twenty LIS programs in the U.S., describes the methodology behind the rankings, and includes links to relevant articles. The *USNO* site can be helpful for those contemplating a degree in a particular specialty, as well, as it also ranks the top ten schools in subcategories such as "Information Systems," "School Library Media," and "Archives and Preservation." While rankings are always subjective, a list such as that available at *U.S. News Online* can be useful in determining the relative regard in which a particular program is held.

If you have an area of concentration in mind when entering a program, examine the educational policy statements of different library-related bodies, collected on the ALA Web site at http://www.ala.org/alaorg/oa/educpol.html. Such policy statements can help you see if these specialties are appropriate to your interests.

Also use sites such as Peterson's (mentioned previously) to help find information on the ethnic makeup of the student body, admissions statistics, and so on. These can be useful in deciding whether a particular program is the right fit for you.

Finding Continuing Education Opportunities

Employers of information professionals overwhelmingly emphasize the importance of continuing education and keeping skills current in an era of ever-changing technology. Each information professional must make a personal commitment to furthering his or her own education by taking advantage of workshops, tutorials, independent study, and formal courses. Even skills recently learned in library school rapidly become outdated in today's information environment. Librarians who want to provide current and useful services to their clients have a responsibility to keep up with developments in the field and to keep their skills fresh.

Academic libraries, in particular, tend to make continuing professional education part of the requirements for advancement within the institution and for receiving tenure. Careers in the field of information technology obviously also require a commitment to continuous education and training. Smaller institutions, however, may find it more difficult to back up their desire for employees with current skills with the financial and time commitment necessary to send their librarians to training. Furthermore, many professional continuing education opportunities are lost because the appropriate professionals fail to find out about their availability in time—as journals or brochures are routed through an institution, the dates for registering often pass by the time the information works its way down to those individuals unlucky enough to be at the bottom of the list.

Those who are proactive about their own education can keep themselves aware of pertinent continuing education opportunities by monitoring a few well-chosen Internet resources in their area of interest. This is another advantage in joining e-mail discussion lists and monitoring current awareness services in the field, as announcements of continuing education opportunities are often posted in such venues.

Make it a point to check the Web sites of local library systems and of your state library on a regular basis. If your system or neighboring systems have Web-based newsletters, see if you can sign up to receive them through e-mail, or be notified via e-mail when a new issue is released on the Web. Such local newsletters often include announcements of workshops or training that can be presented at a lower cost than courses offered by library schools and computer training institutes. The DuPage Library System (DLS) in Illinois is one example of a local system that allows readers of its online semi-monthly *Miscellany* newsletter to register for e-mail notification of new issues (see http://www.dupagels.lib.il. us/pages/miscellany.html). Each issue of *Miscellany* includes a section on "Workshops, Seminars, Meetings, etc." that gives descriptions of and registration information for DLS's and other local programs.

Some state libraries are more active than others when it comes to providing and promoting continuing education opportunities for their state's information professionals. The Wyoming State

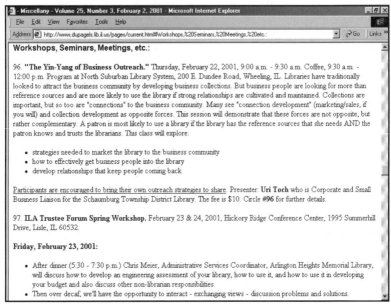

Figure 8.4   DuPage Library System (Ill.) *Miscellany* Newsletter, Local Workshops, Seminars, Meetings, etc.

Library, for example, has a useful "training and programming" Web site (http://www-wsl.state.wy.us/training) that outlines training opportunities, provides online versions of workshop handouts, and describes and provides applications for state continuing education grants for individuals.

Also check for educational opportunities provided by or listed at your professional association. The Medical Library Association is one national association that maintains an online Continuing Education Clearinghouse. This database compiles information on classes that are approved for MLA continuing education credit (http://www.mlanet.org/education/cech/index.php3), and is keyword searchable by subject, location, experience level, instructor, and so on.

If you are serious about maintaining your skills, however, avoid limiting yourself merely to professional education opportunities in the library field. Attending courses or training workshops on related topics from Internet research to Web design to copyright law can supplement a traditional library degree and update your education with current skills that will make you an invaluable asset to your organization. Furthermore, do not limit yourself to taking courses only as they become available at your local library school. You may learn Web design, for example, just as easily through your local community college's continuing education department—and it will probably cost you (or your library) a lot less. (Search for community college sites at Community College Web at http://www. mcli.dist.maricopa.edu/cc.)

Lastly, you may wish to search for continuing education options provided by your library's vendors. Some vendors, such as Follett Software, have even started to offer more general professional development workshops, rather than just courses on the use of their own software packages (http://www.pathwaysmodel.com/ workshops). They will send trainers to particular sites, so, if you are in a smaller library, you might look into bringing such a workshop to your system or consortium.

Acquiring Certification

A variety of institutions offer certificate programs that serve as a complement to or in place of a full MLS degree. Such certificates include school library media certification, nonlibrary computer and software certifications such as the MCSE (Microsoft Certified Systems Engineer), postgraduate certificates of study, state certifications, and short-term intensive certificates in topics such as knowledge management.

Certification can be useful to round out your expertise in a particular subject or to keep your skills current. It can also be useful in convincing an employer of your dedication to personal growth and your value to the organization.

School Library Media Certification

Anyone looking into becoming certified as a school library media specialist should read *School Library Journal's* guide to getting certified in all fifty states (http://www.schoollibraryjournal.com/articles/articles/20000601_7732.asp). This guide is updated every two years and allows potential school librarians to find certification requirements for each state in the U.S. This will also be useful for media specialists interested in moving to a different part of the country, where requirements may differ.

Certification of school library media programs within graduate library schools is usually provided by the respective state board of education and/or the program is accredited by NCATE (National Council for Accreditation of Teacher Education; http://www.ncate.org). Check to see if the program is both ALA and NCATE accredited. This will matter more in certain states, so examine job ads in the area where you are looking for work. If your degree does not have both accreditations, you may be limited as to where you can hunt for employment.

Computer Certification

As the technological requirements for effective librarianship expand, information professionals with computer expertise are increasingly in demand. Those who supplement their library credentials with certification in one or more computer-related topics can find homes as systems and computer services librarians at a variety of institutions. By taking on responsibility for technology, and using their technological expertise to enhance the services an institution can offer, such information professionals often see a concomitant increase in salary and security.

Two of the most useful certificates for librarians are the MCSE (Microsoft Certified Systems Engineer) and A+ (computer technician) certification, although this may vary depending on the hardware and software in use at your institution. Certification in these areas shows your commitment to being an effective systems librarian and allows you to apply for computer-related positions with confidence in your abilities. Do keep in mind that achieving the MCSE is a rigorous and lengthy process, which may be overkill for many systems librarian positions. MCSE holders will be qualified for (generally much more lucrative) positions in private industry. Getting the MCSE or other computer certification, though, is one way to stay within libraries while most likely also being able to improve your salary status.

Computer certifications are one area in which you may wish to have hands-on instruction. Use the Internet to locate local computer training institutes that offer classes toward relevant certificates. A good place to begin your search is at ComputerUser.com's training directory at http://www.computeruser.com/resources/training, which is searchable by state and area of interest.

Post-Graduate Certificates

Post-graduate certificates allow information professionals to gain expertise by intensively studying a specific area of specialty. These certificates are often offered as nondegree programs by LIS schools. Drexel, for example, offers a Certificate in Competitive Intelligence—which can be completely acquired online, as outlined on the school's Web site at http://www.cis.drexel.edu/grad/ci.html. (See the next chapter for more on online distance learning opportunities.)

State and System Certification

States that require or strongly encourage certification of public librarians generally post certification standards and forms online. Check the Web site of your state library, which is often accessible from your state government's home page. Most state government Web addresses are in the format http://www.state.*xx*.us, where *xx* is the two-letter postal abbreviation for that state.

For an example of state certification requirements that can be viewed online, visit the State Library of Iowa's Certification Program page at: http://www.silo.lib.ia.us/Certification/cert_ program.htm. To encourage librarians to apply for state certification, Iowa requires public library directors to be certified in order for their institution to receive state aid. Their site describes different levels of certification, links to the state library's continuing education course catalog, lists continuing education requirements for recertification, and provides a downloadable recertification application form.

State libraries have also begun offering programs for non-MLS library personnel who want to improve their library skills. The Texas State Library, for example, offers a series of workshops geared toward non-MLS Texas library directors. These workshops are intended to provide them with management, collection development, reference, and technical services skills (http://www.tsl. state.tx.us/ld/projects/slmtp/index.html). The Idaho State Library offers an Alternative Basic Library Education (ABLE) program to library workers without a formal library science education in Idaho (http://www.lili.org/isl/cepage/ABLE.htm), and issues a certificate of completion for each course and at the end of the series. Possibly to avoid conflict with ALA, state libraries that offer these alternative programs generally make it very clear that their courses are not meant to replace a formal degree but, rather, are intended to provide basic skills training to non-MLS employees. Non-MLS library workers might, however, consider enrolling in such programs—especially if they are working in states without a library school—as a way to improve their library skills and to show their employer that they are committed to their education.

Some larger or multistate library systems also provide certification programs to employees of their member libraries. NELINET (New England Library and Information Network) allows library staff to earn a "Certificate of Professional Development" by completing a certain number of workshops within an eighteen-month period (http://www.nelinet.net/calendar/tc_info.htm#cert). Their training calendar (http://www.nelinet.net/calendar/train.htm) offers workshop dates and descriptions and identifies which workshops qualify towards completion of the certificate.

Locating a Ph.D. Program

Information professionals seeking a Ph.D. in library science or related fields have somewhat more limited options than those pursuing the MLS. Few schools that grant the MLS degree also offer a Ph.D. program in the information sciences. If you intend to pursue the Ph.D., be prepared to spend more time researching available options and to be willing to relocate, as no institution currently offers a distance learning option to its Ph.D. candidates. An advanced degree is generally necessary if you are interested in teaching in the field and in some cases is helpful when applying for administrator-level positions in certain libraries. Be aware, however, that a Ph.D. in the information field may be perceived as a liability unless you intend to teach or to seek a high-level administrative post; many employers perceive those with a doctorate as overqualified for "regular" librarian jobs and as likely to desert the institution when a "better" position opens up.

Begin researching Ph.D. opportunities at the ALA directory of accredited LIS Masters Programs described in the previous section on locating LIS programs. ALA notes in each description whether the school also offers a Ph.D. in the field. (Be sure to choose "United States" or "Canada" from their directory choices rather than using their "Index to LIS Programs," which does not contain program descriptions.) You can then visit the site of each school to learn more about its doctoral program.

Most schools offering the doctorate maintain detailed descriptions of their program on their Web sites. You should be able to find information on admissions requirements, courses, core reading lists, examinations, and the dissertation process. Previously, such detailed information was only available through printed student handbooks or as disseminated by an advisor, but now Ph.D. candidates can easily keep track of program requirements on the Web. For an example of a detailed description of one school's doctoral process, see UIUC'S GSLIS Doctor of Philosophy Program Stages page at http://www.lis.uiuc.edu/gslis/degrees/phd-stages.html. Emporia has also posted its Ph.D. handbook online in Adobe Acrobat format at http://slim.emporia.edu/phd/phdhandbook.pdf.

Many programs offer online examples of graduate student and faculty research; examine these to see what topics are being covered at the school and whether a faculty member may be doing work in one of your areas of interest. This will be much more important to you as a Ph.D. candidate than it may have been as an MLS student, as you will be working much more closely with your advisor while doing doctoral research. Examine faculty pages as described in the previous section on researching the MLS, but this time pay particular attention to faculty research and writings. Also check the school's Web site for a directory of current doctoral candidates, as this often includes descriptions of their research interests, the names of their advisors, and their dissertation topics.

Make the Internet your first stop in researching educational opportunities. The information you can find online is often more comprehensive and current than that available from any print source or directory.

Endnotes

1. The term MLS (Master of Library Science) is used here to refer to all MLS-equivalent degrees, to avoid confusion over the multiple terms now used at different schools to describe the master's degree achieved by librarians and information professionals.
2. An explanation of the accreditation process and ALA's "Standards for Accreditation" can be viewed online, at http://www.ala.org/alaorg/oa/stanindx.html.

Chapter 9

Distance Education

Degree-aspiring information professionals have a wider variety of options now than in even the recent past, thanks to the availability of distance education programs at several MLS-granting institutions. Those interested in furthering their education through completing continuing education classes or workshops will find that the Internet opens up a wide range of possibilities. "Distance learning" has a variety of meanings, but generally encompasses any courses where the student and instructor are separated by time and/or space. For library schools and organizations today, distance education includes taking classes at off-campus locations in other cities/states, correspondence courses, classes provided by videotape or videoconferencing, and classes offered entirely or largely over the Internet. It is this last meaning of distance learning that we concern ourselves with in this chapter, outlining online degree and continuing education opportunities.

In the summer of 2000, thirty-four information professionals who had either completed an entire MLS degree or taken library coursework online were surveyed via e-mail as to their satisfaction with and reasons for choosing their online learning experience (see sidebar). We refer to quotes and responses from the survey throughout this chapter.

Distance learning is becoming an integral part of library education today. Even professionals who did not receive or are not interested in completing the MLS online may at some point find it useful to take a continuing education class or workshop over the Internet. The cost savings of Internet classes and the ability to

bring together librarians from all over the world in one class provide an unprecedented opportunity.

Distance Education Survey—Summer 2000

1. What is your name/e-mail address/current
   position?
2. At what school(s), and when, did you take your
   online coursework?
3. Why did you decide to take a course(s) online?
4. Did you take your online course(s) toward a library
   degree or as part of your continuing education?
5. How was the course structured? For example, did
   you interact with your professor and fellow students through forums, chat, e-mail, MOO, or any
   combination of the above? Were you required to
   install special software on your machine?
6. Did you experience any difficulties finding or
   accessing required resources for the course?
7. Do you feel that the online coursework prepared
   you as well for library work as more traditional
   courses (would) have?
8. If you have taken multiple online classes, were
   there some topics you felt were more or less suited
   for the online medium?
9. Would you take another online class?
10. If you completed most or all of your degree
    requirements online, have you found that your
    "virtual" degree helps or hinders you when it
    comes to finding employment, or do employers
    seem indifferent to how the degree was acquired?
11. Do you have comments on any distance learning
    issues not covered here?

May we quote you in the book? If so, would you prefer to remain anonymous?

Why Online?

Distance learning offers LIS schools the chance to expand their programs and attract a wider variety of applicants than was previously feasible. Online classes are particularly appropriate for students in these situations:

- Lack of geographic mobility and no nearby LIS institution

- Work and/or family commitments that preclude taking classes at particular times

- Working information professionals who require proof of the degree for career advancement more than they need the socialization into the profession provided by on-campus immersion

- Unable to meet the expense of classes at nearby institutions and need to apply to more affordable schools

- Lack uninterrupted blocks of time to attend formal on-ground classes

Other librarians may take online classes for a variety of reasons, or take a mixture of on- and offline coursework to complete degree requirements or to further their professional education.

The biggest advantage of online education, mentioned by nearly every survey respondent, is the flexibility and convenience it offers to students. Those who face work or family obligations, or who lack a library school within commuting distance, are able to take classes without ignoring their previous responsibility. Survey respondent Tracy Myers explained, "I found the Online MLS Program at SCSU [Southern Connecticut State University] and enrolled there—it has been a godsend for me. I can work, care for my new baby, and go to school." A community college library supervisor mentioned that "A Master's in Library Science was not available at any school in my state (Virginia). Since I had a family, full-time job and didn't want to relocate, I looked into taking courses from home." Online education can also obviate the need to juggle your schedule each semester in order to take required classes that always seem to be offered at the most inopportune times. You can take classes that best meet your needs and interests rather than those that happen to be available at a convenient time slot.

Some survey respondents felt that the online medium forced them to push themselves more than they might have in a traditional classroom, where it is easier to get lost in the crowd and refrain from participating in class discussions. Several respondents mentioned that the need to be self-motivated made them keep up with class readings and assignments. Student Joanne Walsh notes that: "I was inclined to make sure I kept up with the weekly posted classes in terms of reading the class lecture, visiting the linked resources, and checking into the bulletin board, whereas I might tend to delay in my textbook readings even though I always attend classes in the traditional settings. I was more committed, perhaps from fear of not being able to readily ask for clarification in person, to making sure I was attentive to the coursework so as to understand and succeed." This learned self-motivation can also help former online students when they get into the working world!

Online communication often leads to strong bonds between class participants, especially those in the same "cohort" who start and go through an MLS program together. The high level of online interaction allows participants to form an electronic community that lasts even after they complete the program. They have a strong network of peers to draw upon after finishing their degree, similar to the communities that can form on library-related mailing lists, as mentioned in Chapter 2.

Another advantage of the online medium is that electronic communication opens up opportunities for all students to participate equally. Those who may be shy about speaking up in class are often more willing to express their opinions in a chat room or online forum. Professors and peers will have fewer preconceived notions based on visual cues that pertain to classroom interaction—participants' comments have a better chance of being judged purely for their substance and quality. As John Seely Brown and Paul Duguid note in *The Social Life of Information* (225), "Teachers report that online and asynchronous interaction allows students who are reluctant to speak in face-to-face classes to have their say. This can benefit nonnative speakers, the disabled, minorities, and women. (Men are notorious for dominating classroom discussions.)"

The online format may also be particularly suited to library coursework, as librarianship and information technology skills are becoming ever more closely identified. Working online, in a sense, forces students to gain the computer skills that may later be necessary on the job. One survey respondent commented: "In addition to the coursework or assignments for a distance course, you have a lot of other 'learning' to do. You have to figure out the software (WebCT, in my case), how to post to different forums, [and] how to tell if you have e-mail; discipline yourself to keep up with the discussions and the assignments coming up; etc." The online format also requires a good deal of work with electronic databases and other online products, which is useful experience for any librarian. Those who have participated in distance learning courses will also be sympathetic to the needs of other distance learners in their own libraries.

Formats and Requirements of Online Coursework

Before signing up to take coursework online, familiarize yourself with the requirements of the particular school or course. These include both personal and technical requirements, as you must have both the technical ability to participate in the course and the technological comfort level to effectively complete its requirements.

Distance Education Terminology

Asynchronous Communication—Online communication that does not take place simultaneously. Examples of types of asynchronous communication include e-mail and forums.

Bulletin Board—An online message center, where messages left by one participant stay online and can be read and replied to later by other participants. Also referred to as a "forum," "discussion group," or "message board." (See Chapter 2 for more on using online forums.)

Chat—Real-time communication via computer, where everything typed by one participant in the chat can be read and responded to almost instantaneously by the other participant(s).

Cohort—A group of students that starts a distance education program at the same time and goes through classes together.

Courseware—Software intended for use in distance education classes. Usually includes at least a bulletin board component, but may also include chat and other capabilities. Courseware may also be used in on-ground courses to enhance the classroom experience and give students a chance to use the technology.

Forum—An online discussion group. See bulletin board.

MOO—Stands for MUD (Multi-User Dimension [or Dungeon]), Object Oriented. A multi-user, interactive system where participants can chat with and interact with one another in a text-based virtual reality that is spatially organized in "rooms." MOOs differ from chat rooms in that they allow users to manipulate and interact with virtual "objects" in addition to talking with one another.

On-ground—Courses that are taught in the traditional manner, where students have to come and sit in a classroom at a specific time, are on-ground classes.

Synchronous Communication—Online "real-time" communication such as chat is said to be synchronous.

Technical Requirements

Before signing up to take classes online, make sure your computer and software meet the minimum technical requirements specified by Internet course providers. If you have an older computer or an outdated version of Netscape Navigator or Internet Explorer, resist the temptation to squeak by. Many courses, for example, require a Java-capable browser for access to online chats, or expect papers and projects to be submitted in a particular format (usually Microsoft Office 97 or 2000). If you have a slow computer or Internet connection, you will spend a lot of unnecessary time waiting for software and Web pages to load. Especially if you intend to complete an entire degree over a period of several years, ensure that your computer exceeds the minimum technical requirements or that you will be able to upgrade during that time period, as requirements and technologies will probably change during your time in school.

Users of proprietary systems such as America Online (AOL) may experience additional problems, and most universities that offer online coursework advise AOL users at the very least to use external browsers rather than relying on AOL's built-in browser. Many providers of online courses also strongly recommend against using WebTV or similar noncomputer Internet access methods.

In addition to requiring a newer (faster) PC and browser, some courses require that students have or download additional software to complete their online learning experience. Such software may include items such as the freely available RealPlayer audio/video browser plugin, IRC (Internet Relay Chat) software, and software clients that enable students to move more easily around the MOO environment. Additional programs necessary for many classes include the Microsoft Office suite of products, especially Word, PowerPoint, and Access. Also be sure that you have a reliable Internet connection. If you tend to get a lot of busy signals when dialing in to your ISP or your connection is often dropped, you may wish to consider switching to a different provider. (For more information on getting connected to the Internet and choosing an ISP, see Chapter 1.)

Personal Requirements

Learning online provides a variety of advantages, yet the online medium is not for everyone. Learners who are less self-motivated, who are less familiar with Internet technology, or who have a need for face-to-face interaction may be disappointed by the reality of Internet coursework. To help determine whether you have a personality and work style that might mesh with online learning, complete an online questionnaire such as the "Is Online Learning for Me?" self-assessment quiz from the Connecticut State University System (CSU) at http://www.onlinecsu.ctstateu.edu/index.real?action=IsOnline, or the University of Illinois' Self Evaluation for Potential Online Students, at http://illinois.online.uillinois.edu/IONresources/onlineoverview/selfeval.html.

Be sure that you have at least a basic familiarity with the use of the Internet, your computer, and word processing software before considering an online course. In most distance learning environments, you will be required to complete tasks such as attaching files to e-mail and logging into online forums. You must

Figure 9.1   Is Online Learning for Me? From OnlineCSU

be comfortable with the use of this type of technology, or it will become a barrier to a productive educational experience. You should also be fairly confident in basic information retrieval skills such as using online catalogs and periodical databases; most students are able to enhance these skills on-ground over a period of time, but it will be essential for you to start out being able to locate necessary materials from a distance.

Distance education over the Internet is a more comfortable environment for information professionals who are secure in their writing abilities and text-based communication skills. Since most online learning still takes place in a very textual medium of online forums and electronic mail, be sure before applying that you are comfortable expressing yourself in writing in the online medium. (It may also help to brush up on your typing skills, especially if real-time chat will be utilized in your classes.) In many cases, your professor and peers will lack any other opportunity to evaluate your skills and abilities. However, you can also look at online learning as an opportunity to hone those skills so that you are able to effectively express yourself throughout your library career. Corporate librarian Marilyn Geiger noted: "Since my class 'discussions' were posted to a bulletin board, I was careful and thoughtful about what I said. I learned to be concise and direct in my writing."

View your online interaction during class as another form of professional communication, and be sure to share your comments with others in a professional manner. Check your spelling and make sure that your posts add to the discussion. As Library of Congress program assistant Ana Kurland realized, "You have to participate, and it is hard not getting your comments lost in a stream of chatter, so you try to make them count and hope they are seen."

Self-motivation is another essential trait for successful distance learners. Since many online students enter a distance education program because of personal or professional commitments, they must also be determined not to let those commitments interfere with the completion of their online coursework. It can be more difficult to stay on top of assignments and readings when you are not required to face a professor in class every day; the daily demands of a full-time job can easily seem to take precedence over online coursework. The same lack of immediacy will generally affect your interactions with the professor—if you post a question via e-mail or an online forum, for example, you may not receive a response for a couple of days. (Although, on the other hand, professors and peers are in a sense always accessible via e-mail or forums; you will not have to wait for office hours to pose a question.) Be prepared to take on the responsibility for your own learning.

Earning an MLS Degree Online

Those interested in earning an MLS degree over the Internet can start by exploring the offerings of degree-granting institutions that conduct classes online. Some schools have created their own online learning environment or have purchased courseware to help them do so. Others have partnered with online "universities" or other providers that provide the technical underpinnings of the program, while the school's faculty provides the course contents.

Schools That Offer Online Degrees

A good number of library schools have begun offering degrees that can be achieved either partially or entirely online. Keep in mind, however, that several of these universities require that students spend at least a week or two on campus at the beginning of their tenure in the program, at the start of each semester, and/or when beginning particular classes. Do not assume that you will necessarily be able to complete an entire degree without ever setting foot on campus. The following examples of programs that offer online distance education give an idea of the variety of choices out there, but the list is far from comprehensive, and includes only those that offer the majority of the coursework toward the degree online. See the next section on "Choosing a School" for some places to start the search for your perfect online fit. Be sure to thoroughly examine a school's site before applying, as much more information is available online than can be provided in the brief summaries below.

These universities currently offer online MLS degrees:

- *Connecticut State University System* (CSU) OnlineCSU at http://www.onlinecsu.ctstateu.edu. CSU offers Internet coursework through eCollege.com (http://www.ecollege. com), and eCollege awarded CSU a $150,000 grant in late 1999 to expand its OnlineCSU course offerings to include the whole MLS degree. The site includes an "Is Online Learning For Me?" quiz and a demo course to help prospective students see what they are in for. Also useful are video and audio clips of students and faculty that have participated in the program, technical requirements, and an interactive browser test.

- *Drexel University* College of Information Science and Technology at http://www.cis.drexel.edu/grad/online/index.html. Drexel offers both a master's degree in management of digital information and an MS in information systems through its online program. The program is completely online, with no required on-site orientations or residencies. It requires the completion of sixty credits of graduate study. (Note that Drexel's courses are usually four credits rather than the more usual three-credit classes at other schools.) Drexel students enter the program as a cohort and progress through courses with the same group of people, in order to enhance the connections that can be made with other students.

- *Florida State University* (FSU) School of Information Studies at http://www.lis.fsu.edu/Prospects/Grads/DistLearning.cfm. FSU offers a Master of Science in either information studies or library studies that is now fully available online, and the program actually seems to offer more online courses than on-ground classes at this point. The school requires a single three-day on-ground orientation at the beginning of the program, and all succeeding coursework is available entirely online. A demonstration course is also available for prospective students' examination.

- *Syracuse University School of Information Studies* at http://istweb.syr.edu/academic/distance (see sidebar). Syracuse has been offering limited residency distance education courses since 1993, and currently available degrees through its online program include the Master of Library Science, Master of Science in Information Resources Management, and Master of Science in Telecommunications and Network Management. Each group of students that goes through the online program is required to spend at least one week in residence on campus before beginning any coursework. Available courses are then offered either entirely online or as limited residency classes that require a three- to seven-day residency at the beginning of each course.

Interview with Syracuse SIS Coordinator for Academic Services David Pimentel

(Note: Responses do not reflect all distance learning programs at Syracuse University, but only those offered at the School of Information Studies.)

How has the distance learning program at Syracuse evolved since its inception?

The School of Information Studies has been offering master's degrees in a limited residency distance learning format since 1993. This format offers a unique opportunity for those who have schedules that don't allow them to attend regular campus-based courses. (Our students live all over the world, including Central New York.) The program combines brief on-campus residencies with study over the Internet.

Initially, only the Master of Library Science was offered in the distance learning format. Following the success and popularity of the distance MLS, the School's two other graduate degrees were later offered in the distance learning format: the Master of Science in Information Resources Management distance program began in 1996 and the Master of Science in Telecommunications & Network Management distance program was added in 1998.

Limited residency courses meet in Syracuse for two to four days and then are completed from home via continued study and interaction via the Internet. In addition to the limited-residency format, the distance learning program has also evolved to include Internet-only course delivery.

Distance learning and (traditional) on-campus students are now regularly integrated in so-called "joint campus/distance" courses. These offerings are taught in one of the distance learning formats (residency or Internet-only), but are open to both distance learners and main campus graduate students.

What benefits have you found to the brief residency periods that are regularly required of distance learning students?

Students find that the intensive course residencies are invaluable, not only in receiving a significant portion of lecture and instruction, but also meeting and getting to know other students who will be working with them (sometimes in teams) in the online environment. Teamwork in a distributed, asynchronous, online environment benefits greatly from prior face-to-face contact. Students also comment that they enjoy meeting instructors and having a chance to interact with them. The School also uses the residency dates to create opportunities for student social activities as well as academic advising and career counseling.

The residencies are important to the success of the programs for a number of other reasons:

- Students are trained on the technology that will allow them to complete their courses over the Internet.
- Activities that are hard to accomplish at a distance are completed (e.g., hands-on labs).
- Students bond with the other students in their cohort group.

- Students network with each other and faculty members.
- Students are exposed to the atmosphere of the school.
- Students familiarize themselves with the University and develop a sense of identity with Syracuse.

Does the distance learning program seem to attract a different type of student? What are some common reasons prospective students give for wishing to enter the distance learning track?

Distance learning students typically have families, full-time jobs, or are otherwise only able to pursue graduate study in the highly flexible distance learning format.

Many are already working in the field—particularly those that enter our IRM and TNM programs—but some are looking for a career change. The rich backgrounds of the students make each cohort a dynamic group.

Our distance learning applicants also tell us that they have experience as independent learners and are highly self-motivated.

What type of technical requirements are necessary for successful enrollment in one of your Internet courses? What type of computer background is helpful?

The School has developed two specific documents on these topics, both are available online, and are published in the Application for Graduate Study:

Computer Hardware, Software & Internet Access Requirements

http://istweb.syr.edu/prospective/admission/computer_req.shtml

Information Technology Literacy Requirements

http://istweb.syr.edu/prospective/admission/it_req.shtml

Has the distance learning program met with any

resistance from faculty? Do all faculty members teach Internet courses?

Faculty are very enthusiastic about distance instruction. Currently the number of offerings prevents *all* faculty from teaching in this mode, but all would/could if asked.

What kind of reaction have you had from employers of Syracuse graduates? Do potential employers seem indifferent to how the degree was achieved, or do they seem either more or less likely to employ graduates of the distance education program?

Often, we hear that employers of our MLS distance learning graduates are very excited about how students achieved their degree. MLS graduates who have completed a distance learning program are exposed, de facto, to a great deal of technology. Distance learners must be excellent managers and users of technology in order to succeed—so our distance learning students are at an advantage to some main campus students.

But as our Director of Career Planning points out, most employers do not usually ask how a student received the graduate degree. They are interested in Syracuse's graduate program regarding content. Employers are most interested in the skills that the student brings to the table. The MLS provides content that allows for skill development and a broad knowledge of the field, with practical experience in the form of internship. "Our MLS program provides for solid skill development and an excellent fundamental knowledge base—that's what sells the employer."[1]

- *University of Arizona* (UA) School of Information Resources and Library Science at http://www.sir.arizona.edu/viropps. Note that AU requires that all distance learning students complete twelve credits of coursework (of a required thirty-six total) on campus prior to completing the program, so effectively limits online coursework to two-thirds of a student's studies. A minimum of two online courses are available each semester. Useful sections here include a WebCT (courseware) tutorial, a technology guide, and a guide to UA library resources for students.

- *University of Illinois at Urbana-Champaign* (UIUC) Graduate School of Library and Information Science, LEEP (Library Education Experimental Program) at http://alexia.lis.uiuc.edu/gslis/degrees/leep.html. UIUC points out that they no longer consider the program "experimental," yet the acronym has stuck. The LEEP Master of Science program combines brief periods of on-campus study with Internet instruction and independent study. UIUC makes heavy use of interactive technology, using chat, audio, slides, and video to recreate a classroom experience. Their program differs from many others in this way, and courses may require up to two hours per week of "live" Internet interaction at regularly scheduled times. Each LEEP student begins the program with a twelve-day on-campus stay, and is required to spend a brief period on campus at the beginning of each semester thereafter.

- *University of Pittsburgh* (Pitt) FastTrack MLIS at http://fasttrack.sis.pitt.edu. This new (in 2001) offering is a two-year degree program that offers both a public/academic and school media track to students. Pitt requires its distance education students to invest heavily in computer equipment and connectivity, stating on its Web site that it expects its FastTrack students to trade the expense of housing, parking, and transportation for these other

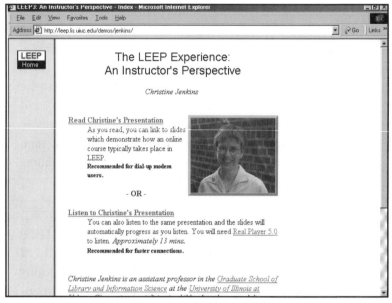

Figure 9.2   The LEEP Experience from the UIUC GSLIS

technological costs. They recommend students acquire (as of 2001) a computer with a Pentium III processor or higher, and require all students to have Microsoft Office 2000 and an Internet account with one of Pitt's "preferred" (high-speed cable or DSL) Internet providers. Pitt's program utilizes a good deal of streaming audio and video to help duplicate the on-ground experience, hence the requirements for a fairly high-end system and fast Internet connection. Students are required to spend some time on campus with their learning cohort the summer before beginning the program, and then to come back to campus for one weekend every semester thereafter.

Our list excludes programs such as Texas Woman's University's "Multi-Site Cooperative MLS Program," which it offers in conjunction with the University of North Texas (http://twu.edu/slis/ls/coopmls.htm). This program differs from the online MLS opportunities mentioned here in that it uses a combination of interactive TV and Internet to offer the MLS at satellite sites throughout Texas. Emporia State University (http://slim.emporia. edu/program/distance/distance.htm) offers a similar satellite program that combines online coursework with intensive week-end sessions (about once a month for each course) at satellite locations in a number of states.

Earning Other Library Degrees Online

Some schools have begun offering LTA (Library Technical Assistant) and other associate degrees online. Library workers who are not inter-ested in earning the MLS or who lack a bachelor's degree may be inter-ested in earning these types of degrees over the Internet. Schools that offer these library technology programs online include the University of Cincinnati's Raymond Walters College (http://www.rwc.uc.edu/ academic/libmedia/lt/index.html). Non-MLS library workers may also be interested in taking continuing education courses online; these are described later in this chapter.

Choosing a School

The previous descriptions of some online programs can help you determine whether you wish to matriculate at one of the above insti-tutions. Since technology, requirements, and focuses change, how-ever, always visit the Web site of each university you are considering. A school's site will tell you whether periods of residency are required, and will provide a fee schedule for online courses, a catalog, and other information to help you make an informed decision. Schools that require residency periods should also explain what arrange-ments they have made to provide students with housing at nearby hotels or in dormitories, and you need to include the cost of this short-term housing (and travel!) in your estimates. Also find out when residency periods will be necessary, and decide whether they will interfere with your work or other obligations.

There are several other questions to ask when browsing information about a school's distance learning opportunities on its Web site. Are online courses largely taught by full-time faculty? Is the school accredited by ALA? Does the program require periods of synchronous instruction such as regularly scheduled chats or video lectures? Will these interfere with your work schedule or family obligations? Does the school's page explain how students obtain access to required resources? Will articles be made available online, will the school fax or mail readings to you, and will you be able to purchase textbooks online and have them arrive in a timely fashion? Another concern at state universities may be the cost of out-of-state tuition, which can be somewhat prohibitive.

Some schools, such as CSU, give Web site visitors the opportunity to view a sample online course (http://www.onlinecsu.ctstateu.edu/Demo_A_C/index.real). If that option is available, spend some time examining the courseware. Is it easy to use? Do the options seem straightforward? Can you see yourself interacting productively this way with your professors and peers? UIUC offers a somewhat less interactive introduction on its page, but you can see what the courses look like through a series of screen shots or online video at http://leep.lis.uiuc.edu/demos/jenkins. Also use a school's Web site to find out what type of technical support will be available as you work your way through the online coursework.

Determine what type of forum or other software will be used in the course. Often, you can search the Web to find interactive demonstrations of and information about popular courseware such as WebCT (http://www.webct.com) to help you decide whether the course environment will be comfortable and productive.

The ALA list of accredited institutions mentioned in the previous chapter (http://www.ala.org/alaorg/oa/disted.html) is one of a number of resources that will help you locate schools that currently offer the ability to take classes online and notes whether each offers distance learning programs. Their list, however, includes programs that offer any type of distance education, including videoconferencing, online classes, satellite programs, and correspondence courses. Read the information carefully to find out what distance learning means in each particular case. You can continue your quest with lists such as LibraryHQ's Distance Learning for Librarians Via the Internet, at http://www.libraryhq. com/distance.html. This list links to a variety of LIS schools that offer online coursework, and notes whether some period of on-campus attendance is required. Also see About.com's distance learning feature, available at http://librarians.about.com/careers/ librarians/bldistlearning.htm.

Continuing Education Opportunities Online

Working librarians interested in updating their skills, filling in gaps in their education, or keeping themselves aware of new developments in the profession can turn to online coursework. Internet education may be even more convenient for degreed librarians in the process of building their careers, who are unable to take time away from their jobs or travel. Information professionals can choose to take Internet courses at library schools or through professional organizations, state libraries, library systems, and other bodies that offer online education. For a searchable guide to all types of online courses, check out the GNA distance learning catalog at http://www.gnacademy.org/ mason/catalog/front.html.

Library School Coursework

Most of the schools offering the online MLS degree welcome part-time students who are interested either in filling in gaps in the coursework offered by their home school or who wish to pursue continuing education opportunities online. Some additional schools offer selected courses or continuing education classes online, although they may not (yet) offer the full degree via the Internet. According to ALISE's *1999 Statistical Report*, forty-five library schools offered a total of 533 distance education classes in the 1997–1998 academic year (*Report* Part III, Distance Education section para. 1). The number of distance education courses is increasing dramatically each year as library schools try to remain competitive. Although not all of these courses are offered online, the Internet is becoming an ever-more-popular method of delivering distance education. Schools that offer some type of library-related online coursework (but nowhere near the entire MLS online) include these:

- *Rutgers University* School of Communication Information and Library Studies at http://www.scils.rutgers.edu/ac offers continuing education courses for librarians, media specialists, and teachers using asynchronous Web-based methods. It also offers a Youth Literature and Technology certificate, which is a 15-credit certificate offered entirely online. Test whether your system meets Rutgers' technical requirements online at http://rutgersonline.net/index.real?action=technical. The site will interactively test your browser and give you instructions on updating your system to meet the school's requirements.

- *University at Buffalo* (UB) School of Information Studies at http://www.sis.buffalo.edu/lis/courses/distancepage.htm. UB offers very few classes via the Internet, but some recent course titles include "Intellectual Freedom" and "Government Information." It utilizes a WebBulletinBoard (WBB) as well as a Discussion Room with regularly scheduled chats with the professor, combining both synchronous and asynchronous teaching methods. Some classes are also offered as independent studies or via interactive video at several extension sites.

- *University of Toronto* at http://ce.fis.utoronto.ca/courses/ webbased.htm offers a number of Web-based continuing education classes. These include courses in competitive intelligence, legal research on the Internet, and mastering Web searching. Most of the courses are not only offered over the Internet, but are also Internet related. The courses listed here are strictly continuing education classes and do not qualify for graduate credit, but they are offered at a reasonable rate.

- *University of Wisconsin*, Madison (UW) School of Library and Information Studies at http://polyglot.lss.wisc.edu/ slis/academic/ces/index.html. They offer a variety of continuing education courses, on-ground, via Internet using WebCT software, and as correspondence courses. Their continuing education course listing notes the method by which each class will be taught. Online courses have included "Virtual Collection Development" and "Basic Cataloging."

Some schools now offer both pre- and post-MLS online certificate programs for information professionals who want to add to their credentials. Drexel, for example, currently offers an online professional certificate in competitive intelligence (http://www.cis.drexel.edu/grad/ci). Their CI certificate can be earned entirely via the Internet in three ten-week modules, and is aimed at corporate information specialists in fields such as competitive intelligence, market research, and strategic planning. Drexel also offers a variety of professional development continuing education courses; see http://www.cis.drexel.edu/grad/continuing_ed.html.

Classes from Professional Organizations

Professional organizations from ALA to SLA to ARL have recently offered online seminars or workshops to help practicing information professionals build their skills in particular areas. ARL

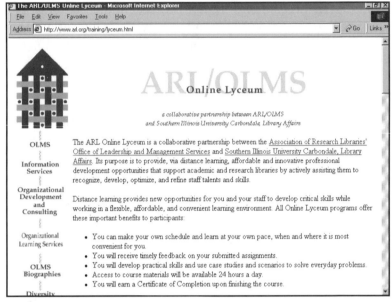

Figure 9.3   ARL Online Lyceum

maintains an online Lyceum at http://www.arl.org/training/ lyceum.html, in collaboration with Southern Illinois University Carbondale's Office of Library Affairs. Courses are discounted for ARL members. ARL offers a combination of self-paced instructional tutorials and collaborative courses that make use of both synchronous and asynchronous methods of interaction, and will mail certificates of completion to each participant who successfully finishes one of their courses. Examples of topics covered in ARL's Lyceum include "Measuring Library Service Quality" and "Training Skills Online."

SLA has a distance learning program to help special librarians further their professional education (http://www.sla.org/ content/learn/learnwhere/index.cfm). Like ARL, SLA includes both self-paced study and "virtual seminars" among its course offerings, and classes are discounted for members. Most of SLA's distance education opportunities seem to be short (one day) seminars rather than full-length courses, and focus around PowerPoint presentations rather than an interactive Web board or e-mail. SLA also has a variety of video and CD-ROM-based courses for sale on its site.

Watch also for online courses offered around special events and/or topics, such as the Fall 2000 e-mail tutorial ALA offered on UCITA (Uniform Computer Information Transactions Act) at http://www.ala.org/washoff/ucita/events.html.

Classes from Local and Regional Groups

Smaller professional organizations, library systems, and state libraries often offer online continuing education classes to members or to library staff working in a particular state/system. Online continuing education classes from Illinois' Suburban Library System (SLS), for example, are offered only to member library staff (and board members!). SLS offers a number of online courses, most focusing on computer skills such as creating Web graphics, JavaScript and CGI programming, and the use of Microsoft Office applications. Get information about their Internet continuing education program at http://www.ed2go.com/sls.

The Colorado Library Marketing Council currently offers an online course on marketing tools for librarians—which, for an additional charge, allows participants to receive graduate credit (http://www.clmc.org/online_course.htm). Check the Web pages of your state library, local system, and local/regional associations for links to such educational opportunities. Often these courses qualify as part of the requirements for state certification.

Other state libraries and groups have begun posting conference and course information. Among these is the Illinois State Library, which sponsors a series of satellite teleconferences that are viewable on certain dates and locations throughout the state. It has begun posting these teleconferences on its Web site in RealPlayer format so that librarians can watch them at their leisure, at http://www.cyberdriveillinois.com/library/isl/training/video.html. (These were previously only available in videotape format through interlibrary loan.)

Related Online Classes

Many working librarians find that they need to update their skills in areas not limited to classes offered by library schools and library organizations. Librarians who are adding "Webmaster" to their job descriptions, for example, may welcome the opportunity to take an online course in using HTML or Microsoft FrontPage. Such classes are often significantly cheaper than those offered by library schools, and can be more convenient for working professionals than on-ground courses at community colleges or computer training centers.

Be careful when choosing an online course, however, that you select one from a reputable educator. With the ease of creating coursework in conjunction with some of the online courseware providers, almost anyone can set up a professional-looking site. Look for sample classes, testimonials from previous students, and brand-name recognition when selecting an online class.

Some librarians that have started their own consultancies have added online training to their repertoire. These consultants often offer both courses for the general public and classes specifically aimed at information professionals. For an example of online classes available from consultants, see Kovacs Consulting at http://www.kovacs.com/training.html. The workshops include topics such as "Designing and Implementing Web-Based Training" and "Genealogical Research on the Internet."

Another useful resource for information professionals interested in online professional development is L.O.S.T. (The Librarians' Online Support Team), at http://www.gnacademy.org/~lost/. L.O.S.T.'s mission is to foster librarians' professional development with a combination of formal and informal online instruction and mentoring. It sponsors a variety of free professional development workshops and seminars that are based on the virtual campus of Diversity University (http://moo.du.org), in a MOO environment.

Lastly, information professionals interested in improving their skills in a particular area, especially skills with a specific computer program, may wish to investigate taking online tutorials on specific topics. These are self-paced, independent tutorials that differ from formal classes in that there is no professor and no interaction with other students—and they are often available for free. To locate such tutorials, start with a site such as Tutorialfind (http://www.tutorialfind.com/tutorials), which is searchable by subject (although heavy on computer-related tutorials). Independent tutorials allow librarians to improve their skills, and the interactivity allowed by the computer medium makes online tutorials more useful for hands-on computer classes than just going through a book might be.

Disadvantages of Online Coursework

Although taking classes online offers many advantages, opening up possibilities for those unable to take on-ground coursework, there are potential pitfalls to consider.

Distance Education and the "Real World"

Online education is a relatively new phenomenon, and many schools and employers have been slow to catch on. In the Lisjobs.com Education Survey mentioned in Chapter 8, for example, twelve of the sixty-eight employers who responded—almost eighteen percent—indicated that they would be less likely to hire an information professional who had earned an MLS degree over the Internet. Although a large majority of respondents said that it was irrelevant how the degree was obtained (as long as it is ALA accredited), several of those who noted that they would be less likely to hire an applicant with an online degree expressed concerns that these librarians would be less prepared to enter the "real world" of work. Some of the distance education students surveyed for this chapter also mentioned that they absorbed more of the culture and philosophy of librarianship in their on-ground courses.

Although relevant work experience is important in being considered for any professional position, it can specifically serve in this case to temper the views of employers who are unsure of the value of distance education. Those who complete their degree online might be wise to ensure that they have a background in library work or have completed an internship to complement the online experience. Your transcripts will not necessarily show that you completed an online program, but it will become apparent to employers if the timing of your tenure at Connecticut State University, for example, overlaps your full-time position working at a public library in Chicago.

Some employers, especially those looking for computer and Internet expertise in their applicants, express the opposite point of view. One distance education survey respondent expanded on the job search experience: "I think it was very impressive to potential employers. It shows you know something about technology, and that you took the initiative to get into something that is different and on the rise in the field of education. I think most employers don't understand much about it, but it looks good on paper to them." Your experience may vary depending on your employer's comfort level with technology and faith in the distance learning process.

Access Problems

Some students enrolled in online courses report having had difficulty accessing required readings, textbooks, and the professional literature necessary for background research. As one

respondent to the distance education survey noted of her experience in a newer online program: "We all bought our textbooks, of
course, but graduate work of necessity requires readings in the literature. Southern [Connecticut State University] did little to make
this available, and most of it was not easily found except at large
academic libraries. I ended up copying what I needed at
Southern's library when I was there for my on-ground courses; I
would then fax the material to my fellow students who lived at a
greater distance from school."

This is becoming less of a problem at schools that have offered
distance learning programs for several years and have had time to
work out the kinks in the delivery of material. Aspiring online students, however, should be sure to inquire as to how the school provides necessary resources to students who are not taking classes
on-ground. Make sure that the available online databases, textbooks, and articles are sufficient for you to complete your coursework. See how proactive the school is in providing resources for
off-campus students. What electronic databases are available? Will
required readings be made accessible, either online, or by fax or
e-mail? Will the school provide technical support in the event of a
glitch? See if the school's Web site or its library's Web site includes
a section outlining the services available to remote students. If
possible, talk to librarians at the school's library to see what services are offered to distance learners. How do they handle interlibrary loan, for example? Do they have reciprocal borrowing
agreements with institutions in your town?

These issues may be even more important for rural students or
those who otherwise do not have easy physical access to a large university library. If you do live in an area where this applies, you will
have to be self-motivated in acquiring necessary materials and allow
time for them to arrive via interlibrary loan or other methods.
University of Arizona Assistant Science-Engineering Librarian
Maliaca Strom mentioned: "Other students who were from more

remote parts of the country sometimes had difficulty accessing research materials for papers, etc. Oftentimes, people only had access to small, public libraries that weren't able to get the needed amount of materials for their research through interlibrary loan on a timely basis." Plan your work ahead of time to avoid such problems.

If you intend to matriculate at a university that offers an online MLS program, see if the school is willing to put you in touch with current students or graduates. Sometimes these contacts are available from a school's Web page. Students may be more open with you about any technical or access problems they may have encountered during their time in the program than the school's official spokespeople will be.

Suitability for the Online Medium

Students who have completed an entire MLS degree online note that a few courses do seem less suited for the online medium than others. The most common types of courses mentioned as being difficult to absorb by respondents to the distance education survey included cataloging and research methods/introduction to reference. Information manager Nancy Brochu noted that "it's more difficult to practice and understand MARC records and how to compile a Dewey Decimal number when it has to be done online."

How well a particular class is suited for the online medium may also depend on the environment in which it is preparing students to work. A reference course that focuses largely on print materials that will be of use in public libraries and one that gives its attention to locating online documents in a corporate environment will be taught very differently, whether provided on- or offline. It may be more difficult to absorb the content of the former course, however, when it is provided via Internet and students lack the opportunity to spend time examining and working with print reference materials. Potential youth services librarians who intend to take classes on topics such as storytelling may also want to think twice about the online medium.

Other respondents felt that any class could be adapted for the online medium, but the difficulties they faced in individual courses were related to the reluctance of particular instructors to thoroughly adapt materials for the Internet or to spend the time necessary to make the class worthwhile. As one respondent who took most of the classes toward her degree online noted: "The quality of the course depends much more on the professor than on the subject matter. I encountered one professor who did not want to be teaching online and was forced into it—and her negative attitude and computer ineptitude was most obvious throughout the course. Other professors took to the online environment like fish to water."

Reluctant and negative professors, of course, are not unique to the online medium, but you might spend some time on the school's Web page to see how extensively its professors have adapted to the Internet. Do they post syllabi, research, or other materials online, or are there testimonials from current faculty about the effectiveness of the distance education program? You want your distance education professors at the very least to have a high level of comfort with Internet tools and online interaction.

As always, research the program before committing your own time and resources. Some time spent now will save you frustration later, whether in the online or offline environment. But if you are just beginning your library education, or if you want to enhance your skills with workshops and classes, look into online education as a way of expanding your options.

Endnotes

1. Interview excerpted with permission from the March 1, 2001 issue of the *Info Career Trends* electronic newsletter. Full interview is accessible online at http://www.lisjobs.com/newsletter/archives.htm.

Works Cited

Brown, John Seely and Paul Duguid. *The Social Life of Information.* Boston: Harvard Business School Press, 2000.

Casado, Margaret. "Delivering Library Services to Remote Students." *Computers in Libraries* Apr. 2001: 32-38.

Daniel, Evelyn H. and Jerry D. Sayes, eds. *Association for Library and Information Science Education: Statistical Report* 1999. Reston, VA: ALISE, 1999. Feb. 11, 2001 (http://ils.unc.edu/ALISE/1999/Contents. htm).

Chapter 10

Show Me the Money! Scholarships, Grants, and Awards

Many grants in the library field are aimed at providing funding for institutional projects, and are available for individual librarians only insofar as they provide financing for carrying out programs that will directly benefit the library. Grant-seeking information professionals, however, should be aware of personal professional development grants and awards that are available to help underwrite the costs of research, writing, and travel. In addition, library associations and other institutions fund scholarships for students interested in pursuing the MLS or taking continuing education classes. Librarians can find funding for activities ranging from personal research to continuing education to the completion of a library degree, or they can nominate themselves and others for awards for their contributions to the profession.

The Internet has made it easier for busy information professionals to research these funding and award opportunities. In many cases, librarians can apply for grants, awards, and scholarships electronically, or can print out an application provided online—saving the time it takes to request a form and wait for it to arrive in the mail. (Be sure that you have the free Adobe Acrobat Reader software installed on your computer, as many of these applications are posted in that format. Download the reader from http://www.adobe.com.) If no application is available online, some organizations at least provide an e-mail address for application requests.

The following sections focus on funding that is specific to study, research, or professional development activities in library and information science. For general financial aid ideas and to start your search for other scholarships and loans, however, a resource such as FinAid (http://www.finaid.org) can be helpful. The University of Washington's graduate school also provides a good list of funding resources online, at http://www.grad.washington. edu/fellow/hotlist.htm, which includes links to sites providing information on all types of fellowships, grants, scholarships, and research funding.

Keep in mind also that the specific grants, awards, and scholarships listed here are only examples of the types of funding available. Scour the Web sites of applicable library-related organizations, schools, and agencies for additional funding opportunities.

Scholarships

A library education can be prohibitively expensive, but librarians can take advantage of a variety of scholarships to help pay for either a full MLS or continuing education opportunities. Realize, though, that most scholarships will only cover part of the cost of a library education. You will either have to pay for the rest out of your own pocket or find supplemental sources of funding such as government loans. If you currently work for a library or related organization, check with your human resources department or administration; many institutions reimburse the cost of classes toward completion of the degree (although this is usually contingent upon your agreeing to stay with the organization for a set period of time after you graduate).

Since scholarships are offered by a variety of associations and groups, funding is available for students of differing backgrounds and interests. Examine the scholarship information available on a number of Web sites to find the one(s) that will be most applicable for you, and remember not to automatically dismiss the possibility of finding funding. Students sometimes have the misconception that scholarship money is available only for students with impeccable GPAs and test scores, but many funding bodies in librarianship are more concerned with your potential contribution to the profession.

MLS

Begin your search for scholarship funding for your MLS education with the online presence of the larger professional associations. Although association-sponsored scholarships are generally available only to members, the cost of membership is much less than the potential savings should you garner one of these scholarship opportunities. For examples of the types of scholarships available from professional associations, examine sites such as SLA's scholarship and awards page at http://www.sla.org/content/

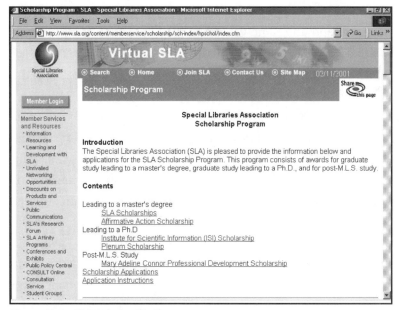

Figure 10.1   SLA Scholarship Program

memberservice/scholarship. Each year SLA awards three general $6,000 scholarships to incoming MLS students and one Affirmative Action scholarship of $6,000 to a member of a minority group, with preference given to those who display an interest in and aptitude for work in special libraries, association members, and those with previous work experience in a special library.

When looking at the scholarships available from SLA, note the detailed application instructions that are posted on the site. Be sure to follow such instructions to the letter when applying for a scholarship from any funding body. Typical requirements include providing the association with a copy of your college transcript, letters of recommendation, demonstration of acceptance by an ALA-accredited institution, and a short essay describing why you qualify for the scholarship and what contributions you expect to make to the profession. Treat your scholarship application as seriously as you would a job application; provide all requested materials completely and professionally. SLA also provides both a printable and an online version of the application form for their scholarships, including instructions on how to fill out each section, how many copies you need to send in, and the due date of the application.

The information provided on the SLA scholarship site serves as a typical example of what you can find when looking for scholarships online. Other associations also post detailed scholarship pages; AALL describes some scholarships for aspiring law librarians at http://www.aallnet.org/services/sch_edu.asp, and descriptions of ALA scholarships are provided at http://www.ala.org/work/awards/scholars.html. For scholarships available through other national associations or subgroups, check the home page of each for a link to "scholarships" or to "scholarships and awards." (A list of associations and their Web addresses can be found in Appendix A.)

Often, scholarships for LIS study are available for students of particular ethnic or cultural backgrounds. The ALA Spectrum Initiative, for example, recruits applicants for graduate study in librarianship and offers fifty $5,000 scholarships yearly to African American, Latino/Hispanic, Asian/Pacific Islander, and Native American/Alaskan Native students. (For information and an online application form, see http://www.ala.org/spectrum.) Such scholarships aim at increasing diversity within the library profession, helping make librarians more representative of the communities they serve. They typically require that the applicant complete the official application form, write a personal statement, and provide three to five references as well as transcripts from their undergraduate institution. The Gates Millennium Scholarship program also provides funding for ethnic minorities, and library science is one of the areas the foundation particularly stresses (http://www.gmsp.org).

Major divisions, roundtables, or caucuses may also provide their own scholarships; check the sites of the ones in your area of interest. REFORMA (National Association to Promote Library and Information Services to Latinos and the Spanish-Speaking), for example, awards a yearly $2,000 scholarship to incoming or current graduate students in librarianship (http://www.reforma.org/schinfo.html). The purpose of the scholarship is to encourage bilingual and bicultural individuals to enter the profession, so this scholarship is awarded to Spanish speakers with a demonstrated desire to serve the Spanish-speaking community in the U.S. Applicants must provide REFORMA with transcripts, two letters of recommendation, a current resume, and a completed application form (which can be printed from the Web site).

When looking for funding for your MLS, also visit the Web site of your state library and state association. Many of these smaller organizations grant scholarships to degree-aspiring students, although the amount awarded may be less than that available from one of the national associations. The Alaska Library Association (AkLA), for instance, provides $2,000 scholarships to students who are beginning or currently enrolled in an ALA-accredited program (see http://www.akla.org/scholarship.htm). Applicants must be Alaska residents and agree to work in an Alaska library for at least one year after graduation, and are required to provide evidence of financial need, an essay describing their professional goals and objectives, and three letters of recommendation. The size of some state scholarships can be significant. The Illinois State Library is an example of a state agency that uses LSTA (Library Services and Technology Act) federal funding to provide up to fifteen yearly $7,500 scholarships to state residents entering library school as full-time students in an Illinois MLS program (http://www. cyberdriveillinois.com/library/isl/training/train00.html). They require recipients to maintain a certain GPA and to sign a contract agreeing to work in an Illinois library for a total of two years within the first three years after graduation. Other state associations and libraries that offer scholarships generally have similar service and GPA requirements; check their respective Web sites for applications, requirements, and instructions.

Lastly, check the Web site of the particular school(s) you are interested in attending to see what scholarships the school itself may provide. For examples of the types of funding that may be available through your school, note that Information School at the University of Washington provides several scholarships based on such factors as financial need, academic achievement, and/or a student's ethnic background (http://www.ischool.washington. edu/mlis/finaiduwscholarships.htm). While checking a school's Web site, also investigate the cost of completing an MLS at that institution; see whether available scholarships will cover the cost. Do not forget to factor in the cost of books, lodging, and fees.

Before applying for any scholarship, understand that there generally are some strings attached. Be sure that you will be able to meet the terms and conditions before applying for any particular source of funding.

Ph.D.

Because the MLS is the main professional degree, fewer funding opportunities are available for librarians who wish to pursue their doctorate. SLA, however, offers two such scholarships (for $1,000 each—see details at their scholarships and awards address listed in the MLS section above). The Medical Libraries Association (MLA) funds a similar $2,000 award for graduate students in the field of health sciences librarianship (http://www.mlanet.org/awards/grants/doctoral.html), but oddly enough their grant must be used for research and/or travel expenses rather than for tuition.

Some associations, although they do not fund the cost of study toward the doctorate, will provide award or scholarship money for dissertation research or to recognize significant doctoral research in the field. ASIST, for one, administers a UMI-sponsored doctoral dissertation award of $1,000 plus an additional $500 to attend the annual ASIST meeting (http://www.asis.org/ awards/docdissumi.htm). The award is available only to those who have recently completed the Ph.D., and is intended to recognize their research and provide a forum for them to present it to the profession at the annual conference.

Often, funding for the Ph.D. is available from individual graduate programs. Check the Web sites of graduate schools offering doctorates in the field for fellowship opportunities and scholarships. If schools do not provide funding for the entire Ph.D., they may at least provide dissertation or research funding for doctoral students. See for example UIUC's list of doctoral grants, at http://alexia.lis.uiuc.edu/gslis/school/awards.html#doctoral, which includes several that are available to UIUC doctoral candidates only. Also check a school's Web site for teaching assistantships and related opportunities that can allow Ph.D. candidates to work their way through graduate school by teaching or by assisting professors with their research.

Continuing Education/Post MLS

Scholarships for post-MLS study in a certificate program or for continuing education classes are also available from professional associations. Start looking for such scholarships at the addresses given above for MLS funding; all types of scholarships are often listed on the same page (other than at ALA, which generally only funds study toward the MLS). SLA, for example, sponsors the Mary Adeline Connor Professional Development Scholarship of up to $6,000 for post-MLS certificate or degree programs; applicants must already possess an MLS and have worked in special libraries for five or more years. See details at http://www.sla.org/ content/memberservice/scholarship/sch-index/hpschol/index. cfm#macscholar.

Associations often provide small continuing education scholarships to defray the cost of a particular class or workshop. One example of this is the Medical Library Association, which awards between $100 and $500 for continuing education activities; see http://www.mlanet.org/awards/grants/ceaward.html. Also check the Web sites of your state and regional associations and state libraries for available workshop funding. The Colorado State Library, for instance, cosponsors continuing education scholarships for Colorado library staff. These scholarships provide up to $200 per year for staff members in libraries that have limited funds for continuing education, and the state library will reimburse tuition, lodging, and travel for qualifying activities (http://www. cde.state.co.us/cdelib/slcescholarships_intro.htm).

Other funding opportunities for MLS graduates include a variety of post-graduate fellowships from individual institutions and universities.

Grants

Grants provide the money for librarians to engage in professional development activities such as research or conference attendance. Some also allow information professionals to study or teach in another state or country. Read the requirements for any grant carefully; many require, for example, that the recipient be a faculty member at an ALA-accredited library school or that a certain research methodology be used.

Research

ALA and other large library organizations often announce grants for librarians doing research in the field. One example of such a grant is the $25,000 ALA Research grant, first announced in September 2000. This grant solicits research proposals from librarians on ways in which library services have a positive impact on the lives of users and what the role of librarians should be in adding value to electronic information. (View the press release at http://www.ala.org/alaorg/ors/research_grant.html.) Descriptions of and applications for other ALA research grants are available online from the Office of Research and Statistics (ORS) at http://www.ala.org/alaorg/ors/orsawar.html. Although many of ALA's more general grants are aimed at institutions, ORS grants are given to individuals doing research in specific areas.

Additional large research grants are available through other larger national organizations. OCLC and ALISE (Association for Library and Information Science Education) have teamed up to offer grants of up to $10,000 to library school faculty interested in independent research. According to the OCLC Web site, this grant is intended to "promote independent research that helps librarians integrate new technologies into areas of traditional competence and contributes to a better understanding of the library environment" (http://www.oclc.org/oclc/research/programs/grants/call.htm).

Other library-related organizations provide fellowship funding for scholars wishing to conduct research at their institution. Chicago's Newberry Library awards both long- and short-term fellowships to researchers, which are intended both to support individual research at the library and to promote participation in its scholarly activities. To this end, fellows are required to participate in a biweekly fellows' seminar. For information about available Newberry fellowships and for online applications and instructions, see http://www.newberry.org/nl/research/L3rfellowships.html. (These grants are not aimed specifically at librarians, but are available to researchers from any relevant field.) The Library of Congress (LoC) has a similar opportunity available, the American Memory Fellows program (http://lcweb2.loc.gov/learn/amfp), which is intended to give humanities teachers, librarians, and school media specialists the opportunity to spend time working with LoC staff and collections in order to study how primary sources can enrich the curricula for grades 4–12. The fellowship provides the funding for participants to attend a six-day summer institute in person at the LoC, and then fellows interact over the rest of the year through online discussion forums.

Some smaller, local library associations also provide funding for library-related research. Such funding, however, is often more limited than that which the larger associations offer. The Mountain Plains Library Association, for example, has a professional development grants program aimed at member librarians who are interested in completing their own research projects (http://www.usd.edu/mpla/committees/profdev/grants.html). The association offers both mini-grants (under $150) and regular grants (up to $600) for research that will benefit the library or associated professions.

Information professionals who are interested in locating grants in the field should also establish a free account at the U.K.-based The Nutshell, at http://www.thenutshell.co.uk. The Nutshell links to LIS funding bodies worldwide, so librarians can browse through the list to see which of the funding bodies may have applicable research grants.

Travel

Other specific grant awards include those available for visiting scholars. Organizations sponsoring such grants generally solicit applications from library science educators and researchers who have distinguished themselves in the field, or who show the potential for making a significant scholarly contribution, either to the sponsoring institution or to the profession as a whole. Grant money is available both for U.S. library practitioners interested in researching and/or lecturing abroad, and for non-U.S. scholars who wish to come to the U.S. to work with researchers here.

Librarians interested in teaching and doing research in another country should look at available Fulbright Scholarships from the Council for the International Exchange of Scholars (CIES) at http://www.iie.org/cies. Each year, CIES awards grants for visiting lecturers and researchers to teach and do research abroad, and the group also brings a large number of foreign academics to the U.S. CIES offers a variety of these grants in the field of library and information science. OCLC has a similar "visiting scholar" position available to bring outside researchers to OCLC and to allow them to collaborate with OCLC staff and use OCLC facilities and resources to conduct research in areas of mutual interest. See http://www.oclc.org/oclc/research/programs/visiting_scholar/about.htm. Figure 10.02 shows the type of information that is generally available on these "visiting scholar" pages.

Librarians outside the U.S. may be interested in the grants IFLA provides for travel to international conferences and study in the

Figure 10.2   OCLC Visiting Scholar Program

U.S. These fellowships are described at http://www.ifla.org/III/members/grants.htm.

Conference Attendance

Library associations such as ALA provide access to grants sponsoring conference attendance for new librarians. Information professionals interested in garnering such conference funding generally are required to apply for the grant in writing and must explain how conference attendance will impact their professional development. This is another case in which the writing skills developed through participating in online discussions or writing for publication can help you create a coherent argument to convince an award committee of the importance of conference attendance to your library career. (For more on conferences, see Chapter 5.)

For examples of the application forms for such grants, look at the EBSCO Conference Sponsorship application, at http://www.ala.org/work/awards/appls/ebscappl.html, and the ALCTS First

Step Award description, at http://www.ala.org/alcts/awards/ firststep.html. Check for information on grants that may underwrite your attendance at an annual ALA conference at the main ALA grants page as well as on the home pages of roundtables of which you are a member.

Other large library associations and vendors also encourage new librarians to attend national conferences by paying their conference fees and travel costs. EBSCO Subscription Services funds an MLA conference attendance grant (http://www.mlanet.org/awards/grants/meeting.html), which requires a similar statement as to how conference attendance will professionally benefit an attendee. Grants are available for both MLS students and Ph.D. candidates; each year ALISE, for example, sponsors attendance at the ALISE national conference for two doctoral students in the LIS field (http://www.alise.org/nondiscuss/award_doc_stud.html).

Often, grants for conference attendance are available to encourage new or student librarians to develop their interest in a particular area of librarianship. An example of this is the Vormelker-Thomas student award (http://www.ibiblio.org/slanews/about/vormelker.html), which allows a $1,500 stipend for a student interested in news librarianship to attend the annual SLA conference. As part of the application process, interested students must submit a 500- to 1,000-word essay addressing an issue in news librarianship and must explain how attending the conference will help them attain their professional goals.

Some organizations even provide funding for librarians to attend international conferences. This can be especially useful if you are responsible for collection development in another language (or languages), or if you are considering a job exchange in another country. International conferences can help you get a feel for the environment and language, and also give you the opportunity to meet colleagues you may never otherwise have the chance to see in person. ALA's International Opportunities and Funding Sources for

Librarians page, at http://www.ala.org/work/international/ircirrt librarysupport.html, includes information on a variety of funding for international conference attendance and other opportunities. Their page includes, for example, information on grants that allow U.S. librarians to attend the Guadalajara and Zimbabwe international book fairs or to attend an international conference (such as IFLA) for the first time. It also lists awards for lecturing and researching abroad.

Awards

If you have written an article or otherwise contributed to the profession through publication, also look at the section in Chapter 7 on locating writing grants and awards. Most awards for published articles or for other contributions to the profession require that those so honored be nominated for the award, either by themselves or, preferably, by one of their colleagues. This is another reason to remain active on professional discussion lists and in other forums, as the name recognition you build up in this way may prompt one of your fellow librarians to nominate you for a relevant award. Or, if a few of your colleagues have distinguished themselves in the field, why not put their names forward?

Some authors may be nominated by their editors for awards in the field. (This is another reason to remain on good and professional terms with your editor!) Some library publishers even offer yearly awards to their own authors and editors, noting recent outstanding papers or books. Emerald, for instance, announces such awards online at its Literati Club (http://www. literaticlub.co.uk).

A variety of awards recognize individual achievement in a certain area of librarianship, and most of these are awarded by associations, roundtables, or vendors in the field. MLA gives awards to individuals who have contributed to the field of medical librarianship, which are described online at http://www.mlanet.org/awards/honors.

ALCTS presents eight awards each year to honor individuals who have contributed to the field of library collections and technical services through research, creativity, leadership, and/or service (http://www.ala.org/alcts/awards2001.html).

Some schools and other bodies have also begun recognizing information professionals who have distinguished themselves in particular areas of librarianship. Syracuse University's School of Information Studies, for one, instituted a 21st-Century Librarian Award in 2001 to recognize "librarians' work in shaping the new information environment that is emerging on a global scale." They seek nominations for candidates who have adapted traditional librarianship to a changing information environment, and reward the winner with $5,000 and recognition at a special ceremony at the school. (Information on the award and how to apply or to nominate others is online at http://istweb.syr.edu/librarianaward.)

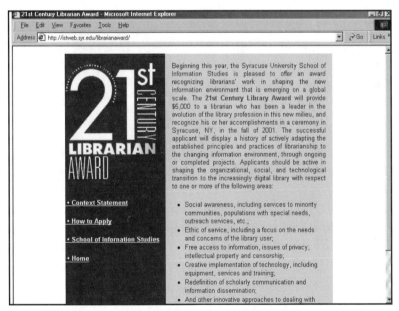

Figure 10.3   Syracuse University's 21st-Century Librarian Award

Besides the monetary benefits that accrue to those who are chosen for these awards, being nominated or selected for an award provides you with professional recognition—and a coup for your resume. Award winners are often listed in relevant professional journals or honored at national conferences, which can greatly increase your name recognition in the field.

As the previous examples demonstrate, funding in the library field is available, although sometimes hard to come by. Use the research skills you have developed as an information professional to ferret out the necessary funding both to help you develop yourself professionally and enable you to contribute to the profession.

Part 4

Employment

Chapter 11

Your Electronic Resume

If at any time you have been out in the job market, chances are that you have had to develop a resume as part of your application for a position. Sending out a resume and cover letter in response to a job posting is the first step in the application process. The content and format of your resume will have a significant impact on whether an employer will decide to interview you, so you want your resume to represent your qualifications in the best and most professional way possible.

If you have created a resume before, chances are that you initially created it in electronic form using a word processing package. However, you most likely had to print it out and send it through the mail in order to formally apply for a job. Over the past few years, electronic submission of resumes has become more accepted in the library world—both in addition to print resumes and as their replacements. In the following sections, we discuss the reasons why, if you are currently job-hunting, you will want to have an electronic version of your resume handy. We also talk about the most appropriate methods of sending your resume to employers, as well as ways to get an online version of your resume noticed.

Although we don't advise you on the actual content of your electronic resume, as this information is readily available elsewhere, we do give you numerous suggestions on why and how you should convert your paper resume into electronic form, as well as on the formats available. This chapter assumes that you have a previously created resume in hand, ready to work with in—or convert into—electronic format.

What Is a Resume?

Most simply described, a resume is an autobiographical document that contains a summary of your professional qualifications. At minimum, your resume should include your contact information, work experience, and education. Many job seekers also include an objective as well as names of professional associations and references. Your resume can take several different forms, chronological (your job history organized by time period) and functional (organized by subject matter) being the most common.

This is necessarily a brief, simplified view of a resume, but most—if not all—of this information should already be familiar to you. If you are new to creating a resume, though, there are numerous books that will take you step-by-step through the process of creating one from scratch. Several of these are noted in the "recommended reading" section at the end of this book. In particular, we highly recommend *Writing Resumes That Work: A How-To-Do-It Manual for Librarians* by Robert R. Newlen (Neal-Schuman, 1998). Not only is it the only book specific to librarian resumes, but it also provides many useful examples of resumes suitable for different position types and locations. In addition, About.com's guide to librarians and library science, Tim Wojcik, has a Web page listing the contents of a typical librarian resume (http://librarians.about.com/careers/librarians/library/weekly/aa021300.htm).

Why Create an Electronic Resume?

An electronic resume has numerous advantages over its print counterpart. It can be sent to employers, or viewed by them, at any time of the day or night. The speed of e-mail also eliminates the inevitable delay of snail-mailing your paper resume to an employer. In addition to this type of online networking, which requires direct action on your part, you can also post your resume online on a Web page, promote the URL appropriately, and let employers approach you. Another option is to post your electronic resume within an online resume bank. (We don't recommend your being too passive, however; in contrast to other fields, online resume banks are not the norm when it comes to traditional library positions.) There are practical advantages, too. If an employer accepts resumes in electronic form, you won't need to bother printing one out on special bond paper, making sure that the watermark is positioned appropriately, and then mailing it off.

As an example, the Web page for Endeavor Information Systems (http://www.endinfosys.com) includes forms through which interested parties can apply for jobs online; the forms include a space to paste in a text-based resume. According to Geri Hernandez, Technical Recruiter for Endeavor, more of their applicants respond to their Web postings than they do to print ads. In addition, she reports that, for Endeavor, resumes received via e-mail have many advantages: "We can distribute the resume with more efficiency to a manager or several managers at one time, and it doesn't matter if [the managers] are on the road or not. It is easier for the HR department to track the resumes if they are in electronic format, and managers tend to respond faster to electronic resumes." This being said, however, it is still the content of the resume, rather than the format, that ultimately determines candidates' eligibility for employment.

When you convert your resume in electronic form (if it is not originally in this form), the actual content stays essentially the same. You still include the same basic information: contact details, employment history, and educational background. The organization of these pieces of your resume can also stay the same, with some additional content for the Web version. What will change, though, will be the resume's file format and presentation.

In order to be read by employers, your resume will need to conform to certain electronic standards. For example, while the Microsoft Word printout used for your paper resume can theoretically use any readable font that is loaded on your computer, you should remember to use only well-known fonts when sending your Word file as an e-mail attachment to an employer. If you get too creative, your resume may come out looking differently on the recipient's end than you intended. For the HTML (Web-based) version of your resume, you need to use standard HTML tags, so that it can be viewed correctly by as many different Web browsers as possible.

The mere fact that you have a resume ready to send, or post, in electronic format can be to your advantage. It indicates a certain degree of technological ability to Net-connected employers, which today comprise the majority within the information field. Even if you hand in a paper resume when you apply for a job, if you include within it the URL for the online version, employers are likely to sit up and take notice—if not pay your online resume a visit. You may be surprised how frequently this occurs. In a 1997 survey conducted by one of the authors of this book, sixty-seven percent of employers who had posted a job opening on the Internet stated that they viewed candidates' online resumes if a URL was provided in the paper version (Nesbeitt, 32).

You may not necessarily be using your resume in an active job search, although this is the most common reason for creating one. If you are an academic librarian, you may be asked to supply your resume or curriculum vitae for an annual evaluation or promotion. (Typically longer than a resume, a curriculum vitae, or C.V., provides a comprehensive summary of your educational background and your career in academia.) Even if you are not actively job hunting, an online resume will broadcast your professional credentials to your peers and colleagues (and if your qualifications happen to meet an employer's needs, you may get inquiries from employers—and professional recruiters—in any case).

One last thing to remember before getting started is that, regardless of format, keeping your resume professional is of prime importance. Although much electronic communication tends toward the casual side, always remember that your electronic resume and your e-mail messages may be an employer's only initial guide to judge your qualifications. The general content and organization of both your print and electronic resumes should be identical. Also, while it is admittedly difficult to get too fancy with a plain text resume, it may be all-too-tempting to go crazy with backgrounds, colors, and fonts in the Web-based version. When it comes to any issue related to possible employment, it is always best to err on the side of caution.

Resume Formats

Let's take a look at the three file formats that are most important for your electronic resume: word processor format (we use Microsoft Word in our examples, as it is the most common program), ASCII (plain text), and HTML (for the Web).

If you are currently job hunting, it is preferable for you to have three separate versions of your resume—one in each format—ready to send or post at any given moment, but this may not be practical due to time constraints. If so, we recommend that you focus your attention on creating your HTML resume. Why? If you already have a resume in word processor format, which is most likely the case, making it conform to electronic standards will be neither difficult nor overly time-consuming. Also, it is relatively easy to convert a resume in MS Word to ASCII if an employer requires it.

Although an HTML-format resume may be the most difficult (technically speaking) to create, your resume's appearance on a Web page will get it out to the largest possible audience. It is also best to have this version done in advance, before you are actively out job hunting, simply because it is the most time-consuming. This way, you will be ready to include its URL in your e-mail signature file or on your print resume when you mail it out.

Each of these three formats will be used in different situations. We evaluate the situations when each is appropriate and provide examples of each, as we continue through the chapter.

Your Resume in MS Word Format

If you have typed up a resume before, it is likely that you used a word processor such as MS Word to create it. If you still have this electronic document, amending it to send via e-mail will be relatively straightforward. On the other hand, if all you currently have is a printout—the paper version, in other words—you will need to re-create it in a word processor before continuing. (And, if you are starting from scratch, consult the resume book for librarians mentioned earlier, or one of the resume books listed in the bibliography at the end of this book.)

We all know the advantages of creating a printed resume using a word processor. Since job seekers typically print out multiple copies at different times, as well as make changes to their resumes over time, it helps to have a master electronic copy on file to refer back to. Most print resumes make full use of features found in all word processing packages, such as different fonts, typefaces (bold, italic, underlining), bulleted lists, word wrap, and centering. The judicious use of these features can help your print resume stand out in a pile—something extremely important when you are out in the market for a job. However, you want to be careful of these very features when e-mailing your electronic resume off to a prospective employer.

Formatting Your MS Word Resume

The hardest part about formatting this version of your resume is being sure that the recipient will receive it in essentially the same form in which it was sent. This means that you should keep to electronic standards as much as possible.

The recipient's word processor will attempt to keep the file in the same format in which it was sent, but his or her version of MS Word may not have all of the same fonts that yours does. For this reason, in your own MS Word resume, change all of the text to a commonly used font. Times New Roman and Arial are always good choices. If you instead keep some or all of the text in an attractive but unusual font such as Centaur or Verdana, you run the risk of having the recipient's word processor use its default font—which may be something that doesn't work well for a resume—instead of what you intended. Or, worse yet, if you use a font that is extremely uncommon, your recipient's version of Word may not know what to do with it and will convert it into garbage characters.

You are also likely to find yourself making frequent use of the Tab key when writing your resume. When you do this, before sending it off to another party, check to see that your tabs are set to the standard half inch. The same principle holds true for margins. Keep to standards here as well: an inch on both sides, as well as top and bottom, is plenty of room. Finally, if your resume is more than one page long, don't rely on "soft" carriage returns (the carriage returns that appear automatically after you have typed a certain amount) to divide your pages. If you do, the pages may be reformatted inappropriately on the recipient's printer. (Within MS Word, a soft return appears as a horizontal dotted line.) Instead, force your word processor to indicate the end of a page by including a hard page break (CTRL-ENTER in Word) where you wish to

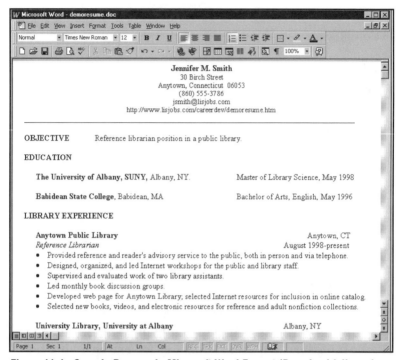

Figure 11.1 Sample Resume in Microsoft Word Format (Download full version at http://www.lisjobs.com/careerdev/demoresume.doc)

divide your pages. As long as your top and bottom margins are adequately long, this will keep the pages of the recipient's copy of your electronic resume looking the same as your version. When you are unsure of what will work best, remember to forsake anything fancy and stick to the standards.

E-Mailing Your MS Word Resume

When you have the go-ahead to e-mail an employer a copy of your resume in word processor format, what is the best way to go about it? In general, there are two ways of e-mailing a document: by cutting and pasting the text directly into an e-mail message or by including the file as an attachment. When it comes to e-mailing your resume in MS Word, the latter is the better option, because you cannot be sure of the e-mail program the person on the other end is using. For example, suppose both you and the recipient are using Microsoft Outlook, an e-mail program capable of displaying formatting tags (such as bold text, italicized text, and margins) appropriately. If you highlight the text from your resume, including all of the special fonts and formatting, copy it, then paste it into an Outlook message, there will be no problem if the recipient is also using Outlook. The resulting message will come through just as you have sent it. On the other hand, if the recipient is using a text-based e-mail program such as Pine, only the words from your resume will come through; all special formatting will be lost. When you e-mail your Word document as an attachment, all formatting will be kept, provided you conform to standard fonts, margins, and so on. Not all e-mail packages can receive attachments, although the majority can.

While we have been using MS Word in this chapter to provide examples, don't forget that there are a number of other frequently used word processors on the market. WordPerfect is another common choice. Each software package also has many different versions, some of which are not backwards-compatible. A computer running MS Word 6.0, for example, cannot read a resume saved in MS Word 97 or 2000. There is no guarantee that the recipient will be using a program that can read the attachment you send.

Most word processing packages, fortunately, let you save a document in a format other than the one in which it was originally created. Within MS Word, choosing File, then Save As, then picking a different version from the drop-down box labeled "Save as Type" will let you convert your MS Word document to another format. If you are unsure what word processor format is best, you can always ask the recipient what format(s) he or she can accept before you attach your file and send it; in many cases, though, this will be noted within the job ad itself. If all else fails, MS Word 97 and 2000 are safe options to choose, as they can be read or converted by most current PC or Macintosh word processor programs.

Last but certainly not least, before sending a Word document to anyone else on the Internet, remember to check your hard drive, and in particular your resume file, for viruses. Microsoft Word "macro" viruses are common, and while many of them are less dangerous than other virus types, they have the potential of "attacking" other Word documents on your hard drive and corrupting all or part of whatever files are subsequently opened. It is true that you will want employers to remember you and your application, but giving them a virus is not the way to do it! Invest in some antivirus software if you have not already done so, and make sure you are running the latest available version. About.com's guide to antivirus software (http://antivirus.about. com/compute/antivirus) provides recommendations of software packages as well as detailed information on what viruses can and can't do.

Your Resume in ASCII (Plain Text) Format

If you have ever come across a file name with the extension ".txt" at the end, chances are that the file is in ASCII format. A document in ASCII (American Standard Code for Information Interchange) format is essentially in plain text format—characters only, with no formatting codes whatsoever. (You may also hear this format referred to as "text only" or "plain text.") This means that these documents won't contain any words in bold, italics, underlining, or any special font. You will not find graphics, headers, footers, or hyperlinks in these documents, either. The only things you see in an ASCII document are the letters, numbers, punctuation marks, and other symbols you would find on a typewriter, including carriage returns. ASCII files, because they contain only text, can be exchanged by all available e-mail packages without anything being lost in the "translation." ASCII files can also be incorporated directly within the text of an e-mail message.

Although plain text documents are not necessarily pretty, they do have a great advantage when it comes to creating an electronic resume. Because employers in the information field use a variety of different e-mail packages, and usually there is no easy way to tell in advance what type of e-mail program your potential future employer will be using, it is best to err on the side of caution and send your resume in ASCII unless otherwise requested.

In the following sections, we provide hints on creating a plain text resume in Notepad, a text editor that comes with all Windows-based operating systems, as well as in MS Word. As with the previous section, apart from the specifics that we give on starting up

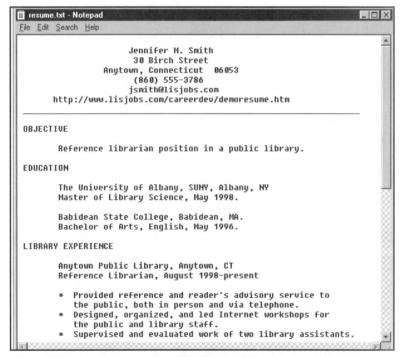

Figure 11.2   Sample Resume in ASCII (Text Only) Format, Created with Microsoft Notepad (View full version at http://www.lisjobs.com/careerdev/demoresume.txt)

both programs, the hints we provide can be applied to any text editor or word processing package.

Creating an ASCII Resume in Notepad

The main reason to start creating a resume from scratch in Notepad—or any other text editor—is if you don't already have a resume in electronic form. If you already do, you will find it much easier to convert your file into "text only" (see the next section) rather than retyping everything.

You can find Notepad on any computer running Windows 95 or higher, by clicking on Start -> Programs -> Accessories -> Notepad. Note that you are only allowed to work with one file in Notepad at any given time. As Notepad is a text editor, once the program is started, all you need to do is begin typing. With a printed copy of your resume (or a resume book) in hand, here are some hints on re-creating your resume in text format.

- Although Notepad will let you select your font, pick a fixed-width font such as Courier or Courier New, 12 pitch. Avoid proportional (TrueType) fonts such as Arial or Times New Roman. With TrueType fonts, not all characters are the same width. While this makes for easier readability in MS Word documents, using them in a text-based resume can result in irregular spacing.

- Use the space bar instead of the Tab key when you indent.

- Include a carriage return at the end of each line, or use Notepad's "word wrap" feature (which will automatically insert hard carriage returns for you as you type).

- Use asterisks or hyphens where you normally would use bullets.

- Type no more than sixty-five to seventy characters on a line. Because margins do not appear in Notepad, this is a safe way of making sure you don't end up with lines that

are too long when you cut and paste your resume into an
e-mail message.

- Because there is no "center" command, use the space bar
  when centering text in relation to the rest of your resume.
  This is one of the reasons it is important to use a fixed-
  width font; if you do not, your centering will be off.

- Use capital letters to highlight words, such as your name
  and resume headings (such as Objective, Experience, and
  Education). Use caps sparingly, though, just as you normally would for bolded text in a regular resume.

When you are done, save your file with the extension ".txt" to
indicate that it is a text file; the filename "resume.txt" is typical.

Creating an ASCII Resume in MS Word

All that we have mentioned in the previous section holds true
when you create a plain text resume in MS Word or another word
processor. Make as many changes as are necessary—such as
changing the font of all text to Courier New 12—within Word itself,
rather than taking the time to fix these things later in Notepad. You
will also have an extra step: after you have a final copy of your
resume typed up in Word, use the Save As command. You will want
to use "Text Only with Line Breaks" as the format. Remember to
use ".txt" as the file extension (this will be the default).

After you have saved this new file, open it up using Notepad.
Make whatever adjustments you need. If there were any characters,
such as bullets, in your original Word file that don't translate into
ASCII, they'll stand out. Proofread your resume carefully to make
sure you have caught all of the problems before sending it via e-mail.

E-Mailing Your ASCII Resume

Unless otherwise specified in a job ad, when e-mailing an ASCII
resume, it is best to include it within the text of a message rather

than as an attachment. Always remember that some people prefer not to deal with attachments, and some e-mail programs are simply unable to handle them—it is better to play it safe when sending a resume to someone you do not know. If the recipient does prefer to receive resumes as an attachment, note that viruses do not attach themselves to text files, so you will have some reassurance on that score.

It is a good idea, though, to see how your electronic resume might look from the recipient's point of view. Try testing out how your resume looks on the other end by first sending a copy to yourself. Try e-mailing a copy to friends as well. Test it out, if possible, with a variety of different e-mail programs, so that you will have your bases covered. If it looks fine, you are ready to send it off. If you see problems in the way that it appears when you receive it, return to Notepad to edit the resume file appropriately.

For more on e-mailing your resume to employers, see the section "When to Send Your Resume Electronically" later in this chapter.

Your Resume in HTML Format

In contrast to its MS Word and ASCII counterparts, the HTML version of a resume is not meant to be sent via e-mail. Instead, the reason you want to create a resume in HTML is so that you can post it on the Web for others to view.

You can be more creative with a Web resume than you could possibly be with its paper equivalent. Not only can you add graphical content, such as a photograph if you so choose (although there is some controversy over this), but you can also jazz it up by adding color. HTML has advantages over plain text in that you can keep the majority of the formatting from your MS Word resume, including bolded text and bullets. With a Web resume, you can also link directly to other Internet sites, in particular to Web pages and other projects that you have created. If you have already created a

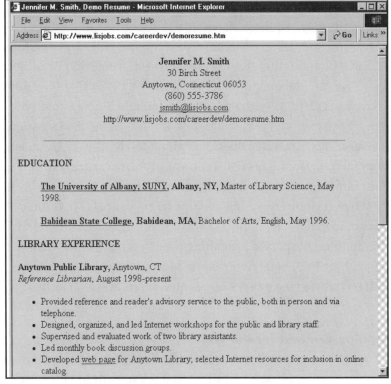

Figure 11.3   Sample Resume in HTML, as Viewed in Web Browser (View complete, full-color version online at http://www.lisjobs.com/careerdev/demoresume.htm)

professional Web page using the guidelines in Chapter 6, a Web version of your resume will complete your online presence.

Creating and Converting your HTML Resume

All of the pointers mentioned in Chapter 6 for creating a Web page as part of your online presence apply to creating a Web-based resume. If you are starting from scratch, use one of the HTML editors recommended in Chapter 6 to type your HTML resume. If you already have a resume written in MS Word, you can use Word's built-in converter to translate your resume into a format suitable for the Web. This feature is available in MS Word 97 and higher, though it may require separate installation (it is an add-on feature), and you will need to have your original MS Word or Office CD-ROM handy. After this feature has been installed in Word, you can save any document in HTML format by choosing File, then "Save as HTML." Give the resulting document a new name, without any spaces, and use either .htm or .html as the file extension. Because this converter doesn't work perfectly (this is an understatement!), you will need to fix up any problems (extra blank lines, for example) that result from the conversion.

When it comes to saving and uploading your HTML resume, it may help to remember that HTML files are, in fact, ASCII files with the addition of specific formatting tags. In other words, when you upload (or FTP) your Web resume to a database or Web site, you will be transferring it in ASCII (as opposed to "binary") format.

Adding Content for the Web

Your Web resume should be more than an exact duplicate of your paper resume translated into HTML. Take advantage of the capabilities of the Web to spice up your resume with additional content.

First, add external hyperlinks to your resume. Link to your previous employers' Web pages and to your educational institutions' Web pages, so that people can jump to view information about places where you have been. Don't go overboard, though; one link per paragraph should be plenty. Include your e-mail address within the contact information at the top of your resume, and make this address a "mailto" link so that employers can click on it to send you e-mail. If you have worked on any Web-based projects, make sure to include them, and add links to these projects' locations on the Web. PowerPoint presentations for workshops you have given can also be converted to Web format (using PowerPoint's built-in HTML converter) and linked from your resume. You may also wish to include separate Web pages containing the texts of articles you have written, and link to these—assuming, of course, that you own the copyright. Alternatively, if articles you have written are already online, such as at a publisher's Web site, it is a good idea to add links to these sites.

It may help to realize that, on the Web, you do not need to be as concerned about resume length as you would be in print. This doesn't mean that you should go all out and include excruciating detail about each of your ten previous jobs, but you can include more information than you would normally have room for on a print resume. If your Web resume ends up being longer than two screens, though, consider adding links at the top of the resume (after your contact details) that lead to sections occurring later within the document. (These are known as "anchor" tags in HTML, or as "bookmarks" if you are using Microsoft FrontPage 2000.)

Although slightly more detail is allowed on the Web version, the overall content of the resume body should remain the same as other forms of your resume. There are some sections, however, that you may wish to consider amending or removing. For example, because your resume will be posted on the Internet for all to see, you may not wish to include your home address or phone number. In this case, your e-mail address will suffice, but you can mention that you will be glad to provide more detailed information to interested parties. You will almost certainly wish to reconsider listing your references' names and contact information in order to protect their privacy. A simple line stating "references available upon request" should do the trick, but even this isn't necessary; it is assumed.

Should you bother including an objective at the start of your resume? This all depends on whether you are currently in the job market, or whether you are just posting your resume online for informational purposes. In the case of the former, including an objective indicates, first, that you are job-hunting, and second, the types of positions you are looking for. Because you can never be

sure who will be looking at your online resume, including a position-specific objective, or any position-specific language at all for
that matter, is generally inadvisable. If you do include an objective,
you will need to strike a balance between the general and the specific. This is not the time to tailor your resume to a particular job
you are interested in; save that for your print or ASCII versions. As
an example, an objective such as "Position as a reference librarian
in an academic library" should suffice.

The jury is still out on whether you should include a photo of
yourself within your online resume. While it can have the effect of
making your resume more personal, your photo can also give
employers clues to your age or ethnic background—which you
may or may not want to reveal before the interview. The same
holds true for other personal information. If your resume is linked
to a personal Web page that provides details on your family background, marital status, or other personal interests, be aware that
this information may influence employers' decisions on whether
or not to interview you.

If you have other versions of your resume available—such as an
MS Word or ASCII version—upload both of these versions to your
Web space, and add links to them toward the bottom of your Web
resume. A downloadable resume in Word can be of particular
interest to employers, because HTML resumes do not always
appear in print as they do on screen. (Remember to upload your
MS Word resume in "binary" format while FTPing.)

Finally, include a "last revised" date at the bottom of your
resume (and update it frequently!), so that employers know that
they are viewing the most recent version.

Presentation and Design

Besides content, of course, presentation and design are critical
in the development of a Web-based resume. Since a well-designed
online resume gets people's attention, you want to make sure that

yours is sufficiently eye-catching. Here are some hints on ways to make your Web resume visually appealing.

Use color, but use it sparingly. While all or the majority of the text in your resume should be the standard black or another neutral color (dark blue or gray, for example), you can use a colored line, for example, to divide sections. Other ways to use color include changing the colors of links from the default blue (unvisited) and purple (visited) to another combination of your choosing.

While the background of your resume doesn't necessarily need to be white, keep it a light, neutral color, just as you would with printed resume paper. Or, instead, you may wish to experiment with a neutral graphic as a background image. Stick to light tans and grays for the most attractive results. Some examples of neutral background graphics and images can be found at http://www.free-backgrounds.com; in particular, check out the "Classic" and "Business" categories. One sample resume, available at http://www.lisjobs.com/jsmith/demoresume.htm, demonstrates the use of neutral background and font colors.

Under no circumstances should you use light text on a dark background (unless your specialty is Web design and you are sure of what you are doing). These resumes can be hard on the eyes, and employers may have difficulty getting them to print correctly.

Unlike your plain-text resume, you can be somewhat creative with fonts on the Web, but stick to commonly used fonts, such as those you would use in your MS Word resume: Times New Roman, Arial, and Geneva, for example. If you don't specify a font, Times New Roman 12 is generally the default. Stay away from Courier and other fixed-width fonts, as these can make your resume look plain. Remember that, although you can be as specific as you want in terms of what fonts to use, the fonts available on the PC of whoever is viewing your resume will be a limiting factor. You should therefore only choose standard fonts. You may also wish to specify alternate fonts, in case the reader doesn't happen to have your preferred font installed.

If your print resume uses columns, you will need to create a table within your HTML resume in order to get the text to display in the same format. When viewing others' online resumes, if you wish to see how a particular file was created, view the HTML source code. Within Netscape, just choose View and then Page Source, or pick View -> Source from Internet Explorer.

If you are knowledgeable about Web design, take this opportunity to show off your skills, but your resume should remain tasteful and readable. In other words, keep overwhelming color choices, animated graphics, and sound for your Web design portfolio—you don't want employers to be distracted from the actual resume content.

Before you are through, make sure that you view your resume using a variety of Web browsers to make sure it displays correctly. At minimum, check its appearance using both Netscape Communicator and Internet Explorer. Does the text line up as you wish? Is the color scheme appropriate? Do the fonts show up correctly? The best way to double check your resume's appearance is to post it online and then have some friends view it with their browsers, monitors, and screen resolutions, particularly if you have included graphics or nonstandard fonts.

Posting Your Resume on the Web

Once you have finished creating your HTML resume, you are ready to start thinking about sites where you can post it online for others to view.

Where should you post your resume? Naturally, if you already have a presence on the Web, you should post your online resume within the same Web space. In addition to other suggestions mentioned earlier in Chapter 6, your home page should contain a link to your resume, so that employers can find it easily. If you use an e-mail signature file that includes the URL for your home page, linking your resume to your Web page will be of prime importance. You never know whether a potential employer will be reading the e-mail messages that you contribute to a discussion list.

As with professional home pages, you have the option of choosing to post your Web resume in space provided by your Internet Service Provider or by a free Web page hosting service such as Yahoo! GeoCities or Angelfire (http://angelfire.lycos.com). Be aware, though, that many of these free services display advertising, and while you may be able to get away with ads within a home page, they are not really suitable within an online resume.

Most employers hiring traditional librarians do not go out recruiting applicants; they advertise their open positions and let candidates approach them. Because of this, if you are searching for a job as a librarian, you may not find it worthwhile to list your resume with a major online service such as Monster.com. Instead, you may wish to stick with posting your resume on your own site, and advertising the address within your home page or signature file.

Resume Sites for Information Professionals

When it comes to resumes, though, you have additional options for sites on which to post them. Seek out resume sites—collections of online resumes—dedicated to information professionals. These sites are generally smaller and not nearly as complex as general sites for job seekers, and they are not usually searchable by keyword. Your library school's Web site is a good place to start. Catherine Collins, a librarian at Texas A&M University-Commerce and a graduate of the library program at the University at Buffalo (SUNY), reported that she found great success with the online resume she posted at her library school's Web site. She explained, "I received nearly a dozen offers to apply for positions from libraries that I had no previous contact with—solely based on my online resume. I believe that much of my success can be attributed to the effort of my MLS program in publicizing new graduates." Buffalo's "Put a Buffalo in Your Library" program is described at http://www.sis.buffalo.edu/lis/studentresources/pab/index.asp.

Many other library programs have Web pages that link to online resumes of both students and alumni. (If you don't know the URL for your alma mater, an index of Web pages of library programs in the U.S. and Canada, with links to Web pages, can be found at http://witloof.sjsu.edu/peo/library.schools.html). The University of Michigan's School of Information (http://www.si. umich.edu/careers/si-resumes.htm), for example, offers such a service, with resumes organized by job category. The University of Texas at Austin's GSLIS program has a similar site (http://www.gslis.utexas.edu/~careers/resume.html), but it is for current students only. Other library schools, even if they don't have a specific page for online resumes, may have a site that lists student or alumni Web pages.

Rachel Gordon's Lisjobs.com (http://www.lisjobs.com/resumes. htm), for a small fee, provides Web space to librarians (and formatting help, if desired) for an electronic resume. In addition, in late 2000, the Special Libraries Association debuted its Career Information Center, which allows all users to create an online version of their ASCII resume using a template (http://sla.jobcontrolcenter. com/apply/advertise.cfm). Librarians may use their electronic resumes, as hosted here, to apply online for jobs. Employers may search the resulting online resume bank for parties who may fit their needs. Applicants can decide whether to keep their resumes confidential or make them available to everyone.

General Resume Sites

If you are looking for a nontraditional position in the information world (such as within the subfields of knowledge management or data mining), or a position as a corporate or special librarian, you may find it worth your time to post your resume with one of the major general online job-search services. Many of these services are even free to job seekers.

Monster.com (http://www.monster.com), for example, lets job seekers create a free account, and with this service you can include up to five different online resumes—which is handy if you are interested in more than one type of position. You can make your resume private (viewable only by you), confidential (which hides your name, contact details, and current employer), or active. Only active resumes appear in the database that employers can search. Unlike the types of online resumes listed in this chapter, however, Monster.com uses its own resume format, which requires you to cut and paste sections from your text-based resume into a template.

Sites such as this are fairly common, and for this reason, it is good to keep a text version of your resume handy. Margaret Riley Dikel, within the Web pages of her Riley Guide for Internet job hunters, presents comprehensive lists of free resume database sites (http://www.dbm.com/jobguide/resfree.html) and fee-based resume sites (http://www.dbm.com/jobguide/resfee.html). Not all, though, are appropriate for information professionals. Of the sites listed, school librarians may have the most luck with education-related sites such as the free Teacherjobs.com (http://www.teacherjobs.com).

Using Keywords Within Your Resume

Most books dealing with electronic resumes advise you to make good use of "keywords" when composing your resume. What does this mean? Are keywords even important for information professionals?

Keywords, in this context, include nouns and phrases that best describe your job-related skills and qualifications. They can be terms that describe your job function (collection development, technical services, bibliographic instruction); your abilities (database searching, teaching, Web design), or industry-specific terms, products, and organizations you are familiar with (Windows NT, DRA, OCLC, ALA). A number of Internet-savvy recruiters, including many working in the computer field, use keywords as terms when searching online resume databanks. In addition, recruiters who scan paper resumes into their company's internal database may use keywords to index and retrieve your resume from their files.

As an information professional, you need to consider what types of jobs you want before you start worrying about whether you need to be conscious of the keywords you use. For example, certain types of positions are more apt to be listed within electronic resume databanks than others. Also, not many employers in the information field scan applicants' resumes. Individual public, academic, and school libraries don't normally have the staff or the time to create an electronic file of all applicants' resumes. Corporations that hire information professionals, though, may maintain such a database.

If you plan to submit your resume to a general site such as Monster.com, however, you want to be conscious of the keywords you use. The catch is that you cannot always be sure which keywords recruiters will be using as search terms, and there is no possible way for you to guess all combinations of these terms. Also, the keywords you choose will depend on your job-related duties and experiences. In general, you should choose keywords that are well known in the field, such as those just mentioned; do not use terms that would not be known outside of your current work environment. Rebecca Smith's Keyword Resume Tutorial (http://www.eresumes.com/tut_keyresume.html) will take you step-by-step through the process of creating what she terms a "keyword resume."

When to Send Your Resume Electronically

When should you use an electronic resume, and when is it best to stick with a print version? Despite all of what we have said about the importance and use of electronic resumes, the fact remains that within librarianship they are still fairly new, particularly in comparison to fields such as computer science. Many library human resource departments, for example, still require a paper resume.

Read the Job Ad

Naturally, the best indication of whether electronic resumes are acceptable is if they are specifically mentioned in a job ad. Some ads mention that electronic applications are preferred, and they typically give an e-mail address where resumes should be sent. If the job ad doesn't specify what format to use—MS Word or plain text, for example—you can't go wrong with a text-based resume. Send both your cover letter and resume via e-mail, within the text of the same message. Include the cover letter first, followed by your ASCII resume. If you also have an MS Word version of your resume available, mention this within your cover letter, or, if you have a Web resume, include the URL.

Similarly, it should go without saying that if you read the statement "no e-mail inquiries" within the ad, you should apply as directed (usually via the traditional paper route). Save your electronic resume for another time.

Query Before Sending

If a postal address is provided within the ad, chances are that the employer wishes to receive print resumes. But if a contact e-mail address also appears within the text of the position announcement, it is a sign that the employer is open to receiving e-mail inquiries. By querying via e-mail, you may end up impressing someone with your technological abilities.

The mere inclusion of an e-mail address within a job announcement should not automatically indicate that this is the time to e-mail a copy of your resume. While most employers, particularly those who post job ads online, are happy to accept e-mail questions from applicants, it is best not to e-mail a copy of your resume without first finding out whether it is an acceptable form of applying for a job. E-mailing library directors or personnel officers a copy of your resume out of the blue can give them an instant negative impression. It takes little or no effort to e-mail a resume to multiple people once it is been created, and employers know this, so you run the risk of appearing desperate, or, at minimum, unfocused. In the online world, there is also the perpetual problem of "spam"—unsolicited, unwanted e-mail that nobody likes to receive. You don't want your electronic resume, as important as it is in the job search process, to be seen as spam by a prospective employer.

Your e-mail query will not be a substitute for a formal cover letter, so within your e-mail message to an employer, briefly discuss your qualifications for and interest in the position, and ask whether he or she would be willing to look at your electronic resume. Ask, also, whether the employer would like you to follow up with a paper resume. This is important for two reasons. First, your electronic resume—particularly if it is in ASCII—may not be aesthetically pleasing when compared with those that other candidates have printed out and mailed in. Second, while employers may be willing to look at your electronic resume, they still may need a print resume for their records. You want to make sure that your application is considered on an equal basis with that of everyone else.

If in doubt, ask first whether it is appropriate to e-mail your resume, and also ask about accepted formats.

Web Sites for Electronic Resume Help

Not surprisingly, there are a variety of Web sites that provide suggestions on the format and content of an electronic resume (as well as when and when not to use them). Although most of these sites are not aimed specifically at information professionals, much of the advice holds true for all applicants.

Rebecca Smith's *eResumes and Resources* (http://www.eresumes.com) is one of the premier Web sites on the subject, with useful how-to advice and a gallery of examples to follow.

Margaret Riley Dikel's *The Riley Guide*, mentioned earlier, has a specific section on composing an electronic resume and writing cover letters to go with them (http://www.dbm.com/jobguide/letters.html).

The Web Resume (http://icdweb.cc.purdue.edu/~mcgrady/webresume/ webresume.html), a site run out of Purdue University, focuses on the HTML version of your resume: how to create it, what it should contain, and how to format it using Netscape's Page Composer. It also provides links to a variety of sites that illustrate good Web design. Even though some of the directions found here are Purdue-specific, you will find some general hints here as well.

Once you have created an electronic resume, you have completed the first part of the online job search. In the next two chapters, we take you through the next two steps: looking for online job postings in the information field and using the Web to research employers.

Works Cited

Nesbeitt, Sarah L. "Trends in Internet-Based Library Recruitment: An Introductory Survey." *Internet Reference Services Quarterly*, 4.2 (1999): 23–40.

Chapter 12

Library Job Hunting Online

The Internet is a natural place to begin searching when you are in the market for a new job. Not only can you can scan online job postings at your leisure, but announcements from halfway across the country are as easily accessible as those from your local area. Most online job sites are free to job seekers, and a number of these same sources are free to the employer as well, making it cheap, easy, and fast for ads to be disseminated. Employers looking to quickly fill positions look first to the Internet, because the turnaround time for posting can be immediate. In many cases a job ad appears online before it ever appears anywhere in print, giving you the chance to respond immediately and get your application noticed first.

The Internet abounds with online job banks, professional recruiters, industry-specific sites, and job search tips, plus meta-indexes to them all. Without guidance to this plethora of online employment sources, it can be hard to decide where to look first. In December 2000, Yahoo.com listed over 800 sites containing job announcements. Only four of these, however, were specifically geared toward librarians. From this, you may deduce that there aren't many relevant online sources for our profession, but your assumption would be far from correct. The authors' Web sites, Library Job Postings on the Internet (http://webhost.bridgew.edu/snesbeitt/libraryjobs.htm) and Lisjobs.com (http://www.lisjobs.com) link to more than 300 individual Web sites, placement firms, and electronic mailing lists aimed at helping information professionals find employment. Most take the form of online classifieds. Not all, of course, will be relevant for your particular needs. In this chapter, we

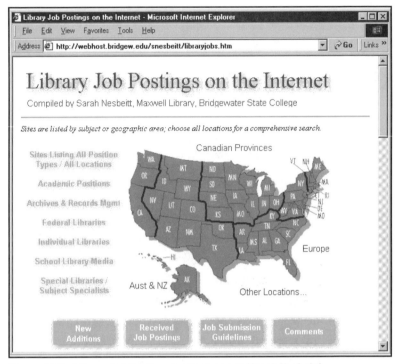

Figure 12.1   Library Job Postings on the Internet (Sarah Nesbeitt)

recommend the best places to look on the Web for job announcements, whether you are looking for a traditional library position or
wish to branch out into a related field. We also cover sites where you
can find advice on job-hunting and the interview process.

Pros and Cons of the Online Job Search

We have already mentioned some of the advantages of job hunting online: speed, access, and timeliness. Before we get into the
real "meat" of this chapter by telling you how and where to look for
the jobs, here are some additional issues you will be facing when
you conduct your job search online.

Figure 12.2   Lisjobs.com's Job Postings Page (Rachel Singer Gordon)

Online Anonymity

You have the opportunity to be almost completely anonymous on the Internet. There is nothing preventing you from obtaining an e-mail address from one of the free sources mentioned in Chapter 2 and responding to job ads that way. If you are currently employed, and you don't want your employer to know that you are job hunting, you may wish to use a free e-mail service. It may also be a good idea for you to hide your home phone and mailing address from public display on the Web, for privacy reasons.

When it comes to job hunting, though, anonymity isn't necessarily a good thing; keeping your identity a secret can easily backfire. First, some employers may look down on free e-mail accounts, mainly because many "spammers" hide behind such addresses. If you use such an address and post to discussion lists with it, make sure you sign the messages with your real name. (And if you do end up using a free e-mail account or AOL, don't choose a "cutesy" username, because it can indicate a less-than-serious attitude to employers.)

Will you be barraged with e-mail from employers if you indicate on a resume board or discussion group that you are looking for a job? Most likely not, so you shouldn't be afraid on that score. But if you do want to keep the fact that you are job hunting from your current employer, be discreet. Your employer may have rules against personal use of the Web during work time or use of the employer's resources for your own purposes. The information profession can be a small world, so if this is true for you, surf only during off-hours, and take care not to mention your job situation on public discussion lists.

Technological Advantages

Because technological skills are so highly prized in today's libraries, employers will be impressed with the degree of technological ability you demonstrate by job hunting online. Indicate in your cover letter that you are responding to a job ad that was posted on the Web or on a discussion list, and mention the specific source. On your print resume, indicate the URL of your Web resume or professional Web page, especially if you have added links to projects you have worked on. If you are a strong candidate, there is an excellent chance that the employer or a search committee member will take the time to go online to find out more about you. No matter what type of library position you are applying for, the more technological expertise you can demonstrate, the better off you will be in the job market.

The Global Internet

In the online job market, geography can work both for you and against you. On one hand, you can easily locate job ads in libraries thousands of miles away, via sources you might not otherwise have access to. Employers frequently advertise online in order to widen the applicant pool, particularly if a local search failed to attract good candidates. They know that if they advertise online, librarians around the country will be reading their ads. One children's librarian, writing from North Carolina, found her current position via the Internet while she was living in New York. As she explains: "When I received my MLS twelve years ago, my search for work was hit or miss, costly, and localized. When I started searching for a new job a few years ago, it was like the world had opened up. Online job listings are one of the best things to happen in library circles in the past ten years!"

On the other hand, many library jobs are posted online without the employer's direct knowledge. The director of a small public library in Colorado, for example, may post a job ad in the local library consortium newsletter, intending to attract local candidates. What this employer may not realize, though, is that the newsletter will be posted on a Web page for anyone around the world to view. Employers in this situation may be surprised to receive inquiries and applications from librarians outside the local area. If you do get an interview invitation from such an employer, there is also a good chance that you will have to pay your own way. This is not to discourage you from applying for remote jobs listed in local advertising sources such as newsletters and regional joblines, though. If you are a strong candidate, your current location may not matter. And if you have definite plans to relocate to the area where you are applying, don't forget to mention this in your cover letter.

Speed and Currency

One advantage to Web-based job ads is speed and currency; many ads, particularly those posted in electronic discussion groups, appear online before in print. Also, once you apply, employers can choose to respond to you just as quickly. As one Colorado librarian reports, "Recently I submitted an online application, sent my resume via e-mail and was called the following day for an interview. It was easy and amazingly quick!"

A disadvantage with some online job announcements is that they may not list the date when they were posted. If there is no obvious clue, such as a job closing date or posting date, be wary of the ad. This is particularly true when you are searching online mailing list archives, which may contain ads from anytime within the past few years. Because it is better to be safe than sorry, it will benefit you to contact the employer either by e-mail or phone to check whether the position you want is still open.

Online vs. Traditional Job Hunting

Can you use the Internet as your sole source for job announcements in the library field? Of course you can. But the more appropriate question may instead be: Should you? Because you will be able to find many more jobs online than you possibly could in print (or via telephone), and because it has so many other advantages for the library job seeker, the Web is easily the best single source when it comes to finding job announcements. If you are familiar with the best Web sites for your needs and check them on a regular basis, and if you are signed up for the most appropriate discussion groups, you may not ever need to consult any other sources for job ads. Still, when you are job hunting, you cannot afford to ignore any possible leads. In this case, it can help you to be aware of what job sources aren't online. *American Libraries*, for example, regularly publishes lists of library telephone joblines in its classified section, and the *Bowker Annual* does the same. Most joblines these days have online equivalents, but some states and regions still have not caught up to others this way. Keep your eyes open for jobs posted on bulletin boards at your local library or library school, and read your local library newsletter, looking for position announcements as well as for clues (such as retirement announcements) that jobs may soon be opening up.

There is more to job hunting than simply finding ads to apply for, though. Networking is just as important in person as online, which is why conference and meeting attendance is imperative for job seekers. Getting yourself known as someone who is professionally involved is helpful at any stage of your career, but particularly if you are looking for a position. Also, you never know whether the colleague you meet at a professional conference will be able to connect you with a job opportunity at some point in the future.

Online Job Listings for Librarians

Within the library field, relevant job listings may be found online in a variety of different places, including the following:

- Joblines posted by library associations, consortia, and state libraries

- Newsletters posted by library associations and consortia

- Placement services posted by library associations

- Classified ads from trade journals

- Job announcements and placement bulletins posted by library schools

- Ads and services from placement services and employment agencies

- Online newspaper classifieds

- Jobs posted on electronic mailing lists

Each has particular advantages for both the employer and the job seeker, but when you are doing a comprehensive job search, the actual format is not important. What is essential is that you consult all of the possible listings for your particular interests.

Focusing Your Search

Where would you like to work? This is best decided before you begin the online job search, if at all possible. While in theory there is nothing wrong with being undecided about location or library type, the fact remains that the more undecided you are, the more sites you will have to consult—and that can increase the amount of time you spend going though online classifieds. More specifically, here are some questions you will want to consider as you begin the process:

- In which type of library or organization do you want to work?

- What type of position are you looking for?

- In what geographic area would you prefer to live?

- Are you looking for a traditional library position, or something more nontraditional, such as a position within the field of knowledge management?

Think about your answers to these questions as you read through the following sections, as some sections will be more applicable to you than others, and the Web sites that you consult the most often will depend on your employment preferences. Because in the interest of space it is not feasible for us to outline every library job site that we have come across, we recommend that you consult either of our respective Web pages for a comprehensive list of these sites.

General Sites for Librarians

If you are not sure where you would like to work, or if you would just like to get a feel for the types of jobs that are currently available, start with general sites. Trade journals in librarianship that post their job ads online can be reliable general sources. In most cases, you still have to wait until a new print issue is published (occasionally weekly, but usually monthly or bimonthly) before new job ads appear online. While these sources are wonderful for those who wish to view a wide range of available jobs, not all libraries can afford to advertise in these publications.

All members of ALA should be familiar with Career Leads, the classified ad section published at the end of each issue of *American Libraries*. For the benefit of all job seekers, the last several months' worth of these ads are available online at ALA's Web page (http://www.ala.org/education). As with the print ads, the online ads are organized by library type. Public and academic library positions predominate. Also at this site are *American Libraries*' Late Job Ads, which are posted as received, usually every weekday. Employment classifieds from the other main trade journal in the field, *Library Journal*, are also online (http://libraryjournal.reviewsnews.com; choose Jobs-Library at left). Here you have the option of viewing all ads or doing a search for specific terms.

The LIBJOBS mailing list, sponsored by IFLA, is a high-traffic e-mail list dedicated exclusively to library job ads. Employers take advantage of this free advertising method to contribute anywhere from a few to several dozen messages per day—when we say "high traffic," we mean it! To receive job ads from LIBJOBS as e-mail messages, it is easiest to sign up via the Web gateway (http://listserv.nlc-bnc.ca/cgi-bin/ifla-lwgate.pl/LIBJOBS). However, you and your mailbox may find it more convenient to view a month's worth of postings all at once via the monthly archive (http://infoserv.nlc-bnc.ca/cgi-bin/ifla-lwgate.pl/LIBJOBS/archives).

Most library schools receive job announcements from local employers and post these jobs internally for students to view. Some take this one step further and offer placement bulletins to current students and alumni, and a number of these present online versions freely to all via the Internet. Despite their apparent regional nature, many online placement bulletins from library schools are also good sources for job ads nationwide. Although a portion of the ads may be most applicable to candidates from the area surrounding the school, don't forget to consult these sites in your overall job search. Some of the best placement bulletins to visit include SLISJobs, a searchable database from Indiana University (http://www.slis.indiana.edu/cfdocs/slisjobs); the Southern Connecticut State University Library Jobline (http://scsu.ctstateu.edu/~jobline), organized geographically and by library type; JobFinder, from the University of Michigan School of Information (http://intel.si.umich.edu/cfdocs/si/jobs/postings); and the weekly job listings from the College of Education, University of Missouri-Columbia (http://www.coe.missouri.edu/~career). At the latter site, choose the category "library science."

Employment Sites by Library Type or Position Type

You may already know that you would like to work for a particular type of library or in a particular type of position. If so, a number of online employment sources, such as those from subject-specific library associations or trade journals, await your attention. By focusing your search within these subject-specific Web pages, you can save yourself some time; still, don't forget also to consult the general sources mentioned above.

Academic and Research Libraries

Academic librarians already know the best print publications for job ads: *College & Research Libraries News* (*C&RL News*) (monthly except in summer) and *The Chronicle of Higher Education* (weekly). Advertisements from these three sources have translated well into the online format. Postings from *C&RL News* can be found online via the ALA employment Web page (http://www.ala.org/education). Not only does this Web site include postings from the last three months of print publications, but it also provides the text of ads set to appear in future print issues and online-only postings.

Librarians searching for ads in the online *Chronicle* should search by keyword using terms such as "library or librarian." If you subscribe to the print version, you will have an advantage in that you will be able to access, via password, the job ads from the following week's *Chronicle* (http://chronicle.com/weekly/jobs).

If you are looking for a position in library education, in addition to the *Chronicle* you should also check the Web page of ALISE, the Association for Library and Information Science Education. Its job site (http://www.alise.org/cgi-bin/jobssee.cgi) has sections for dean/director positions as well as positions as for teaching faculty. A similar mix of positions can be found via the EDUCAUSE Job Posting Service (http://www.educause.edu/jobpost/jobpost.asp), which includes all types of faculty positions. Try searching by the keyword "library" for good results. Many library positions listed here are in upper management.

If your interest is in large research libraries, check out the Association of Research Libraries' career resource page (http://db. arl.org/careers/index.html). Here you can search by region, state, and job category, and new librarians can choose to see only entry-level positions.

Electronic discussion lists can also be good sources for academic library job announcements. Relevant places to look include COLLIB-L (ACRL College Libraries Section Discussion Group) and BI-L (Bibliographic Instruction Discussion Group).[1] In addition, your local ACRL chapter may have a mailing list for its members, and this will be a good place to find job ads for the area. For details, check your ACRL chapter's Web page (a listing of these is available at http://www.ala.org/acrl/policy/ch2poly.html#2ten).

Finally, if you are a library school student or recent graduate who is interested in academic or research librarianship, consider applying to a residency program. These programs help guide a new librarian's career by combining on-the-job training with mentorship. Most of these assignments last for one to two years, and some may have specific requirements (minority status or a minimum amount of post-MLS experience). Interested librarians can browse the Association of Research Libraries' Research Library Residency database at http://db.arl.org/residencies/review.html.

Public Libraries

Public librarians might feel at an initial disadvantage in the online job search simply because there are no large national databases dedicated to posting just public library jobs. However, there are plenty of relevant sources—it is just a matter of knowing where to look.

Aside from looking at all-encompassing sites, such as the online versions of *American Libraries* and *Library Journal* mentioned earlier, consult the Web pages and online newsletters of library networks and consortia. Many list employment opportunities at libraries within the region. Examples include Career Central (http://www.sls.lib.il.us/consulting/ccentral/index.html), a service that distributes resumes of interested parties among libraries belonging to any one of five library systems in the metro Chicago area. A large number of the postings in their searchable database originate from public libraries. As it is not plausible for us to list all such Web sites here, we recommend that you consult either of our library employment sites or another, such as Ann's Place (http://aerobin.www7.50megs.com/libjob) or Library Job Resources, sponsored by the ALA chapter of University at Buffalo (http://wings. buffalo.edu/sils/alas/usamap), and look for regionally based job sources. Web sites containing listings within a particular state or region are also good choices for public librarians. We discuss these sites some more under "sites by geographic location" on the following page.

The principal e-mail list for public librarians, PUBLIB, is naturally a good source for job announcements. PUBLIB is a high-traffic list, so if you lack the time to subscribe directly,[2] you can view the online archives at your leisure (http://sunsite.berkeley.edu/ PubLib/archive.html). These are both searchable and browsable by date. Try searching using the phrase "job or position," but be warned that the search results do not necessarily appear in chronological order; you may have better luck browsing the archives by month.

School Libraries

School librarians and library media specialists can find online job listings both in traditional "library" venues as well as within employment sites for educators. *School Library Journal*, like other trade publications in the field, posts its classifieds on the Web (http://www.slj.com/classifieds/index.asp). General education employment sites include K12jobs.com (http://www.k12jobs.com), which lists positions available at elementary, secondary, and vocational schools across the country. Teacherjobs.com is another such site (http://www.teacherjobs.com), although free registration is required in order to search the database. Both of these education sites also allow you to include your resume in an online databank.

For budgetary reasons or to attract mostly local candidates, many library media positions are advertised only locally or statewide rather than nationally. Those in search of school media positions may have the best luck viewing jobs from statewide and regional joblines or online newspaper classifieds. Some local school library media associations provide job ads through their sites as well. Examples include the Florida Association for Media in Education (http://www.firn.edu/fame/joboard.htm) and the California School Library Association (choose "CSLA Job Hotline"

from http://www.schoolibrary.org). A comprehensive list of professional associations for school librarians worldwide, which
include school library divisions of state associations, can be found
at the International Association of School Librarianship Web page
(http://www.hi.is/~anne/slibassoc.html).

Web pages of state education departments, in addition to listing
job openings, will help you find more information on licensure or
certification for school librarians (if required). The National Teacher
Recruitment Clearinghouse (http://www.recruitingteachers.org), in
addition to providing information on educational job banks for
each of the fifty states and all U.S. territories, provides such a list
online (direct address http://www.recruitingteachers.org/doe.
html).

Special Libraries and Subject-Specific Positions

The natural place for special librarians to begin searching is the
"Virtual SLA," the SLA Web page, which in late 2000 opened up
access to its employment classifieds to nonmembers (http://sla.
jobcontrolcenter.com). Candidates may view all jobs in the database
or search by numerous categories: keyword, job location (U.S. and
international), job category, experience level, and more. You may
also post your resume online here. Individual SLA chapters and divisions (http://www.sla.org/content/chdiv/index.cfm) occasionally
have Web pages with job openings; others have mailing lists for the
discussion of SLA business, on which job ads may be posted.

Besides SLA, national associations for different types of special
library interests frequently post employment opportunities online.
Examples include the American Association of Law Libraries
(http://www.aallnet.org/services/hotline.asp), the Medical Library
Association (http://www.mlanet.org/jobs), and the American
Theological Libraries Association (http://www.atla.com/member/
job_openings.html). Appendix A provides a comprehensive list of
library association Web pages.

Many special library jobs fit into the "nontraditional" category, and for these types of jobs—information managers, knowledge specialists, researchers, and other "nonlibrary" titles—you may have luck searching through general online job banks, such as those described at the end of this chapter.

Alternatively, you may wish to search for employment within a particular subject specialty. The sources you use can be the same as those mentioned earlier in this section; these employment pages typically include not only positions within special libraries, but also subject-specific positions within academic or public libraries. Some additional examples include the Art Libraries Society of North America's job postings (http://www.arlisna.org/jobs.html), the Music Library Association Joblist (http://www.musiclibraryassoc.org/services/se_job.htm), and the North American Serials Interest Group's job listings http://www.nasig.org/jobs/index.htm. Subject-specific mailing lists are also good sources for job postings.

Employment Sites by Geographic Location

When you are applying outside of your current location, keep in mind the problems of the global Internet mentioned earlier. If the ad is clearly geared to local candidates, or if you see the ad in a source with a limited regional audience, mention in your cover letter that you saw the notice online, and that you are looking to relocate.

United States

Library associations and consortia frequently collect job ads of interest to their membership, and these announcements may be posted online individually or as part of a regular newsletter. State libraries often offer a similar service, disseminating job ads for librarians living within state boundaries or within the surrounding area. In the past, you may have had to phone a telephone jobline for the same information. While these telephone services are con- venient for employers, they are not nearly as useful for applicants. With phone-based joblines, if you hear an advertisement you are interested in, you have to scramble to write all of the information down correctly, and you have to listen to all the announcements in order to find one of possible interest. The online versions of these postings save you this trouble; they also eliminate potential long-distance charges.

Most state library associations (see Appendix A) and/or state libraries have Web-based joblines. These sites, in addition to listing positions in the state that they represent, also occasionally list job ads from nearby states. Examples include the Oregon Library Association Jobline (http://www.olaweb.org/jobline.shtml) and the Florida Library Jobline (http://dlis.dos.state.fl.us/fllibjobs/ Jobs.html), from the State Library of Florida. Some states, such as Texas, even have more than one appropriate library employment source: This state boasts both the Texas Library Association Jobline (http://www.txla.org/jobline/jobline.html) and the Texas State Library Jobline (http://www.tsl.state.tx.us/ld/jobline/index.html).

Local library consortia may either post their jobs online on a separate page, or list available jobs in their online newsletters. Since these sites can be hard to locate on an individual basis, meta-indexes to library employment sites, such as those run by the authors, can serve as good starting points for locating all of these different varieties of job sources.

Besides state associations, Web pages of Special Libraries Association regional chapters (see under "Special Libraries and Subject-Specific Positions" above) are also good sources for job ads. Although their focus is special libraries, academic and public library positions may be posted on these sites as well. For example, for additional job ads within Texas, check out the Texas Job Bank from the Central Texas SLA Chapter (http://www.txsla.org/jobs.htm).

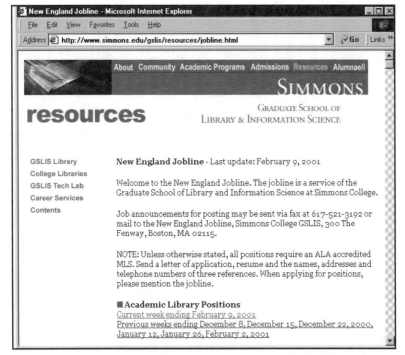

Figure 12.3   New England Jobline, Simmons Graduate School of Library & Information Science

Regional joblines, listing jobs in a larger geographic area, are popular sources as well. Examples of this include the New England Jobline (http://www.simmons.edu/gslis/resources/jobline.html), for the New England states, and the Mountain Plains Library Association Jobline (http://www.usd.edu/mpla/jobline), listing jobs in twelve western states.

International Sources

The advice just presented holds true for Canada as well as the U.S. Provincial library associations, such as the Foothills Library Association in Calgary (http://www.fla.org/jobline.html), are good sources for job postings. (A comprehensive list of Canadian library associations can be found online at http://www.nlc-bnc.ca/services/ecanassc.htm.) Placement bulletins from Canadian library schools are good choices as well. Some useful sites include JobSite, from the Faculty of Information Studies at the University of Toronto (http://www.fis.utoronto.ca/resources/jobsite/index. htm) and FIMS Jobs, from the University of Western Ontario (http://www.fims.owu.ca; click on "Career and Employment Opportunities").

Among English-speaking countries outside of North America, the United Kingdom, Australia, and New Zealand each have numerous sites for librarian jobs. For the U.K., the best site is the Bulletin Board for Libraries, or BUBL (http://bubl.ac.uk/news/jobs), which also lists postings from elsewhere. Those who wish to relocate to Australia should consider the Web page of the Australian Library and Information Association (http://www.alia.org.au/aliappointments), and the LIANZA Web page lists jobs in New Zealand (http://www.lianza.org.nz/employment.htm). Information on library organizations that promote international job exchanges and other non-U.S. library employment sites can be found online via Rachel Gordon's Web pages (http://www.lisjobs.com/nonus.htm) and ALA's International Relations Office (http://www.ala.org/work/international).

Additional Employment Sources for Librarians

In order to do a truly comprehensive search, you will want to make sure you have all your bases covered. This means moving from the very general to the most specific. Be sure to consult all possible sources for employment, including as many of the following sources as are appropriate.

Individual Library Web Pages

For one reason or other, you may be most interested in finding employment at one particular library or company. While it would be most helpful in this case to have a contact who is willing to keep you informed about openings, you may also wish to periodically peruse a library's Web page to see if any open positions are listed. As an example, Stephanie Willen Brown, Database Services Librarian at Hampshire College Library, found her current position posted on the library's Web site several weeks before it was advertised in the local newspaper. Advertising on a library's Web page is most effective for large libraries simply because they employ the greatest numbers of people, but also because they are most likely to have personnel departments that regularly update their pages. For an index to library Web pages worldwide, consult Libweb (http://sunsite.berkeley.edu/Libweb). It may help to remember that for academic libraries, jobs may be listed at the institution level, and for public libraries, at the city/town/village level. For colleges and universities, try looking for Web pages using a site such as Peterson's Education Center (http://www.petersons.com). For local government employment pages, look for links that lead from a public library's page, or try browsing Yahoo! Local (http://local.yahoo.com).

Online Newspaper Classifieds

Newspaper ads have always been the mainstay of the classic job hunt. In the online world, searching the classifieds has become even more convenient, as many papers have made their ads keyword searchable at no charge to the user. You now also have the option of searching job ads from newspapers around the country, depending on where you wish to relocate, and papers may keep more than just last Sunday's edition online. Newspaper classifieds are good sources for all types of jobs in the field, including nontraditional positions. Paraprofessional positions in particular may be advertised in the local paper and nowhere else.

You can find a comprehensive list of links to newspapers with online editions through sites such as NewsDirectory

(http://www.newsdirectory.com) or Online Newspapers
(http://www.onlinenewspapers.com). At the home page for
each paper, look for the link to its classified ad section (not all
have such a link, but many do). Employers tend to place ads in
the local paper with the largest circulation so that they can get
the word out to the most people. For this reason it is best to
favor major newspapers, such as the *Boston Globe*, over smaller
town or county papers. Also, read the search tips for each
paper's database before you begin, because each has its own
quirks. What search terms should you use? Consult the sidebar
on online job databases for a list of suggested keywords to try.

Placement Services from Associations

Many professional associations offer placement services at their
national conferences. These services benefit both employers and
applicants by bringing them together in a single location for the
sole purpose of recruitment. For example, at the ALA national conferences, the Placement Center (sponsored by the Office of Human
Resource Development and Recruitment) provides listings of both
open positions and candidate resumes. Physical space is set aside
for tables where interviews may take place.

Association Web pages (see Appendix A) frequently provide
information on and forms for registering for conference placement services, and some even allow you to register online and/or
view the job openings. It is best to begin consulting these sites
approximately three months before a conference will be held.

Some larger association Web pages, such as ALA's, display jobs
listed at their placement service around the same time that their
conferences are held. Beginning with ALA Midwinter 2001, ALA is
providing both job seeker information and job openings in a
searchable online database, accessible to anyone via the Internet
(http://www.ala.org/hrdr/placement.html). Employers attending
ALA may tend to register their open positions with the Placement

Center and nowhere else. If you plan to visit the Placement Center at an ALA conference, it is good to consult this site several months in advance; this way you will have enough time to research jobs and employers before you interview. Other smaller associations may post similar information on their Web pages, or they may simply display information about the placement service or allow you to register online.

Although it may be possible for you to participate in a placement center solely via the Internet, it will benefit you greatly to follow up your online research with in-person networking. In other words, you should make the effort, if at all possible, to meet with employers in person at the conference. (For more details about finding conference information online, see Chapter 5.)

Electronic Discussion Lists

We have already named some specific electronic discussion lists that you may want to join, depending on what type of position you are seeking. These lists can be particularly useful in the job search process. Librarians regularly contribute job ads at their own institutions to subject-specific lists as a way of reaching an audience already focused on a particular subject within the field. In this way, they can also find librarians who may not be actively looking for a new job, but who may find an opportunity too good to pass up. These lists are free to join and free for employers as well, making e-mail discussion lists a not-to-be-missed source for librarians in the job market. Wei Wu presents a comprehensive list of library mailing lists, Library-Oriented Lists and Electronic Serials, at http://www.wrlc.org/liblists. (Additional information on electronic mailing lists can be found in Chapter 2.)

Employment Agencies and Placement Firms

Placement firms and employment agencies in the information field frequently have a Web presence, in order to advertise their services to the largest possible audience. These organizations can help you in your job search, whether you are looking for permanent or temporary employment. Some require you to register first in order to view the lists of open jobs, while some list all open positions for all to view. Others may simply provide information and/or an application form but not list any jobs online at all. Also, while some placement services have a national focus, others place information professionals only in certain local metropolitan areas. Lisjobs.com offers a comprehensive list of library employment agencies with Web pages (http://www.lisjobs.com/temp.htm).

Sources for Nontraditional Library Positions

The job sources that we have mentioned thus far are most appropriate for finding a job within a library. If you are looking for a position in a corporation, or if you are looking for an information-related position in another type of institution, you will want to consider looking in Internet job banks with a more general scope.

General Job Banks

The number of job sites on the Internet is vast, and it can be hard to decide where to start. To begin, we recommend you consult one of the meta-indexes to Internet job sites, such as Margaret Riley Dikel's The Riley Guide. The section labeled "Job Listings" (http://www.dbm.com/jobguide/jobs.html) takes you straight to a table of contents for various types of jobs. Begin with the most general sources listed under "Job Banks and Recruiting Sources." The Riley Guide's recommended sites for information professionals include these:

- America's Job Bank (direct link at http://www.ajb.org)

- Excite Employment Classifieds (http://www.classifieds 2000.com)

- Headhunter.net (http://www.headhunter.net)

- HotJobs (http://www.hotjobs.com)

- Monster.com (http://www.monster.com)

- Flipdog.com (http://www.flipdog.com)

Within the menus for each of these sites, look for an option that lets you search by keyword (unless the site surprises you by having a separate listing for information-related positions). See the sidebar in this chapter for recommended keywords to try. When searching general job banks, it helps to remember that many nontraditional positions don't include the word "librarian" in the job titles. You may end up retrieving ads for positions such as "tape librarian" or "software librarian," but these will be false hits, as these job titles are normally used for positions within the computer science field. Read the job ads carefully. Many of these sites also allow you to submit your resume into their databank, but registration (and/or payment) may be required.

Personalized Job Agents

Personalized agents (see more in Chapter 3) save you time by scouring the Net—or a particular database—and alerting you to resources related to your particular interests. In a similar fashion, a number of general job banks provide agents that e-mail you when jobs matching your keywords are inserted into their database. To register for these services, you need to create an account and fill out a profile describing the types of jobs you are looking for. At Monster.com, for example, the agent My Monster (http://my.monster.com) e-mails you when jobs matching your criteria are added to the database; this feature can also alert you to news and articles you are interested in. My CareerBuilder (http://my.careerbuilder.com) lets you create up to five profiles and e-mails you with keyword matches from the CareerBuilder database. If you are looking for a nontraditional library position and can't chance being caught "surfing" during work time, this may be a good option.

Online Job Databases:
Searching by Keyword

Whether you are searching for positions in a database of newspaper classifieds or in an online job bank, you will have to tell the database what keywords to search for. Some, like CareerBuilder (http://www.careerbuilder. com) may make the job easy for you and let you search by category, such as "library science." If they do, take advantage of it, but most do not offer this option. Keywords commonly used as job titles for information professionals and related terms (such as "library") are listed here. Those marked with an asterisk (*) are most frequently used in nontraditional library settings or information-related positions outside libraries. For additional terms and suggestions, consult Michelle Mach's page on searching for real job titles for librarians and information professionals (http://alexia.lis.uiuc.edu/~mach/realjobs.html). Use quotes to search job titles as a phrase.

archivist
bibliographer
cataloger
data mining
document delivery
*documentation manager
indexer
*information analyst
*information architect
*information manager
*information officer
*information professional
*information scientist
*intelligence specialist

*knowledge manager
librar* (if truncation allowed)
librarian
library
library assistant
library science
library technician
media specialist
preservationist
records manager
*research analyst
*research scientist
*researcher
*taxonomist

The Application Process

Once you have found appropriate job ads, you will have completed the first step in your online job search. Naturally, there are
some parts of the employment process that you will not be able to
do via the Web—the interview is an obvious example. However, in
some situations, you may find it appropriate and even helpful to
conduct other job-related activities online. Chapter 11 covers the
best ways to compose an electronic resume and forward it to
employers. In the next few sections, we continue this discussion
with regard to communicating with employers and applying online.

The "Hidden" Job Market

When you are looking for a job, you cannot afford to pass up any
possible leads. Networking, both online and offline, is a crucial
part of the job search process. You can use the net to find out about

conferences that will give you the chance to network with others who share your professional interests. You also never know whether the colleague you first "meet" on an electronic mailing list will be in a position to tell you about a job opening sometime down the road.

For this reason, you should always be on your best behavior whenever you are online. Follow the advice mentioned in Chapter 2 with regard to online networking, join appropriate electronic discussion lists, and always observe "netiquette." Avoid flaming others, and be careful to follow the rules of the list. Keep the tone and content of your posts professional. Eliminate all political and social commentary from your signature file. Remember, also, that although you may be desperately looking for a new job, it is best not to appear desperate. For example, posting your cover letter or electronic resume to an entire discussion list is a no-no (unless you are posting on a Usenet newsgroup exclusively for resume postings). Messages asking whether anyone on a discussion list can help you find a job are also to be avoided. Finally, never e-mail your resume to any individual unsolicited. Hold off sending application materials until you know whether it is appropriate to do so.

On the other hand, you do want to make yourself visible to others on a discussion list—lurking won't get you anywhere if you are job hunting. Make intelligent contributions to discussion lists. Or write separate replies to others' postings, if you are not sure whether your topic or question is appropriate for the group as a whole.

Querying Employers

Approaching an employer about obtaining a job is always an awkward situation, even under the best of circumstances. The Internet can make this process a bit smoother, because you will avoid much of the nervousness that comes with making phone calls or introducing yourself in person. With e-mail, you can take your time in composing an appropriate introductory message. Of course, you will have to be patient and wait for the employer to respond to you.

If you see a job posted online and the employer's e-mail address is provided, it is acceptable for you to drop him or her a brief e-mail note asking a question about the position. You may also wish to inquire whether an employer would be willing to accept an electronic version of your resume. (If you are replying to a list posting, though, make sure that you are addressing your question to an individual, and not to the entire list!) Keep your message simple, polite, and professional, and remember to follow netiquette.

Applying Online

If an employer gives you the go-ahead to send your electronic resume, or if it is already stated in the ad that you should send your resume electronically, include a brief cover letter as part of your message. You would never send a print resume without an accompanying cover letter, and the fact that you are using the Internet instead should make no difference.

For example, Marilyn Jenkins, Manager of Library Cooperation and Networking at the Saskatchewan Provincial Library in Regina, Saskatchewan, has found that a large number of her library's applicants make use of the Internet to some degree, as her library's open positions are advertised widely on electronic job boards. At her library, electronic and print applications are equally acceptable, provided that formatting is retained in the electronic transmission. Applications submitted via e-mail are printed out and included in a pile alongside those received through regular mail. "It is not acceptable to forego the formality of a cover letter and the inclusion of the pertinent information that it would normally contain, just because it is an application in electronic format," she advises.

Since numerous books have been written on both resumes and cover letters, we merely make the following recommendations for your online cover letter. Before you send an electronic cover letter to an employer for the first time, try sending a copy first to yourself to make sure that it arrives in a readable format.

- Keep the overall content of your electronic cover letter the same as you would in print.

- Include the date as well as the employer's name and address at the very top of your message, just as you would do in print. Because the employer may print out both your cover letter and resume, you want to keep the format similar.

- As with all other e-mail communication, keep the tone professional, and address the employer by "Ms." or "Mr.," not by his or her first name.

- Mention within the text of the letter where you found the job ad (the title of the source itself, such as the online *Chronicle of Higher Education*, not the specific URL).

- Conclude the cover letter with a closing statement, such as "Sincerely yours," and type your full name.

- If you include a signature file, make sure that it has your full contact information: name, address, phone, and e-mail address, at minimum. If you do not have a signature file, include this information at the bottom of the message after your name.

- After your signature, include your electronic resume. As mentioned in Chapter 11, an ASCII version is preferred if you are not sure what format to use.

A number of Web sites provide additional tips on what to include in a cover letter. Two of the more useful sites are Rebecca Smith's eResumes and Resources (http://www.eresumes.com/tut_ecoverletters.html), which is geared to the electronic environment, and "Writing Effective Letters Guide," from the Florida State

University Career Center (http://www.fsu.edu/~career/write_
eff.html), which provides good general suggestions.

Interview Follow-Up

E-mail is also a good tool to use to follow up with an employer
after you have had a job interview. If you know that an employer
will be making a decision in the near future, an e-mail follow-up
note is a good way of making sure that your message reaches him
or her in time. Remember to thank the employer for his or her time
and consideration, and reiterate your interest in the position. You
may also use e-mail at this time to ask any additional questions
you had about the position; this will indicate your continued interest. If you are simply sending a thank-you note, though, and if your
interview was with a search committee rather than one person, it
is a nice touch to send separate messages to each individual who
interviewed you. E-mail can save you money on postage if you
interviewed with a large number of people!

Job-Hunting Advice and Interview Questions

The Web abounds with interview tips and general job-hunting
advice, most of it aimed at the general public. A number of library
organizations, graduate programs, and career centers, however, offer
tips for job hunters and interviewees on their Web pages. A number
of these are provided on Lisjobs.com's "Advice, Statistics, and
Articles" page (http://www.lisjobs.com/advice.htm). Among the
most useful is Priscilla Klob's (now Priscilla Shontz) "First
Impressions, Lasting Impressions: Tips for Job Interviews," at the
New Members Round Table Web site (http://www.ala.org/nmrt/
footnotes/interview.html). The Topica e-mail list LibraryJobHunt
(http://www.topica.com/lists/LibraryJobHunt) can serve as an

online sounding board for librarians interested in discussing employment-related issues with others in the field. Those contemplating becoming a public or academic librarian should read more about the interview process at these locations. Consult the library job information page posted by the Association of Graduate Library and Information Science Students (AGLISS) at the Catholic University of America (http://studentorg.cua.edu/agliss/libjobs.htm).

No matter what type of environment you choose, though, you should always take the time to research the background of the employer before you interview. We discuss how the Internet can help with this stage of the job hunt in the next chapter.

Endnotes

1. To subscribe to COLLIB-L, send the e-mail message "subscribe COLLIB-L Firstname Lastname" to listserv@willamette.edu. To subscribe to BI-L, send the e-mail message "subscribe BI-L Firstname Lastname" to listserv@listserv.byu.edu.
2. To subscribe to PUBLIB, send the e-mail message "subscribe PUBLIB Firstname Lastname" to listserv@sunsite.berkeley.edu.

Chapter 13

Researching Employment Situations

Creating a resume and searching for job ads are two essential steps in the employment process for which the Internet can be a valuable tool. In trying to decide whether a job is a good match for you, though, you also want to take some time to find out as much as you can about your possible future employer and employment environment. Not only does this involve doing some research on the library or other organization where the job is located, but it means finding out about the town or region (especially if you are not a local candidate) as well as whether the salary is reasonable. Online tools to investigate the types of jobs you are best suited for can help you gain a better idea of whether your potential future workplace would fit your skills and personality.

Career Planning and Self-Assessment

Before diving into reading job ads, you may first wish to take a closer look at your own career preferences. This is particularly useful if you are a new graduate out in the job market for the first time or if you are contemplating a career change. Not sure exactly what type of work within the information profession you would be best at? Would you prefer a job that has direct contact with the public? Would you rather work behind the scenes? How do you react in certain work-related situations? If you are unsure of the answers to these questions, consider completing a skills inventory, personality test, or other career assessment tool. While you can easily take one of these tests on your own initiative, you may also be asked to do a formal self-assessment by your employer, particularly if you work in a corporate setting.

A number of these tools are available online. The Job Hunter's Bible (http://www.jobhuntersbible.com), in addition to general career-planning advice, includes links to personality tests on the Web. This site, compiled by Richard Bolles, author of the well-known career guide *What Color Is Your Parachute?*, was designed to be a supplement to his book, though a considerable amount of information is freely available online. Among the tests he lists is the Keirsey Temperament Sorter (direct link at http://www.keirsey.com), which gives results similar to the Myers-Briggs Type Indicator—both tests measure whether you are more an introvert or an extrovert, whether you more frequently use your judgment or perception, and so on.

The online version of the *Occupational Outlook Handbook* (http://stats.bls.gov/ocohome.htm) is another valuable site to check if you are unsure about whether to begin a library career in the first place, or if you are simply interested in reading about where the profession is heading. Each profile within the *Handbook* describes typical job duties, the total number of people employed in the field, their typical schedules, the training (including degrees) that is required, the outlook for the profession, related occupations, and additional resources to consult. Jobs in the information field are mostly located in the "Professional and Technical" section, and separate outlooks are available for librarians, library technicians, and archivists. Under the "Administrative Support" section, which covers clerical positions, you can find a separate profile on the positions of library assistant and bookmobile driver (direct link http://stats.bls.gov/oco/ocos147.htm). According to the *Handbook*, although the number of overall positions in the traditional library setting may to go down over the next few years, growth can be expected for information-related positions outside libraries. In addition, more positions are likely to open up toward the end of the decade, as many librarians reach retirement age. Although this view may seem pessimistic, the *Handbook* neglects to mention the ways in which librarians are specially trained to help people deal with "information overload," especially these days when the common belief is that everything is available for free on the Internet. The *Handbook* is updated annually, both in print and online.

Other online articles take a more positive attitude toward the value that librarians add in this technological era. "Librarians in the 21st Century," from the Syracuse University School of Information Studies (http://istweb.syr.edu/21stcenlib/index.html), discusses career possibilities and overall trends among various information-related professions. The Winter 2000–01 issue of *Occupational Outlook Quarterly* presents librarians as "experts in the information age" (http://www.bls.gov/opub/ooq/2000/Winter/art01.pdf). Also of particular note is "The Modern MLS Degree" (http://www.usnews.com/usnews/edu/beyond/grad/gbmls.htm) by Marissa Melton, which recounts how the "cyber-revolution" has transformed the library profession.

Employer Background

A job search is always a two-way process. Not only must an employer determine whether your skills are a match for his or her open position, but you must learn enough about an organization to decide whether you would feel comfortable working there. Have you seen an ad for a job you are interested in, but aren't sure whether you should apply? Have you gotten a call for an interview at a library and want to go in prepared? Doing research on employers on the Web can be a great benefit in these and other situations. Dan Longley, Manager of Product Support/Information Specialist at Community of Science, Inc., reports that not only did he find his current job through an online library/information science job site, but he also researched the company extensively before his phone and in-person interviews; this additional information aided in his final decision to work there. Knowing background on a library or company in advance can help you make a more informed employment decision.

Investigating Library Web Pages

The majority of libraries in the U.S. have an online presence, and individual library Web pages provide an enormous amount of detail that can be useful to you in making employment decisions.

Figure 13.1   Libweb, Index to Library Web Pages Around the World (Berkeley Digital Library SunSITE)

Granted, you can (and should) always look up library employers within the *American Library Directory* for the basics, but as its listings are the results of surveys and space is limited, it will not have the quantity of information—or the personal touch—that library Web pages can provide.

Libweb (http://sunsite.berkeley.edu/Libweb) at the Berkeley Digital Library SunSITE provides links to more than 4,000 library Web pages worldwide. This comprehensive site should be your starting point. (If you do not find your desired library page here, try searching for it using a search engine, such as AltaVista or Google.)

You can learn quite a bit just from a five-minute browse through a library Web page. As an example, take a look at the Web site of the Washington-Centerville Public Library in Centerville, Ohio, at http://www.wcpl.lib.oh.us. From the professional-quality graphics, the link to the Web catalog, and the e-mail reference service, you could make an educated guess that the library itself is technologically

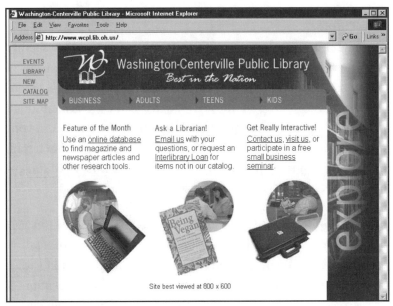

Figure 13.2   Washington-Centerville Public Library Home Page (Centerville, Ohio)

progressive. Naturally, though, you won't want to limit yourself to the first page when looking at sites; take the time to click on all links. In the case of large libraries or library systems with multiple locations, such as that for the New York Public Library (http://www.nypl.org), you will want to look through the site to find a link to the particular library or branch where the job you are applying for is located. A site map can be of help in this instance.

What if a library has no Web site? This, too, can aid in your employment decision. Perhaps the library is actively looking for an incoming librarian to take on this role. If this is not the case, as a technologically involved information professional you may wish to question whether you would feel comfortable working for an organization where the Internet seems of such low importance. (At the same time, though, be aware that many school, special, and small public libraries, while connected to the Internet, may not have the resources to maintain a separate Web presence.)

Site Content

While browsing through a library Web site, look to see whether you can find the following information. Knowing these pieces of information can help you make a better-informed employment decision. Also, finding out the answers to the questions mentioned below can suggest other questions for you, in turn, to ask at your interview. And if you do use a library's Web site as a research tool, be sure to mention this when you reach the interview stage—chances are that the search committee will be impressed.

- *Size and names of staff.* How many people does the library employ? Look for links labeled "about the library" or "staff directory." What is the library director's name? If a job ad doesn't give a contact name to address your application to, you may be able to find this information online; you can also find out an e-mail address to write to if you have questions about the position. Depending on the site, you may be able to discover background information on the people with whom you will be interviewing.

- *Name of the online catalog vendor.* Does the library have a Web-based (or telnet-based) catalog? If so, take the time to familiarize yourself with basic search strategies. If the library has no Internet-accessible online catalog at all, this is a topic that you could bring up in your interview. Do they plan to purchase a new system in the future? Does the library share a catalog with any other libraries? Does it belong to a union catalog project?

- *Available online databases.* Does the library subscribe to InfoTrac, Ovid, EBSCOhost, SIRS, FirstSearch, or similar products? If you are familiar with any of these vendors' databases yourself, take the time to point this out in your cover letter and interview.

- *Special collections.* Does the library have interests in any particular subject areas? Are there any unique departments, such as local history, genealogy, or particular archival collections?

- *Photographs.* While this may be obvious, don't forget to browse a library's Web site to see if any photos of the building or interior are included. You may not find them on the initial page. While photographs may not be the part of a library's site that makes or breaks your decision, you may be reassured to learn that the building was constructed within the past few years (a sign of recent funding), or dissuaded by the fact that its decor has not changed since the 1960s.

Site Presentation

In addition to looking at the actual content of a site, pay attention to the site's presentation. Are the links well organized? Is it made up of a single page or multiple pages? Are the graphics of professional quality, or are they fairly basic (or even amateurish)?

While the quality of the site can reflect the abilities of the library's technical staff, it is also true that many libraries outsource the initial design of their Web pages. Still, as Web design can be expensive, this can reflect on the library's budget for technology. Beth Roberts, Reference Librarian at the Office of Prevention, Pesticides and Toxic Substances Chemical Library of the U.S. Environmental Protection Agency, summarizes this concept well when she states: "Before I apply for a job online I always see if the company or library has a Web site. Usually they do. The quality of the Web site can often be indicative of how seriously an organization takes itself, how big of a budget they have, and/or how much they value the Internet. All very important things to know before working for an organization!"

Additional Sources

Besides the Web pages presented by libraries themselves, you can find (or deduce) additional information about a library environment through other online sources. The sites you consult will depend on the type of library you are interested in—academic, public, school, special, or corporate. In all cases, for employment purposes it is helpful to learn not just about the organization/library itself, but also about whatever larger organization it is part of.

Academic Libraries

Librarians in academia know that, in the course of their jobs, not only will they have to interact with library staff and students, but they will also have to work with the administration of the college or university. If you are considering applying for or accepting an academic library job, it can be beneficial to know background information about the institution as a whole in addition to specifics about the library.

Many meta-indexes to college and university Web pages exist, and you can choose any of them to find a link to the institution that the library belongs to. Places to start include Peterson's Education Center (http://www.petersons.com), CollegeNET (http://www.collegenet.com) and CollegeView (http://www. collegeview.com). In most cases you can also find a link to the institution's Web page directly from the library's page.

What should you look for? Pay attention to the course listings (which may be within a catalog), the mission statement (if available), and the academic calendar. Make a point of noticing exactly where the library is placed hierarchically within an institution. Is it a separate academic department? How close are its ties to the institution's information technology department or computer center? Do you see any clues as to whether librarians are given faculty status and are eligible for tenure? If individual librarians have Web pages, look at their online resumes. What committees are they involved in? Do they publish frequently?

If technology is important to a campus, the quality of an institution's Web site will reflect this. Chances are that a campus-wide emphasis on technology will be carried over into the library. You can get an idea about the administration's impression of the library by looking at where the library is mentioned on the institution's Web site. Is the library prominently displayed on the main page, or do you have to hunt it down through layers of links? From the main campus page, you should also be able to find a link to a page for the college or university's human resources department. Here, take a look for information on general college-wide employment policies, such as tuition reimbursement and union documents (if unions are present on campus), not to mention salary schedules, benefits information, and hiring policies.

Public Libraries

For those interested in public libraries, a library Web site can also indicate where the library fits hierarchically into the town, village, or city government. More often than not, you will be able to find a link to the local government site from a public library Web page. You may also be able to deduce how the library gets its funding, and what its relationship is with its Board of Trustees. If Libweb does not list an address for the public library you want, try stepping up one level to find a site for the community where it is located; Yahoo! Local (http://local.yahoo.com) is a good place to begin.

While researching a public library site, you may be interested in answers to questions that may help you decide whether you would like to work there, such as whether a residency requirement is imposed on employees or what the Internet access policies are. You may wish to take a look at the library's online calendar of events, just to give you a sense of what community groups it works with, as well as what happens in the library on a daily basis. Some public libraries put their annual reports online, giving you an idea of their overall circulation, staffing, and budget. And if the job ad you are interested in gives some indication of the duties involved (leading book groups or teaching Internet classes, for example), you may be able to find information about these programs online.

School Libraries

Just as public librarians will be curious about the city or town where the job is located, school librarians and media specialists will be interested in the school district or in the school itself. Some school librarians have taken the initiative of creating Web pages for their libraries; a number of these are linked via Peter Milbury's Network of School Librarian Web Pages (http://www.school-libraries.net). Although many schools—and most school libraries—do not have Web sites to call their own, you will be able to go online to find basic information on the school or school district.

The American School Directory (http://www.asd.com) provides information on all 108,000-plus K-12 schools within the U.S. Included are names of officials, the number of students, contact information, and the number of Internet-connected computers—as well as a link to the official school Web site, if one exists, and the Web page of the state's Department of Education (DOE). Certification information for media specialists can typically be found at a DOE site. The National Public School Locator (http://nces.ed.gov/ccdweb/school), from the National Center for Education Statistics, provides the name of the district to which a school belongs, whether the district is independent, its locale (rural or urban), the number of teachers, the number of minority students (broken down by race/ethnicity), and the student-teacher ratio.

Special Libraries, Corporate Libraries, and Nonlibrary Employers

Like school libraries, special and corporate libraries may not have public Web sites of their own. (Many corporate Web sites are on an intranet that is inaccessible to outsiders, for privacy or security reasons.) If they are not listed in Libweb, try a general search on the library name (or, more likely, the name of the larger organization) using Dogpile, AltaVista, or another major search engine.

Special librarians working in corporate libraries, or information professionals working outside the library setting, may be able to find information on corporations using an online business directory such as Lycos Companies Online (http://www.companiesonline.com) or Hoover's Online (http://www.hoovers.com). For large, well-known corporations, you may be able to find the Web address simply by guessing that the URL is of the form http://www.companyname.com. Also, if you happen to be interested in working at a publicly held company, you may be able to locate its annual report online. This information can typically be found via a corporate Web site or a site such as EDGAR (http://edgar.sec.gov), which lists reports that companies file with the U.S. Securities and Exchange Commission. Many of these reports contain company histories as well as financial data.

Salary Information

You no doubt will be curious about whether the salary range listed in a job ad—or the salary offered to you as the chosen candidate—is reasonable, both for the type of position as well as for the region of the country. Many state library associations establish minimum salary guidelines (which are frequently, though not always, followed by member libraries). Check the Web page of the library association for the state where the job is located (refer to Appendix A of this book) to see if a salary minimum for librarians is listed. A specific figure may be listed within the online state library jobline, if available online. The Connecticut Library Association, for example, recommends a minimum annual salary of $36,546 as of July 1, 2001, based on a 35-hour workweek (http://www.lib.uconn.edu/cla/jobline. html). (Librarians in all other states should be so fortunate!)

Large library associations such as ARL, SLA, and AALL (American Association of Law Libraries) post their salary surveys—or at least portions thereof—online on a regular basis. Ann Robinson, within her Library Job Hunting Web pages, provides lists of links to national and statewide salary surveys as well as to library salary guides in general (http://aerobin.www7.50megs. com/libjob/salary.html). Of particular interest are the following:

- *The Salary Calculator* (http://www.homefair.com/calc/ salcalc.html). Use this form to compare the cost of living from one U.S. city to another. According to this calculator, an annual salary of $36,546 in Hartford, Connecticut, the statewide minimum, equates to approximately $34,000 in

Charleston, West Virginia, $47,200 in Los Angeles, or $98,600 in the heart of Manhattan!

- *ARL Annual Salary Survey* (http://www.arl.org/stats/ salary). This site includes salary statistics from more than 12,000 positions in all types of research libraries—academic, law, medical—in the U.S. and Canada for the past five years. Not all tables are available online.

- *"Better Pay, More Jobs" by Vicki L. Gregory & Sonia Ramirez Wohlmuth* (http://www.libraryjournal.com/placements). This article contains most of the text from the article published in the October 15, 2000, issue of *Library Journal*. The journal's yearly October 15 issue includes LJ's report on placements and salaries.

- *SLA Salary Survey* (http://www.sla.org/category.cfm? catid=21). Selected tables, mainly national average salaries for special librarians, are available via the SLA Web page, though you must purchase the entire book to see all statistics.

Moving and Relocation

Information professionals applying for jobs in another part of the country will face more than just a salary adjustment; they will eventually have to deal with the prospect of relocating to a new area. In addition to the employer's background and the salary range, the geographic location can also play a strong role when you are deciding whether a job would be right for you. Fortunately, there are a number of online resources that can help you find out in advance what to expect in an area and also help you to physically move your household to a new location.

Though a few years old, Paula Hammett's WebWatch article
(1999) on online resources for relocation is a good place to begin.
An online version of her article is available via the *Library Journal*
WebWatch archive at http://www.libraryjournal.com/articles/
multimedia/webwatch/19990401_4432.asp. Specific Web sites to
aid in the moving process, both those mentioned in the article as
well as others, include the following:

- Monstermoving.com (http://www.monstermoving.com)—
  One stop-shopping site for relocation

- Homefair.com (http://www.homefair.com)—Community
  reports, crime statistics, school reports, and real estate listings

- The School Report (http://www.schoolreport.com)—
  Detailed information on school districts. Be aware,
  though, that you need to submit your personal information in order to get a free report.

- Mapquest (http://www.mapquest.com)—Driving directions and street maps for the U.S. and Canada.

- NewsDirectory (http://www.newsdirectory.com)—Links
  to local newspapers from around the country

Summary

The Internet can be a great help whenever you need to find out
more on the background of libraries or other information-related
organizations, including the general work environment, their
focus on technology, typical salaries, and background information
about the geographic area. In all, no matter whether you are
searching for your first job out of library school or searching to
switch to a new position, finding employment can be an awkward

process. In all but a few stages of the game, doing your job search using Web-based resources can help smooth your way.

Works Cited

Hammett, Paula. "Relocating Resources on the Web." *Library Journal*, Apr. 1, 1999: 26–27.

"Librarians." *Occupational Outlook Handbook*. Sept. 29, 2000. Bureau of Justice Statistics, U.S. Dept. of Labor. Jan. 16, 2001 (http://stats.bls. gov/oco/ocos068.htm).

Conclusion

Putting It All Together

Successful information professionals will integrate the use of the Internet into all aspects of their careers. This book only begins to describe the wide range of resources available to all librarians.

Those focusing on career development will also want to check out the various library portals, which include links to sites devoted to all aspects of librarianship. Topical portals differ from general portals such as Yahoo! in that they attempt to be less a comprehensive conglomeration of popular "things to see and do" on the Web than a guide to useful library-related resources. Resources available through such portals range from professional development sites and opportunities, such as those described throughout this book, to Web pages, lists, and contacts that will be helpful in completing work-related projects. They are maintained by a variety of vendors, companies, universities, and organizations:

- *BUBL LINK*—http://bubl.ac.uk/link/l/librarians.htm. A good resource for browsing; BUBL includes links to e-mail discussion lists, journals, and training resources for both U.K. and international librarians.

- *Digital Librarian: Librariana*—http://www.digital-librarian.com/librariana.html. A somewhat random list of links relating to librarianship; many are relevant to professional development.

- *Internet Library for Librarians*—http://www.itcompany. com/inforetriever. Fairly commercial (even including topical banner ads on many subject categories). Both browsable by subject and searchable; each resource is briefly annotated.

- *Internet Public Library (IPL) Services for Librarians*— http://www.ipl.org/svcs. Broken up into broad sections such as Library Employment, Organizing the Web, On the Job, Advocacy, and Fun Facts, IPL provides an annotated guide both to online professional development resources and to sites focusing on the use of the Internet in library settings

- *Librarians' Resource Centre*—http://www.sla.org/chapter/ctor/toolbox/resource. Examine their Professional Development section for a number of relevant links.

- *LibraryHQ*—http://www.libraryhq.com. Somewhat commercial, but useful sections for professional development include Speaker Source, where librarians can list themselves as speakers or find speakers for their events, and conference listings.

- *LibrarySpot*—http://www.libraryspot.com. The free e-mail newsletter is a good current awareness resource, and also check out the section titled "The Librarian's Shelf" for career development links.

- *Library Resource List*—http://www.dpi.state.wi.us/dltcl/pld/lib_res.html. Look at the section on The Library Profession for a lengthy list of links.

- *The List of Library and Information Sciences & Telecommunications Resources on the Web*—http://www.pitt.edu/~inscilib. Links to a good mix of professional development and on-the-job resources for librarians.

Each portal offers its unique perspective and links. Note, however, that the majority of the links in most portals relate to "on-the-job" and library issues rather than to professional development per se, and be prepared to dig for relevant resources. Use the links in this book to point you toward many of the most relevant professional development resources online, and also visit its companion Web site at http://www.lisjobs.com/careerdev for updated links and information.

Throughout this book, we have shown you how online professional development opportunities abound. Given that the Internet is still a relatively new medium, and that schools, associations, and individual librarians are still exploring the best ways to use online resources, we expect such Internet opportunities to proliferate in the years ahead. Many areas are in a state of transition: Conferences are just beginning to move to the electronic environment, employers are using a mix of online and print venues to post job advertisements, and library schools are beginning to venture into using distance education to expand their offerings. Print professional development resources are moving online, such as ACRL's *InPrint*, focusing on publishing opportunities for college librarians. As broadband Internet access becomes more widespread, we can expect to see more use of videoconferencing and other online uses of technology to bridge the distance between librarians worldwide.

Those who now take advantage of the potential to build their own careers using Internet resources will be prepared as the Internet becomes the only way to participate in certain library-related activities. As you see new ways to use technology for professional development, welcome the opportunity to be on the forefront of the library future.

The Internet and the library profession go hand-in-hand. Make the Internet the first stop on the road to your career development, yet always remember that the Internet is a tool, not a replacement for the principles and practices of our profession. Use it as you would any other tool at your disposal, integrating your online expertise with the rest of your training and knowledge.

Part 5

Appendices

Appendix A

Professional Organizations and Conferences with an Online Presence

National Associations in the U.S.

American Association of Law Libraries (AALL)
http://www.aallnet.org

American Association of School Librarians (AASL; division of ALA)
http://www.ala.org/aasl

American Indian Library Association (AILA)
http://www.nativeculture.com/lisamitten/aila.html

American Library Association (ALA)
http://www.ala.org

American Society of Indexers (ASI)
http://www.asindexing.org

American Society for Information Science and Technology (ASIST)
http://www.asis.org

American Theological Library Association (ATLA)
http://www.atla.com

Art Libraries Society of North America (ARLIS/NA)
http://www.arlisna.org

Association for Educational Communications and Technology
(AECT)
http://www.aect.org

Association for Information and Image Management
http://www.aiim.org

Association for Library and Information Science Education (ALISE)
http://www.alise.org

Association for Library Collections and Technical Services
(ALCTS; division of ALA)
http://www.ala.org/alcts

Association for Library Service to Children (ALSC; division of ALA)
http://www.ala.org/alsc

Association for Library Trustees and Advocates (ALTA; division of
ALA)
http://www.ala.org/alta

Association of Christian Librarians (ACL)
http://www.acl.org

Association of College and Research Libraries (ACRL; division of ALA)
http://www.ala.org/acrl

Association of Independent Information Professionals (AIIP)
http://www.aiip.org

Association of Jewish Libraries (AJL)
http://www.jewishlibraries.org

Association of Moving Image Archivists
http://www.amianet.org

Association of Records Managers and Administrators (ARMA)
http://www.arma.org

Association of Research Libraries (ARL)
http://www.arl.org

Association of Specialized and Cooperative Library Agencies (ASCLA)
http://www.ala.org/ascla

Bibliographic Society of America
http://www.bibsocamer.org

Catholic Library Association
http://www.cathla.org

Chinese American Librarians Association (CALA)
http://www.cala-web.org

Church and Synagogue Library Association
http://www.worldaccessnet.com/~csla

Coalition for Networked Information (CNI)
http://www.cni.org

Council on Library and Information Resources
http://www.clir.org

EDUCAUSE
http://www.educause.edu

LOEX Clearinghouse for Library Instruction
http://www.emich.edu/public/loex/loex.html

Library Administration and Management Association (LAMA; division of ALA)
http://www.ala.org/lama

Library and Information Technology Association (LITA; division of ALA)
http://www.lita.org

Major Orchestra Librarians Association
http://www.mola-inc.org

Medical Library Association (MLA)
http://www.mlanet.org

Music Library Association (MLA)
http://www.musiclibraryassoc.org

National Association of Government Archives and Records Administrators
http://www.nagara.org

National Association of Media and Technology Centers
http://www.namtc.org

National Federation of Abstracting and Information Services
http://www.nfais.org

North American Serials Interest Group
http://www.nasig.org

North American Sport Library Network
http://www.sportquest.com/naslin

Public Library Association (PLA; division of ALA)
http://www.pla.org

REFORMA (National Association to Promote Library Services to
Latinos and the Spanish-Speaking)
http://www.reforma.org

Reference and User Services Association (RUSA; division of ALA)
http://www.ala.org/rusa

Society of American Archivists
http://www.saa.org

Theatre Library Association
http://www.brown.edu/Facilities/University_Library/
beyond/TLA/TLA.html

Urban Libraries Council (ULC)
http://www.clpgh.org/ulc

Young Adult Library Services Association (YALSA; division of ALA)
http://www.ala.org/yalsa

National (English-Language) Associations Outside the U.S.

Aslib, the Association for Information Management (U.K.)
http://www.aslib.co.uk/aslib/index.html

Australian Library and Information Association
http://www.alia.org.au

Canadian Library Association
http://www.cla.ca

The Library Association (U.K.)
http://www.la-hq.org.uk

Library and Information Association of New Zealand (LIANZA)
http://www.lianza.org.nz

U.S. State and Regional Associations

Alabama Library Association
http://allaonline.home.mindspring.com

Alaska Library Association
http://www.akla.org

Arizona Library Association
http://azla.org

Arkansas Library Association
http://www.arklibassn.org

California Library Association
http://www.cla-net.org

Colorado Library Association
http://www.cla-web.org

Connecticut Library Association
http://www.lib.uconn.edu/cla

Delaware Library Association
http://www.dla.lib.de.us

Florida Library Association
http://www.flalib.org

Georgia Library Association
http://wwwlib.gsu.edu/gla

Hawaii Library Association
http://www2.hawaii.edu/hla

Idaho Library Association
http://www.idaholibraries.org

Illinois Library Association
http://www.ila.org

Indiana Library Federation
http://www.ilfonline.org

Iowa Library Association
http://www.iren.net/ila/web

Kansas Library Association
http://skyways.lib.ks.us/kansas/KLA

Kentucky Library Association
http://www.kylibasn.org

Louisiana Library Association
http://www.leeric.lsu.edu/lla

Maine Library Association
http://mainelibraries.org

Maryland Library Association
http://www.mdlib.org

Massachusetts Library Association
http://www.masslib.org

Michigan Library Association
http://www.mla.lib.mi.us

Minnesota Library Association
http://www.lib.mankato.msus.edu:2000

Mississippi Library Association
http://www.lib.usm.edu/~mla/home.html

Missouri Library Association
http://www.mlnc.com/~mla

Montana Library Association
http://www.mtlib.org

Mountain Plains Library Association (MPLA)
http://www.usd.edu/mpla/index.html

Nebraska Library Association
http://www.nol.org/home/NLA

Nevada Library Association
http://www.nevadalibraries.org

New England Library Association
http://www.nelib.org

New Hampshire Library Association
http://www.state.nh.us/nhla

New Jersey Library Association
http://www.njla.org

New Mexico Library Association
http://lib.nmsu.edu/nmla/index.html

New York Library Association
http://www.nyla.org

North Carolina Library Association
http://www.nclaonline.org

North Dakota Library Association
http://ndsl.lib.state.nd.us/ndla

Ohio Library Council
http://www.olc.org

Oklahoma Library Association
http://explorer3.pioneer.lib.ok.us/ola

Oregon Library Association
http://www.olaweb.org

Pacific Northwest Library Association
http://www.pnla.org

Pennsylvania Library Association
http://www.palibraries.org

Rhode Island Library Association
http://nick.uri.edu/library/rila/rila.html

South Carolina Library Association
http://www.scla.org

South Dakota Library Association
http://www.usd.edu/sdla

Tennessee Library Association
http://toltec.lib.utk.edu/~tla

Texas Library Association
http://www.txla.org

Utah Library Association
http://www.ula.org

Vermont Library Association
http://www.vermontlibraries.org

Virginia Library Association
http://www.vla.org

Washington Library Association
http://www.wla.org

West Virginia Library Association
http://wvnvms.wvnet.edu/~wvla

Wisconsin Library Association
http://www.wla.lib.wi.us

Wyoming Library Association
http://www.wyla.org

Canadian Provincial and Regional Associations

Association of Professional Librarians of New Brunswick
http://www.umoncton.ca/abpnb-aplnb/ind_98a.html

Atlantic Provinces Library Association
http://www.stmarys.ca/partners/apla

British Columbia Library Association
http://web.ucs.ubc.ca/bcla/bcla.html

Corporation of Professional Librarians of Quebec
http://www.cbpq.qc.ca

Foothills Library Association
http://www.fla.org

Library Association of Alberta
http://www.laa.ab.ca

Manitoba Library Association
http://www.mla.mb.ca

Newfoundland and Labrador Library Association
http://www.infonet.st-johns.nf.ca/providers/nlla

Nova Scotia Library Association
http://rs6000.nshpl.library.ns.ca/nsla

Ontario Library Association
http://www.accessola.org

Quebec Library Association
http://www.abqla.qc.ca

Saskatchewan Library Association
http://www.lib.sk.ca/sla

International Associations

International Association of School Librarianship (IASL)
http://www.hi.is/~anne/iasl.html

International Council on Archives
http://www.ica.org

International Federation of Library Associations and Institutions (IFLA)
http://www.ifla.org

Internet Library Association
http://www-org.usm.edu/~ila

Special Libraries Association (SLA)
http://www.sla.org

Appendix B

English-Language Library-Related Publishing Outlets with an Online Presence

The following list gives a brief description of the focus of the publishing house or journal, and then provides the general Web site for the publisher, and for author/submission guidelines, if available. Given that new journals emerge regularly and the sheer scope of material available, this is not a complete list. It is intended to give an idea of the variety of outlets available for your library-related article and book ideas. If a publication is described on its Web site as peer-reviewed, this is noted in its description here.

Monographs

ALA Editions: The publishing arm of the American Library Association. Looking for projects that will be of practical use to large segments of the library community.
http://www.ala.org/editions
http://www.ala.org/editions/proposal.html

ARL SPEC: SPEC Kits examine current research library practices and policies. SPEC authors are expected to create, tabulate, and analyze a survey on their suggested topic and bring together

other information to create the kit. ARL pays a small honorarium to each author.
http://www.arl.org/spec/index.html
http://www.arl.org/spec/specfaq.html

ARL Transforming Libraries: Seeks proposals reporting how individuals or institutions are using technology to transform library operations and services.
http://www.arl.org/transform/index.html

CLIP Notes (ACRL College Libraries Section): CLIP Notes authors compile survey results, literature reviews, and sample documents from surveyed libraries to explain trends and/or practices and procedures in small and midsized academic libraries.
http://abell.austinc.edu/CLS/cls6.html#publications
http://abell.austinc.edu/CLS/clipguide.html

Greenwood Publishing Group: Publishes books on librarianship, library management, information management, and children's/young adult literature.
http://www.greenwood.com
http://www.greenwood.com/author/index.asp?SectionID=
contactus@Location=author_page

The Haworth Press, Inc.: A publisher of both books and journals, The Haworth Press publishes textbooks and reference books in librarianship.
http://www.haworthpressinc.com
http://www.haworthpressinc.com/AuthorInfo

Highsmith Press: Handbooks and other practical professional books for librarians. Includes a link to its Upstart Books imprint,

which publishes resources for school library media specialists and children's librarians.
http://www.hpress.highsmith.com
http://www.hpress.highsmith.com/submiss.htm

H.W. Wilson: Reference books for librarians and researchers. Also publishes some professional resources.
http://www.hwwilson.com

Information Today, Inc.: Publishes books on libraries and information technology, as well as material on how to do online research. Also publishes monthly trade journals, magazines, and newsletters for librarians and other information professionals.
http://www.infotoday.com

Libraries Unlimited: Aimed at practicing librarians, media specialists, and library educators, this press publishes library science textbooks and handbooks.
http://www.lu.com/lu
http://www.lu.com/lu/manu.html

Library Association Publishing: The British national association's publishing arm.
http://www.la-hq.org.uk/directory/publications.html
http://www.la-hq.org.uk/directory/publications/lap/yourbook.html

McFarland & Company, Inc., Publishers: Publishes books on librarianship as well as reference works for librarians.
http://mcfarlandpub.com
http://mcfarlandpub.com/book_proposals.html

Neal-Schuman Publishers, Inc.: Publishers of "How-To-Do-It Manuals for Librarians" as well as other practical books for librarians and information professionals.

http://www.neal-schuman.com
http://www.neal-schuman.com/submission.html

Oryx Press: Among its specialties is library and information science.
http://www.oryxpress.com
http://www.oryxpress.com/auguide.htm

Scarecrow Press: A scholarly, academic publisher. One of its publication focuses is "Library and Information Science."
http://www.scarecrowpress.com
http://www.scarecrowpress.com/SCP/Submission

National and International Journals

American Libraries: The official publication of the American Library Association, which is disseminated monthly to all members.
http://www.ala.org/alonline/index.html
http://www.ala.org/alonline/guide/mss.html

The Australian Library Journal: Quarterly publication of the Australian Library and Information Association.
http://www.alia.org.au/alj
http://www.alia.org.au/alj/contributor.notes.html

Book Links: Connecting Books, Libraries, and Classrooms: An ALA publication containing bibliographies and articles for those serving preschool through eighth grade.
http://www.ala.org/BookLinks
http://www.ala.org/BookLinks/writing.html

Catholic Library World: Official quarterly publication of the
Catholic Library Association.
http://www.cathla.org/cathlibworld.html

Computers in Libraries: Monthly theme issues, practical information for librarians on computer-related topics.
http://www.infotoday.com/cilmag/ciltop.htm
http://www.infotoday.com/cilmag/contrib.htm

EContent Magazine (formerly *Database*): Intended for hands-on
searchers and directors of information facilities. Reviews and
compares information sources and software.
http://www.ecmag.net
http://www.ecmag.net/ECforms/authors.html

Information Outlook: The monthly professional journal of the
Special Libraries Association.
http://www.sla.org/content/Shop/Infomation/ioarticles/index.cfm
http://www.sla.org/content/involved/shareknowledge/
writingforio.cfm

Information Today: Monthly, combines news articles with topical
articles describing developments in the field, emphasizing electronic information.
http://www.infotoday.com/it/itnew.htm

International Leads: Published by ALA's International Relations
Round Table, focuses on international librarianship.
http://www.ala.org/irrt/leadsissues.html
http://www.lita.org/ital/infoauth.htm

Intranet Professional: Case studies and how-tos for libraries and
research centers.

http://www.infotoday.com/IP/default.htm
http://www.infotoday.com/IP/ipsubs.htm

JOYS: Journal of Youth Services in Libraries: Published by ALSC and YALSA, focuses on continuing education of librarians dealing with youth.
http://www.ala.org/alsc/joys/index.html
http://www.ala.org/alsc/joys/guidelines_authors.html

Law Library Journal: Official publication of the American Association of Law Libraries; publishes both scholarly and practice-oriented articles.
http://www.aallnet.org/products/pub_journal.asp

Libraries & Culture: Explores the significance of collections of recorded knowledge in social and cultural historical context.
http://www.utexas.edu/utpress/journals/jlc.html

Library Administration and Management: Practical articles and interviews of use to library administrators.
http://www.ala.org/lama/la&m/index.html
http://www.ala.org/lama/la&m/author.html

Library Journal: National journal, feature articles, news, and reviews.
http://libraryjournal.reviewsnews.com

Library Mosaics: Focuses on support staff issues.
http://www.librarymosaics.com

LQ: The Library Quarterly: Research in all areas of librarianship.
http://www.journals.uchicago.edu/LQ
http://www.journals.uchicago.edu/LQ/instruct.html

MultiMedia Schools: For librarians, teachers, and technology coordinators, focuses on use of electronic information resources and integrating them into the curriculum.
http://www.infotoday.com/MMSchools/default.htm
http://www.infotoday.com/MMSchools/MMSforms/authors.html

Online Magazine: Focuses on electronic information topics, directed at hands-on searchers and information managers.
http://www.infotoday.com/online

The Progressive Librarian: Critical perspectives in librarianship, progressive perspective, published twice yearly.
http://www.libr.org/PL
http://www.libr.org/PL/submissions.html

Public Libraries: The official bi-monthly journal of the Public Library Association.
http://www.pla.org/mag-index.html
http://www.pla.org/mag-instructions.html

Searcher: The Magazine for Database Professionals: Issues of interest to professional database searchers.
http://www.infotoday.com/searcher/default.htm

The Shy Librarian: Both e-mail and print, focuses on marketing and PR for libraries.
http://www.shylibrarian.com
http://www.shylibrarian.com/hotstoryidea.htm

Today's Librarian: A glossy, more "popular" magazine devoted to public librarians.

http://www.todayslibrarian.com
http://www.todayslibrarian.com/writing.html

The U*N*A*B*A*S*H*E*D Librarian: Seeks practical articles on "How I run my library good."
http://www.unabashedlibrarian.com
http://www.unabashedlibrarian.com/contribute.php3

VOYA (Voice of Youth Advocates): Addresses the informational needs of teenagers.
http://www.voya.com
http://www.voya.com/voyasubmit.html

Peer-Reviewed Journals (With a Print Counterpart)

The American Archivist: Refereed publication of the Society of American Archivists; publishes research articles, case studies, bibliographies, and reviews.
http://www.archivists.org/periodicals/aa-toc.html

Behavioral and Social Sciences Librarian: Focuses on the production, collection, organization, dissemination, retrieval, and use of information in the social and behavioral sciences.
http://libweb.sdsu.edu/genref/mstover/bssl.htm
http://libweb.sdsu.edu/genref/mstover/bsslguid.htm

The Bottom Line: Managing Library Finances: Quarterly. Information on helping libraries deal with financial constraints.
http://www.emeraldinsight.com/bl.htm
http://www.emeraldinsight.com/journals/bl/notes.htm

Bulletin of the Medical Library Association: International, peer-reviewed. Articles on health sciences librarianship.
http://www.mlanet.org/publications/bmla/index.html
http://www.mlanet.org/publications/bmla/bmlainfo.html

Campus-Wide Information Systems: Information for large academic institutions on purchasing, installing, and running campus-wide computer networks.
http://www.emeraldinsight.com/cwis.htm
http://www.emeraldinsight.com/journals/cwis/notes.htm

Collection Building: Quarterly. Mix of practical and theoretical papers on collection building.
http://www.emeraldinsight.com/cb.htm
http://www.emeraldinsight.com/journals/cb/notes.htm

Collection Management: Focuses on all aspects of collection development.
http://html.ulib.csuohio.edu/CollectionMgmt/about.html
http://html.ulib.csuohio.edu/CollectionMgmt/authors.html

College & Research Libraries: Double-blind refereed. A scholarly research publication of ACRL focusing on academic and research librarianship.
http://www.ala.org/acrl/c&rl.html
http://www.ala.org/acrl/instruct.html

The Electronic Library: Peer-reviewed. Addresses all aspects of computerization in libraries.
http://www.emeraldinsight.com/el.htm
http://www.emeraldinsight.com/journals/el/notes.htm

Government Information Quarterly: Cross-disciplinary and refereed. Analyzes government information policy and practices, new

development, and policies for managing government
information.
http://www.elsevier.com/locate/govinf

Health Libraries Review: Peer-reviewed. Encompasses all health-
care information and librarianship.
http://www.blackwell-science.com/~cgilib/jnlpage.bin?
Journal=hlr&File=hlr&Page=aims
http://www.blackwell-science.com/~cgilib/jnlpage.bin?
Journal=hlr&File=hlr&Page=authors

The Information Society: Refereed. Deals with information technologies and their impact on society.
http://www.slis.indiana.edu/TIS
http://www.slis.indiana.edu/TIS/basic_info/instructions.html

Information Technology and Libraries: Refereed quarterly journal
published by LITA. Focuses on all aspects of libraries and information technology.
http://www.lita.org/ital/index.htm
http://www.lita.org/ital/infoauth.htm

International Information and Library Review: Quarterly. Focuses
on developments in the information field.
http://www.academicpress.com/iilr
http://www.academicpress.com/www/journal/lr/lrifa.htm

Internet Research: Research and practical advice on the Internet
as an information resource.
http://www.emeraldinsight.com/intr.htm
http://www.emeraldinsight.com/journals/intr/notes.htm

Journal of Academic Librarianship: International, refereed. Focuses on research relevant to academic librarianship.
http://www.elsevier.com/inca/publications/store/6/2/0/2/0/7/index.htt
http://www.elsevier.com/inca/publications/store/6/2/0/2/0/7/620207.pub.istaut.shtml

Journal of Documentation: Peer-reviewed. Focuses on the recording, organization, management, retrieval, dissemination, and use of information.
http://www.aslib.co.uk/jdoc
http://www.aslib.co.uk/jdoc/notes.html

Journal of Internet Cataloging: Peer-reviewed. Focuses on organization, access, and bibliographic control of Internet resources.
http://www.haworthpressinc.com:8081/jic
http://www.haworthpressinc.com:8081/jic/jicinau.html

Journal of Knowledge Management: Quarterly, peer-reviewed. Focuses on knowledge management strategies and business solutions.
http://www.emeraldinsight.com/jkm.htm
http://www.emeraldinsight.com/journals/jkm/notes.htm

Knowledge Quest: Bi-monthly, September–June, parts refereed. For school library media specialists.
http://www.ala.org/aasl/kqweb/index.html
http://www.ala.org/aasl/kqweb/kqguidelines.html

Library Hi Tech: Quarterly. Combines in-depth articles, case studies, and scholarly literature reviews on current and emerging technologies.
http://www.emeraldinsight.com/lht.htm
http://www.emeraldinsight.com/journals/lht/notes.htm

Library Resources and Technical Services: Quarterly, peer-reviewed. Supports the profession of collection development and management.
http://www.ala.org/alcts/lrts
http://www.ala.org/alcts/lrts/guide.html

Library Review: International communication link between librarians, educators, and information professionals in all types of settings.
http://www.emeraldinsight.com/lr.htm
http://www.emeraldinsight.com/journals/lr/notes.htm

Library Trends: Theme issues on a single aspect of professional activity or interest.
http://www.lis.uiuc.edu/puboff/catalog/trends
http://www.lis.uiuc.edu/puboff/catalog/trends/#manuscript

New Library World: On the changing role of the library.
http://www.emeraldinsight.com/nlw.htm
http://www.emeraldinsight.com/journals/nlw/notes.htm

Portal: Libraries and the Academy: Refereed. Focuses on how technology affects academic librarianship and scholarship.
http://www.press.jhu.edu/press/journals/informat/portal.html

Reference & User Services Quarterly: Double-blind refereed. Official RUSA journal, addresses all aspects of library services to adults.
http://www.ala.org/rusa/rusq/index.html
http://www.ala.org/rusa/rusq/rusq_aut.html

Public Services Quarterly: A Haworth journal addressing service issues in the changing academic library environment.
http://lclark.edu/~dorner/psq

Reference Services Review: Dedicated to the enrichment of reference knowledge and the advancement of reference services.
http://www.emeraldinsight.com/rsr.htm
http://www.emeraldinsight.com/journals/rsr/notes.htm

Research Strategies: Refereed. Publishes research on instructional services and the educational mission of the library.
http://www.elsevier.com/locate/lcats

School Library Media Research: Scholarly, refereed. Research on management, implementation, and evaluation of school library media programs.
http://www.ala.org/aasl/SLMR/index.html
http://www.ala.org/aasl/SLMR/mspolicy.html

The Serials Librarian: International serials management journal.
http://www.serialslibrarian.com
http://www.serialslibrarian.com/instructions.html

Serials Reference Services Quarterly: Haworth Press journal focusing on reference work and serials librarianship.
http://www2.msstate.edu/~doll/instr.htm

Urban Library Journal: Refereed. Deals with all types and aspects of urban libraries.
http://lacuny.cuny.edu/ulj/
http://lacuny.cuny.edu/ulj/ms.htm

WebNet Journal: International, features are peer-reviewed. Quarterly for researchers, focuses on Internet and network technologies, applications, and services.
http://www.aace.org/pubs/webnet/
http://www.aace.org/pubs/webnet/guidelines.htm

Electronic Journals and Newsletters (General and Refereed)

ALA TechSource: Seeks 500-word feature articles on library news and technology trends.
https://www.techsource.ala.org
https://www.techsource.ala.org/submissions.shtml

Ariadne: For information professionals in academic libraries; U.K. focus but applicable in the U.S. and elsewhere. Evaluates Internet resources and gives news about digital libraries.
http://www.ariadne.ac.uk
http://www.ariadne.ac.uk/mail/intro-new.html

Associates: The Electronic Library Support Staff Journal: Library support staff issues, including technology, downsizing, staff development, how-tos, profiles, and so on.
http://www.ukans.edu/~assoc
http://www.ukans.edu/~assoc/submit.htm

Bulletin of the American Society for Information Science and Technology: Bi-monthly, seeks short articles, generally reports of practice, reviews, and public policy/legislative issues.
http://www.asis.org/Bulletin
http://www.asis.org/Bulletin/sumit.html

D-Lib Magazine: Monthly, intended for a technical and professional audience, focuses on innovation and research in digital libraries.
http://www.dlib.org/dlib.html
http://www.dlib.org/dlib/author-guidelines.html

Info Career Trends: Bi-monthly e-mail newsletter focuses on career development issues for practicing information professionals.
http://www.lisjobs.com/newsletter
http://www.lisjobs.com/newsletter/theme.htm#contrib

Information Research: An International Electronic Journal: An international, scholarly journal that publishes both refereed and working papers in the fields of information science, information management, information systems, information policy, and librarianship. Note that it requires submissions in HTML format.
http://www.shef.ac.uk/~is/publications/infres/ircont.html
http://www.shef.ac.uk/~is/publications/infres/author1.html

Issues in Science and Technology Librarianship: Includes refereed and nonrefereed sections. Published quarterly by the Science and Technology Section of ACRL.
http://www.library.ucsb.edu/istl
http://www.library.ucsb.edu/istl/guidelines.html
http://www.library.ucsb.edu/istl/guidelines2.html

JoDI: Journal of Digital Information: Peer-reviewed. Focuses on management, presentation, and uses of information in digital environments.
http://jodi.ecs.soton.ac.uk
http://jodi.ecs.soton.ac.uk/sec.php3?content=submit

Journal of Library Services for Distance Education: Peer reviewed, international. Focuses on challenges of providing library service

to distance education students. In frames, so click on "About" for submission guidelines.
http://www.westga.edu/~library/jlsde

Library Philosophy and Practice: Refereed. Seeks articles that show the connection between library practice and the philosophy/theory behind it.
http://www.uidaho.edu/~mbolin/lp&p.htm
http://www.uidaho.edu/~mbolin/authors.htm

Libres: Library and Information Science Research: Includes refereed and nonrefereed sections. Published twice yearly to communicate scholarly thought on library and information science.
http://aztec.lib.utk.edu/libres
http://aztec.lib.utk.edu/libres/authors.html

MC Journal: The Journal of Academic Media Librarianship: Peer-reviewed, practical and scholarly information relating to academic audiovisual librarianship.
http://wings.buffalo.edu/publications/mcjrnl
http://wings.buffalo.edu/publications/mcjrnl/edit.html

SIMILE: Studies in Media & Information Literacy Education: Peer-reviewed. Covers the connections between information instruction, media literacy, and information literacy.
http://simile.fis.utoronto.ca
http://simile.fis.utoronto.ca/instructions.html

Transforming Traditional Libraries: Peer-reviewed. Focuses on exploring how librarians integrate new technologies and services with their traditional role.
http://www.lib.usf.edu/~mdibble/ttl
http://www.lib.usf.edu/~mdibble/ttl/call.html

Related Publications Outside the Library Field

Elementary School Journal: Data about school and classroom practices in elementary and middle schools.
http://www.journals.uchicago.edu/ESJ/home.html
http://www.journals.uchicago.edu/ESJ/instruct.html

First Monday: Peer-reviewed, online only. Seeks articles of interest to the Internet community and scholarly research articles about the Internet.
http://www.firstmonday.dk
http://www.firstmonday.dk/idea.html#submit

Link-Up: For users of online services, CD-ROMs, and the Internet.
http://www.infotoday.com/lu/lunew.htm

T.H.E. Journal: Technical Horizons in Education: Focuses on integrating technology throughout campuses and curricula.
http://www.thejournal.com
http://www.thejournal.com/business/cp

Reviewing Opportunities

Booklist: Reviews of books and electronic media for librarians in all types of libraries.
http://www.ala.org/booklist/index.html

Choice Magazine: An ACRL publication that evaluates materials for academic libraries. Reviewers must be teaching faculty or librarians at academic institutions.
http://www.ala.org/acrl/choice/home.html
http://www.ala.org/acrl/choice/revguide.html

Counterpoise: Alternative journal reviewing alternative publications and independent media worldwide.
http://www.liblib.com/Cpoise/Cpoise.html

Journal of Academic Librarianship: Books relevant to academic librarians.
http://www.elsevier.com/inca/publications/store/6/2/0/2/0/7/index.att
http://www.elsevier.com/inca/publications/store/6/2/0/2/0/7/620207.pub.istaut.shtml

Library Journal: Reviews of all types of material for libraries.
http://libraryjournal.reviewsnews.com

LQ: The Library Quarterly: Reviews books on librarianship and library issues.
http://www.journals.uchicago.edu/LQ
http://www.journals.uchicago.edu/LQ/instruct2.html

Reference Reviews: Reviews of reference publications and subject bibliographies as well as of electronic resources/Web sites.
http://www.emeraldinsight.com/rr.htm
http://www.emeraldinsight.com/journals/rr/notes.htm

The Serials Librarian: Reviews publications related to serials work.
http://www.serialslibrarian.com/reviews.html

Video Librarian: Comprehensive video review guide for libraries.
http://www.videolibrarian.com

VOYA (Voice of Youth Advocates): Reviews literature and media for young adults; reviewers should be youth-serving professionals.
http://www.voya.com
http://www.voya.com/voyarevwr.html

State/Local Journals

Arkansas Libraries
http://pweb.netcom.com/~ronruss/Publications.html
http://pweb.netcom.com/~ronruss/PubGuide.html

Florida Libraries
http://www.flalib.org/library/fla/florlibs/florlibs.htm
http://www.flalib.org/library/fla/florlibs/flguide.htm

Georgia Library Quarterly
http://www.library.gsu.edu/gla/glq/index.htm

The Idaho Librarian
http://www.idaholibraries.org/idaholibrarian/index.htm

Louisiana Libraries
http://www.leeric.lsu.edu/lla/bulletin/index.htm

Mississippi Libraries
http://www.lib.usm.edu/~mla/publications/ml/main.html
http://www.lib.usm.edu/~mla/publications/ml/about.html

Nebraska Library Association Quarterly
http://www.nol.org/home/NLA/nlaq.html

New England Libraries
http://www.nelib.org/publicat.html

North Carolina Libraries
http://www.esn.net/tnt/NCL/NCL.htm
http://www.esn.net/tnt/NCL/manuscripts.htm

Ohio Libraries
http://www.olc.org/ohio_lib.html

Oregon Library Association Quarterly
http://www.olaweb.org/quarterly/index.shtml
http://www.olaweb.org/quarterly/authors.shtml

The Tennessee Librarian
http://toltec.lib.utk.edu/~tla/pubtoc.html
http://toltec.lib.utk.edu/~tla/tlainst.html

Texas Library Journal
http://www.txla.org/pubs/pubs.html
http://www.txla.org/pubs/manguide.html

Virginia Libraries
http://scholar.lib.vt.edu/ejournals/VALib/index.html
http://scholar.lib.vt.edu/ejournals/VALib/submission.html

Appendix C

Recommended Reading

General Sources for Librarianship, Career Development, and the Internet

Crosby, Olivia. "Librarians: Information Experts In the Information Age." *Occupational Outlook Quarterly*, Winter 2000–01. Dec. 30, 2000 (http://www.bls.gov/opub/ooq/2000/Winter/art01.pdf).

Eberhart, George M., comp. *The Whole Library Handbook 3*. Chicago: American Library Association, 2000.

Gause, Sharon, and Daria Carle. "Time to Shift Gears: From Libraries to Librarians." *Leadership, Performance, Excellence: Information Profesionals in the Driver's Seat*. Washington, D.C.: Special Libraries Association, 1998: 8–28.

Gordon, Rachel Singer, and Sarah Nesbeitt. "Who We Are, Where We're Going: A Report From the Front." *Library Journal*, May 15, 1999: 36–39.

Hayes, Jan E., and Julie Todaro. *Careers in Libraries: A Bibliography of Traditional and Web-Based Library Career Resources*. Chicago: American Library Association Office for Human Resources Development and Recruitment, 2000.

Jana, Varlejs. "On Their Own: Librarians' Self-Directed, Work-Related Learning." *Library Quarterly*, 69.2 (1999): 173–201.

"Look It Up: Not an Endangered Career." *CNN.com*, Nov. 28, 2000. CNN, Nov. 29, 2000 (http://www.cnn.com/2000/CAREER/trends/11/28/librarians/index.html).

Monty, Vivienne, and P. Warren-Wenk. "Using the Internet as a Professional Development Tool: An Analysis." *Education Libraries*, 18.1 (1994): 7–10.

Mount, Ellis, ed. *Expanding Technologies—Expanding Careers: Librarianship in Transition.* Washington, D.C.: Special Libraries Association, 1997.

O'Leary, Mick. "Grading the Library Portals." *Online*, Nov./Dec. 2000: 38–43.

Pantry, Sheila, and Peter Griffith. *Your Successful LIS Career: CVs, Interviews, and Self Promotion.* London: Library Association Publishing, 1999.

Poulter, Alan, Debra Hiom, and Gwyneth Tseng. *The Library and Information Professional's Guide to the Internet.* 3rd ed. London: Library Association Publishing, 2000.

Rubin, Richard. *Foundations of Library and Information Science.* New York: Neal-Schuman, 2000.

Shontz, Priscilla K. *Jump Start Your Career in Library & Information Science.* Lanham, MD: Scarecrow Press, 2001.

Stover, Mark. *Leading the Wired Organization: The Information Professional's Guide to Managing Technological Change.* New York: Neal-Schuman Publishers, Inc., 1999.

Tillman, Hope N., ed. *Internet Tools of the Profession: A Guide for Information Professionals.* 2nd ed. Washington: Special Libraries Association, 1997.

Chapters 1–3: Learning and Growing Online

Agre, Phil. "Networking on the Network." Phil Agre: 1993–2001. Feb. 25, 2001 (http://dlis.gseis.ucla.edu/people/pagre/network.html).

Balas, Janet. "Online Treasures: Staying Afloat in the Net Sea." *Online,* May 1997: 41–43.

Bell, Steven. "To Keep Up, Go Beyond: Developing a Personal Professional Development Plan Using E-Resources Outside the Bounds of Library Literature." *College and Research Libraries NewsNet,* 61.7 (2000). Jan. 4, 2001 (http://www.ala.org/acrl/keepup.html).

Benson, Allen C. *Neal-Schuman Complete Internet Companion for Librarians.* 2nd ed. New York: Neal-Schuman, 2001.

Berry, John N., and Paul Kaplan. "E-mail Blues." *Library Journal,* Feb. 1, 1997: 6.

Cartwright, Glen Phillip, and Diane Kovacs. "Beyond E-mail." *Change,* May/June 1995: 50–53.

Dillon, Karen. "Finding the Right Mentor for You." *Inc.,* June 1998: 48.

Fourie, Ina. "Empowering Users—Current Awareness on the Internet." *The Electronic Library*, 17.6 (1999): 379–388.

George, Mary W. "Monitor as Mentor: Internet's Role in Professional Growth." *College and Research Libraries News*, March 1994: 142–3.

Gordon, Rachel Singer. "Online Discussion Forums: Finding Community, Commentary, and (Hopefully) Answers." *Link-Up*, 17.1 (2000). Feb. 25, 2001 (http://www.infotoday.com/lu/jan00/gordon.html).

Hammond, Michael. "Professional Learning and the Online Discussion." 2nd National Symposium on Networked Learner Support, June 23–24, 1997, Sheffield, England. Nov. 2, 2000 (http://www.shef.ac.uk/%7eis/publications/infres/paper34.html).

Jones-Quartey, Theo. "Mentoring—Personal Reflections of a Special Librarian." *Information Outlook*, 4.7 (2000): 26–30.

Jossie, Frank. "Mentoring in Changing Times." *Training*, Aug. 1997: 50–54.

Kassel, Amelia. "Web Monitoring and Clipping Services Round-Up." *Searcher*, Jul./Aug. 2000: 26–31.

Levine, John R., Carol Baroudi, and Margaret Levine Young. *The Internet for Dummies*. 7th ed. Indianapolis: Hungry Minds, 2000.

McMahon, Kenneth. "BUBL Bits: Current Awareness Services." *Computers in Libraries*, Apr. 1995: 79–80.

"Mentoring: A Key Resource to Develop Professional and Personal Competencies." *Information Outlook*, 3.2 (1999): 12.

Mountfield, H. M. "Electronic Current Awareness Service: A Survival Tool for the Information Age?" *The Electronic Library*, 13.4 (1995): 317–323.

Murray, Laura K. *Basic Internet for Busy Librarians: A Quick Course for Catching Up*. Chicago: ALA Editions, 1998.

Notess, Greg R. "On the Net: Internet Current Awareness." *Online*, Mar./Apr. 1999: 75–78.

Robinson, Kara, and Diane Kovacs. "LibRef-L: Sharing Reference Expertise Over the Academic Networks." *Wilson Library Bulletin*, Jan. 1993: 47–48, 50.

Roselle, Ann. "Internet-Related Work Activities and Academic Government Documents Librarians' Professional Relationships." *Government Information Quarterly*, 16.2 (1999): 149–168.

Schneider, Karen. "The Committee Wore Pajamas: ALA Debuts Online Chat."*American Libraries*, Dec. 2000: 62.

Stenstrom, Patricia F., and Patricia Tegler. "Current Awareness in Librarianship." *Library Trends*, Spr. 1988: 725–739.

Tedd, Lucy A., and Robin Yeates. "A Personalized Current Awareness Service for Library and Information Services Staff: An Overview of the NewsAgent for Libraries Project." *Program*, 32.4 (1998): 373–390.

Tolson, Stephanie. "Mentoring Up the Career Ladder." *Information Outlook*, 2.6 (1998): 37–38.

Tudor, Jan Davis. "Using Droids and Agents to Treat Information Overload." *Online*, Nov./Dec. 1997: 51–58.

Wildemuth, Barbara, et al. "What's Everybody Talking About? Message Functions and Topics on Electronic Lists and Newsgroups in Information and Library Science." *Journal of Education for Library and Information Science*, 38.2 (1997): 137–156.

Wordsworth, Anne. "MLS Students Find Internet the Virtual Link to Mentors." *Wilson Library Bulletin*, Apr. 1995: 16.

Chapters 4–7: Professional Involvement

Bahr, Alice, ed. *InPrint: Publishing Opportunities for College Librarians*. Chicago: ACRL, 2001. Feb. 4, 2001 (http://acrl.telusys. net/epubs/inprint.html).

Block, Marylaine. "If You Give It Away for Free Will He Still Marry You? Or: Building a Business by Giving Away Free Internet Content." Nov. 8, 2000. Jan. 2, 2001 (http://marylaine.com/il2000. html).

Borei, Karin Begg. "The Rewards of Managing an Electronic Mailing List." *Library Trends*, 47.4 (1999): 686–698.

Burch, Sue. "Professional Library Associations: An Ally for the 21st Century." *Kentucky Libraries*, 63.4 (1999): 14–17.

Day, Abby. "How to Write Publishable Papers." Bradford, England: MCB University Press Literati Club, March–May, 2001. Mar. 9, 2001 (http://www.literati.club.co.uk/writing/publishable.html).

"Directory of Associations." *Library Journal Buyer's Guide.* Dec. 2000: 12–17.

Dominick, Joseph R. "Who Do You Think You Are? Personal Home Pages and Self-Presentation on the World Wide Web." *Journalism & Mass Communication Quarterly,* 76.4 (1999): 646–658.

Frank, Donald G. "Activity in Professional Associations: The Positive Difference in a Librarian's Career." *Library Trends,* 46.2 (1997): 307–319.

Glendenning, Barbara J., and James C. Gordon. "Professional Associations: Promoting Leadership in a Career." *Library Trends,* 46.2 (1997): 258–277.

Haines, Annette. "Librarians' Personal Web Pages: An Analysis." *College & Research Libraries,* 60.6 (1999): 543–550.

Info Career Trends (theme issue on writing for publication). Nov. 1, 2000. Feb. 4, 2001 (http://www.lisjobs.com/newsletter/archives.htm).

Li, Xia, and Nancy Crane. *Electronic Styles: A Handbook for Citing Electronic Information.* Medford, NJ: Information Today, Inc., 1996.

Litwin, Rory. "Creating Library Juice." *Info Career Trends,* Nov. 1, 2000. Dec. 29, 2000 (http://www.lisjobs.com/newsletter/archives/nov00rlitwin.htm).

Price, Gary. "Marylaine Block: A Librarian with All but Walls." *Searcher,* June 2000. Jan. 13, 2001 (http://www.infotoday.com/searcher/jun00/price.htm).

Schwartz, Candy, and Peter Hernon. "Editorial: Professional Associations and LIS Research." *Library and Information Science Research*. Stamford, CT: Ablex, 1999. 141–151.

Shontz, Priscilla K. "Tips for Enjoying Your First ALA Conference." *American Libraries*, Jun./Jul. 1999: 108.

Virgo, Julie Carroll. "The Role of Professional Associations." *Library and Information Science Research*. Stamford, CT: Ablex, 1991. 189–96.

Weaver, Angela. "Personal Web Pages as Professional Activities: An Exploratory Study." *Reference Services Review*, 28.2 (2000): 171–177.

Weller, Ann C. *Editorial Peer Review: Its Strengths and Weaknesses*. American Society for Information Science and Technology. Medford, NJ: Information Today, Inc., 2001.

Chapters 8–10: Education

Bjørner, Susanne. "Online On Point: CE 101: Continuing Education." *Online*, Sept. 1997. Nov. 2, 2000 (http://www.onlineinc.com/onlinemag/SeptOL97/online9.html).

Carr-Wiggin, Anne. "Rothstein's Baby: Continuing Professional Education for Librarians." University of Alberta SLIS: 1996, revised March 30, 1998. Dec. 1, 2000 (http://www.slis.ualberta.ca/cap98s/acarr).

Chepesiuk, Ron. "Learning Without Walls." *American Libraries*, Oct. 1998: 62–65.

Ellison, John. "Distance Learning for Today's Librarian." *Library Review*, 49.5 (2000): 240–242.

Gibbons, W. J. "From Dungeons to Degrees." 1997. Jan. 2, 2001 (http://www.kcc.hawaii.edu/org/tcc_conf97/pres/gibbons.html).

Info Career Trends (theme issue on distance education). Mar. 1, 2001. Mar. 9, 2001 (http://www.lisjobs.com/newsletter/archives.htm).

Mangan, Katherine S. "In Revamped Library Schools, Information Trumps Books." *The Chronicle of Higher Education*, Apr. 7, 2000: A43–A44.

National Education Assocation (NEA). "Confronting the Future of Distance Learning—Placing Quality in Reach." NEA: June 14, 2000. Nov. 19, 2000 (http://www.nea.org/nr/nr000614.html).

Paris, Marion. "Beyond Competencies: A Trendspotter's Guide to Library Education." *Information Outlook*, Dec. 1999: 31–36.

Sitze, Amy. "Faculty Gives e-Learning a Thumbs Up." *Online Learning*, Oct. 2000: 14.

Small, Ruth V. "A Comparison of the Resident and Distance Learning Experience in Library and Information Science Graduate Education." *Journal of Education for Library and Information Science*, 40.1 (1999): 27–47.

Smith, Duncan. "What Is the Shelf Life of the MLS?" American Library Association Congress on Professional Education. Oct. 26, 2000 (http://www.ala.org/congress/smith.html).

Turlington, Shannon R. *How to Find a Scholarship Online.* New York: McGraw-Hill, 2001.

White, Herbert. "The Changes in Off-Campus Education." *Library Journal,* Feb. 15, 1999: 128.

Chapters 11–13: Employment

Bolles, Richard. *What Color Is Your Parachute? 2001, A Practical Manual for Job-Hunters & Career-Changers.* Berkeley, CA: Ten Speed Press, 2000.

Criscito, Pat. *Resumes in Cyberspace: Your Complete Guide to a Computerized Job Search.* Hauppauge, NY: Barrons Educational Series, 2000.

Dikel, Margaret F., and Frances Roehm. *The Internet Guide to Job Searching 2000–01 Edition.* Lincolnwood, IL: NTC/Contemporary Publishing, 2000.

Dolan, Donna R., and John E. Schumacher. "Top U.S. Sources for an Online Job Search." *Database,* Oct./Nov. 1994: 34–43.

Foster, Janet B. "Jobs on the Net for Librarians." *Public Libraries,* Jan./Feb. 1999: 27–29.

Heacox, Stephanie. "Information Job Hunting Through the Internet." *Searcher,* Mar. 1996: 8–12.

Lorenzen, Elizabeth A. "Librarian for Hire: Internet Searching for Job Search Success." *Technicalities,* Jan. 1995: 11–14.

Nesbeitt, Sarah L. "Trends in Internet-Based Library Recruitment: An Introductory Survey." *Internet Reference Services Quarterly*, 4:2 (1999): 23–40.

Newlen, Robert R. *Writing Resumes That Work: A How-To-Do-It Manual for Librarians.* New York: Neal-Schuman, 1998.

Riley, Margaret. "Riley's Guided Tour: Job Searching on the Net." *Library Journal*, Sep. 15, 1996: 24–27.

Singer, Rachel. "Neglected Networking: Why (And How!) Not to Overlook the Internet in Your Library Job Search." *Illinois Libraries*, Fall 1997: 174–176.

Smith, Rebecca. *Electronic Resumes and Online Networking.* Franklin Lakes, NJ: Career Press, 2000.

Van Tassel, Debra S. "Job Searching on the Internet." *Colorado Libraries*, Fall 1996: 44–46.

Weathers-Parry, Patte. "The Librarian's Portfolio." *Info Career Trends*, Jan. 1, 2001. Jan. 13, 2001 (http://www.lisjobs.com/newsletter/archives/jan01pparry.htm).

Weddle, Peter. "Job Searching Confidentially: Internet Job Agents Can Help You Get a Lot Closer to Your Dream Job." *CNN.Com*, Dec. 4, 2000. CNN, Dec. 19, 2000 (http://cnnfn.cnn.com/2000/12/04/career/q_weddle).

Yate, Martin John. *Resumes that Knock 'Em Dead.* 4th ed. Holbrook, MA: Adams Media, 2000.

About the Authors

Sarah L. Nesbeitt is Reference/Systems Librarian at Maxwell Library, Bridgewater State College, Mass. Since 1995, she has compiled "Library Job Postings on the Internet," a Web-based guide to help librarians find employment. She also works as the North American editor for the library journal *Reference Reviews*. Among her nontechie interests, Nesbeitt serves as the U.S. coordinating editor for the *Historical Novels Review* and writes a bimonthly column on historical fiction for NoveList.

Rachel Singer Gordon is Head of Computer Services at the Franklin Park Public Library, Ill. She is the Webmaster of the library career site Lisjobs.com and the founding editor of the *Info Career Trends* electronic newsletter, which focuses on career development issues for information professionals (http://www.lisjobs.com/newsletter). Her published work includes *Teaching the Internet in Libraries* (ALA Editions, 2001).

Index

A

AALL (American Association of Law Libraries)
discussion list, 36
job ads, 294
Law Library Journal, 350
mentorship program, 40
scholarship information, 238
Web site, 102, 333
AASL (American Association of School Librarians), 333
ABLE (Alternative Basic Library Education), 198
About.com, 43, 254
Academic Libraries of the 21st Century Project, 47
Academic Newswire, 72
Accreditation, 79, 181–184
ACL (Association of Christian Librarians), 334
ACQNET discussion list, 34
ACRL (Association of College and Research Libraries), 81, 148–149, 329, 334, 346
Adobe, 44–45, 191, 235
AECT (Association for Educational Communications and

Technology), 334
Agee, Phil, 26
AGLISS (Association of Graduate Library and Information Science Students), 310
AIIP (Association of Independent Information Professionals), 96, 335
AILA (American Indian Library Association), 333
AJL (Association of Jewish Libraries), 335
ALA (American Library Association)
accreditation requirements, 79, 181
ALA discussion lists, 36
ALA Editions, 152–153, 345–346
ALA roundtables, 36
ALA TechSource, 358
Booklist, 361
Career Leads, 289
Choice Magazine, 361
Directory of Accredited LIS Masters Programs, 180–181, 222–223

Divisions, Units, and
Governance page, 86
educational policy statements
of library-related bod-
ies, 192
employment Web page, 291
EMPTF (Electronic Meeting
Participation Task
Force), 114–115
Events and Conferences page,
113
Frederick G. Kilgour Award for
Research in Library and
Information Tech-
nology, 171–172
grants and awards, 171–172
grants sponsoring conference
attendance, 246
International Opportunities
and Funding Sources,
247–248
International Relations Office,
298, 349
Library and Information
Technology Association
(LITA), 63
Library History Round Table,
107
Library Job Resources, 292
NMRT (New Members Round
Table), 114, 309
NMRTWriter discussion list,
147, 169
Office of Research and
Statistics (ORS), 243
online chat rooms, 48
Open Stacks section, 175
Periodicals list, 150
Placement Center, 300–301
scholarship information, 238
Spectrum Initiative, 239

"Standards for Accreditation",
201
Web site, 92–95, 333
ALA Symbols (Olson's Library Clip
Art), 129
ALA TechSource, 358
Alabama Library Association, 338
Alaska Library Association (AkLA),
240, 338
ALCTS (Association for Library
Collections and
Technical Services)
First Step Award, 246–247
Web site, 334
ALCTS First Step Award, 249
Alerting services, 59, 60–61
ALISE (Association for Library and
Information Science
Education)
1999 Statistical Report, 224
conference attendance grant,
247
job site, 291
research grants, 243
Web site, 334
ALSC (Association for Library
Services to Children),
334
ALTA (Association for Library
Trustees and
Advocates), 334
AltaVista search engine, 85, 315,
321
Amazon.com Alerts, 60, 71
America Online
AIM (AOL Instant Messenger),
46
built-in browser, 209
The American Archivist, 352
American Geographical Society, 53

American Libraries, 65, 120, 286, 289, 292, 348

American Libraries Online Web site, 74, 113

American Library Directory, 14, 315

American Memory Fellows program, 244

American Psychological Association, 174

American School Directory, 321

America's Job Bank, 302

Amigos' Conference Calendar, 113–114

Angelfire, 273

Ann's Place Web site, 292

ANYBrowser Web site viewer, 129

Ariadne, 358

Arizona Library Association, 338

Arkansas Libraries, 363

Arkansas Library Association, 338

ARL Annual Salary Survey, 323

ARL (Association of Research Libraries)
  Online Lyceum, 226
  Transforming Libraries, 346
  Web site, 335

ARLIS/NA (Art Libraries Society of North America), 334

ARMA (Association of Records Managers and Administrators), 335

Art Libraries of North America, 295

Articles. *See also* Professional literature
  alerting services, 60–61, 71
  online collaboration, 172–173
  online research, 167–169

ASCII (American Standard Code for Information Interchange), 262–266, 278

ASCLA (Association of Specialized and Cooperative Library Agencies), 335

ASI (American Society of Indexers), 333

ASIST (American Society for Information Science and Technology), 95–96, 112–113, 333

Aslib (Association for Information Management), 53, 70, 338

Associates: The Electronic Library Support Staff Journal, 358

Association for Information and Image Management, 334

The Association for Librarians and Information Managers, 100–101

Association of Moving Image Archivists, 335

Association of Professional Librarians of New Brunswick, 343

Association of Research Libraries
  career resource page, 291
  Research Library Residency, 292

Associations and Organizations Related to Information Studies, University of Toronto, 86

Asynchronous communication, 208

AT&T Broadband, 16

ATLA (American Theological Library Association), 334

Atlantic Provinces Library Association, 343

Atomz.com, 130
Australian Library and Information
    Association, 36, 98–99,
    298, 338
The Australian Library Journal, 348
Author guidelines, 150–151, 163
AUTOCAT discussion list, 34
Awards
    locating, 171–172
    opportunities, 248–250
    researching, 236–236

B

Bahr, Alice, 148–149
Bare Bones Guide to HTML, 128
Begg Borei, Karen, 140
*Behavioral and Social Sciences
    Librarian*, 352
Bell, Colleen, 134
Bell, Steven, 70
Benedicto, Juanita, 134
Berkeley Digital Library SunSITE,
    315
Berners-Lee, Tim, 133
Best of LRTS Award, 171
"Better Pay, More Jobs", 323
BI-L discussion list, 34
Bibliographic Society of America,
    335
Blackwell's Book Srvices, 61
Block, Marylaine, 73, 125–126
Blogger Web site, 136
Bobby Web site, 130
Bolles, Richard, 312
*Book Links: Connecting Books,
    Libraries, and
    Classrooms*, 348
Book Magazine, 158
The Book of IRC, 46
Book publishers, 152–154
The Bookdragon Review, 138–139

Booklist, 361
Bookmark files, 69–70
Books. *See also* Professional
    literature; Publishing
    outlets
    about the Internet, 18–19
    alerting services, 60–61, 71
    clip art, 129
    international book fairs, 248
    online collaboration, 172–173
    reviewing opportunities, 139,
        157–158, 361–363
*The Bottom Line: Managing
    Library Finances*, 352
*Bowker Annual of Library and
    Book Trade Information*,
    85, 286
Breeding, Marshall, 109
Bridgewater State College, Web
    publishing guidelines,
    131, 132
British Columbia Library
    Association, 343
Brown, John Seely, 207
Brown, Stephanie Willen, 299
Bruce, Bertram C., 188
BUBL (Bulletin Board for
    Libraries), 59–60, 150,
    298, 327
Bulletin boards, 208. *See also*
    Forums; Mailing lists
*Bulletin of the American Society for
    Information Science and
    Technology*, 358
*Bulletin of the Medical Librarian
    Association*, 353
Burns, Shelly, 164
BUSLIB-L discussion list, 34

C

Cable Internet access, 16

CALA (Chinese American
Librarians Association),
335
California Library Association, 338
California School Library
Association, 102,
293–294
*CALL. See Current Awareness—
Library Literature*
Calls for presenters, 111–113,
158–159
*Campus-Wide Information
Systems*, 353
Canadian Library Association, 338
Canadian library associations, 85,
297–298
Career Central Web site, 292
CareerBuilder Web site, 303
CARL UnCover. *See* Reveal, from
Ingenta
Carver, Blake, 65, 66–67, 134, 136
Castro, Elizabeth, 128
CataList discussion list, 35
Catholic Library Association, 335
Catholic Library World, 349
Catholic University of America,
310
Central Texas SLA Chapter, Texas
Job Bank, 296
Centre for Studies in Teacher-
Librarianship of New
South Wales, Australia,
115–116
CERN (European Organization for
Nuclear Research), 133
"Certificate of Professional
Development", 198–199
Charalabidis, Alexander, 46
Chat rooms, 45–49, 208
Chicago Library System, "CLS
Online", 44

The Chicago Manual of Style FAQ,
174
*CHOICE: Current Reviews for
Academic Libraries*, 81
Choice Magazine, 361
The Chronicle of Higher Education,
43–44, 62, 72, 290–292
Church and Synagogue Library
Association, 335
Cites and Insights: Crawford at
Large, 74
CityNet. *See* Excite Travel Web site
CLA (Canadian Library
Association), 99
CLENERT discussion list, 36
Clip Art Searcher, 129
Clip art Web sites, 129
CLIP Notes, 346
"CLS Online" Web site, 44
CNI (Coalition for Networked
Information), 335
CNN.com, 68
Cohen, Stephen M., 134
Cohort, 208
Collection Building, 353
Collection Management, 353
College & Research Libraries, 353
College & Research Libraries News,
120, 290–292
CollegeNET, 319
CollegeView Web site, 319
COLLIB-L discussion list, 34
Collins, Catherine, 273
Colorado Library Association, 339
Colorado Library Marketing
Council, 227
Colorado State Library, 242
Community College Web, 195
Community of Science software,
113
comp.info.www.announce, 143

Computer certification, 196–197
Computers in Libraries, 349
Computers in Libraries conference, 107–108
ComputerUser.com, 197
Conferences. *See also* Professional associations
  documenting, 120
  electronic meetings and, 114–117
  focus, 105–106
  grants for, 246–248
  online listings, 113–117
  presentations and poster sessions, 110–113, 144
  registration, 117–119
  sponsored by organizations, 106–107
  sponsored by publishers, 107–108
  travel planning, 119
  vendors, 108–110
Connecticut Library Association, 322, 339
Connecticut State University System (CSU)
  "Is Online Learning for Me?" quiz, 210, 211, 213
  OnlineCSU, 213–214
  sample online course, 222
Continuing education opportunities, 192–195, 223, 242
"Cookie cutter" sites, 131
Copyright, on images, 129
Corporation of Professional Librarians of Quebec, 343
Council for the International Exchange of Scholars (CIES), 245

Council on Library and Information Resources, 336
Counterpoise, 362
Courseware, 208
Crawford, Walt, 74
Creating Web-Accessible Databases, 173
Current awareness
  information overload, 51–53, 68–75
  services, 56–68
Current Awareness Abstracts, 53, 70
Current Awareness—Library Literature (CALL), 53
Current Cites, 63, 72
Current Contents, 53
Current Contents: Social and Behavioral Sciences, 71
Current Geographical Publications, 53
Cyber Cafés, 15–16

D

D-Lib Magazine, 359
Danish Royal School of Library and Information Science, 185
Data Research Associates (DRA), 108
Datebook, American Libraries Online, 113
DeCandido, GraceAnne, 158
Deja.com. *See* Google Groups
Delaware Library Association, 339
Dialog
  alerting services, 61
  Web site, 45
Dialog: Customer Alerts, 71
Digest format, 30, 31
Digital Librarian: Librariana, 327
Digital libraries, 47

Dikel, Margaret Riley, 275, 279, 302
Discussion lists. *See* Mailing lists
Distance education programs
  advantages, 203–207
  choosing a school, 221–223
  considerations, 45
  continuing education
    opportunities
    advantages, 223
    disadvantages, 229–233
    library school coursework,
      223–225
    from local and regional
      groups, 227–228
    from professional organiza-
      tions, 225–227
    related online classes,
      228–229
  definition, 203
  format and requirements of
    online coursework,
    207–212
  online MLS degree
    considerations, 212–213
  schools offering online
    degrees, 213–221
  other library degrees online,
    221
  technical requirements,
    209–210
  terminology, 208–209
Distance Education Survey—
  Summer 2000, 204
Doctor HTML Web site, 130
Documents in Information
  Science, 168
Dogpile search engine, 321
Domain name registration,
  132–133
Dominican University, 188
Drexel University

College of Information Science
  and Technology, 214
  continuing education courses,
    225
  MOO environment, 229
  online professional certificate
    in competitive intelli-
    gence, 225
DSL (Digital Subscriber Line),
  16–17
Duguid, Paul, 207
Duncan, Melanie, 138, 141
DuPage Library System (DLS), 193,
  194

E

E-mail. *See also* mailing lists; Web-
  based discussion
  groups; Web-based
  newsletters
  alerting services, 59, 60–61
  chat rooms, 45–49
  contacting colleagues, 25–26
  discussion lists, 26–39
  electronic newsletters, 61–63,
    71–72
  employment opportunities, 39
  folders, 69
  forums, 41–45
  free accounts, 283–284
  mentoring opportunities,
    39–41
  technical considerations, 22–25
EBSCO
  ALA conference sponsorship
    grant, 172
  Conference Sponsorship appli-
    cation, 246
  EBSCOAlert, 58, 71
  Library Reference Center
    (LRC), 167

EBSCO *(cont.)*
   online research, 169
   Subscription Services, 247
eContent conference, 108
EContent Magazine, 349
EDGAR Web site, 321
Education decisions. *See also*
      Distance education
   acquiring certification, 195–199
   considerations, 179–180
   continuing education opportu-
      nities, 192–195, 223
   international degrees, 185
   LIS programs, 180–184
   MLS programs
      applying for, 191
      decision process, 186–192
      Ph.D. programs, 199–200
      post-graduate certificates, 197
      researching, 191–192
EDUCAUSE Job Posting Service,
      291, 336
Electronic Journal Miner, 143
Electronic journals, publishing
      opportunities, 154–156
Electronic Libraries Programme,
      U.K., 63
The Electronic Library, 57, 59, 353
Electronic mail. *See* E-mail
Electronic mailing lists. *See*
      Mailing lists
Electronic meetings, 114–117
Electronic newsletters, 61–63,
      71–72, 136–142
Electronic resumes
   considerations, 253
   definition, 254
   formats
      advantages, 255–257
      ASCII (plain text), 262–266,
         278

considerations, 257–258
guidelines, 279
HTML, 266–271
MS Word, 258–262
sending electronically,
      277–278
on the Web, 272–276
general Web sites, 274–275
keywords, 275–276
Elementary School Journal, 361
The Elements of Style, 174
Emerald E-Mail Alert, 59, 60, 71,
      166–167, 248
Emoticons, 30
Employment agencies, 301–302
Employment opportunities. *See*
      also Electronic resume;
      Professional
      associations
advice and interview ques-
      tions, 309–310
application process, 305–309
considerations, 39
job announcements, 281
nontraditional positions,
      302–305
online job searches
   advantages, 285–286
   career planning, 311–313
   compared to traditional job
      hunting, 286–287
   considerations, 284–285
   employer background,
      313–314
   job listings for librarians,
      287–302
   library Web pages, 314–322
   online anonymity, 283–284
   relocation considerations,
      323–324
   salary information, 322–323

technological advantages,
284
Endeavor Information Systems,
108, 109, 255
Ensor, Pat, 52, 69, 74
EoMonitor Web site, 74
eResumes and Resources, 279, 308
Eudora Pro Web site, 23
Excite Employment Classifieds,
302
Excite Travel Web site, 119
ExLibris, 125–126

F

Faculty information, 186–188
FastTrack MLIS, 219–220
Faxon Web site, 113
Feinburg Library, SUNY University
at Plattsburgh, 47
FinAid Web site, 236
"First Impressions, Lasting
Impressions: Tips for
Job Interviews", 309
First Monday, 361
First Search, 168
Flames, 30, 31
Flipdog.com, 303
Florida Association for Media in
Education, 293
Florida Libraries, 363
Florida Library Association, 339
Florida Library Jobline, 296
Florida State University (FSU)
Career Center, 308–309
School of Information Studies,
214
Follett Software, 195
Foothills Library Association,
Calgary, 297, 343
Forums, 41–45, 208
Fourie, Ina, 57

Fox, Lynne, 27
Frederick G. Kilgour Award for
Research in Library and
Information
Technology, 171–172
Free Pint Web site, 73
Fulbright Scholarships, 245

G

Gale Research, InfoTrac database,
169
Geiger, Marilyn, 212
Georgia Library Association, 339
Georgia Library Quarterly, 363
Google Groups, 42
Google Image Search, 129
Google search engine, 85, 315
Gordon, Rachel Singer, 274, 283,
298. *See also*
Lisjobs.com
*Government Information
Quarterly*, 353–354
Grants
locating, 171–172
for research, 243–245
researching, 236–236
travel, 245–246
Graphics software, 128–129
Greenwood Publishing Group, 346
Gregory, Vicki L., 323
"Grey literature", 55
GrokSoup Web site, 136
Guadalajara international book
fair, 248

H

Hammett, Paula, 324
Hampshire College Library, 299
Hawaii Library Association, 339
Haworth Press, 151, 153–154, 346

Headhunter.net, 302
Health Libraries Review, 354
Heriot-Watt University Library, 71
Hernandez, Geri, 255
Hexadecimal Colour Numbers
    Web site, 130
Highsmith Library Literature
    Award, 172
Highsmith Press, 346–347
Himmel and Wilson Library
    Consultants, 86
Homefair.com, 324
Hoover's Online, 321
HotJobs Web site, 303
Hotmail, 22–23
HotMetal, 127
"How to Write a Decent Book
    Review", 158
HTML (HypterText Markup
    Language)
    in e-mail messages, 31
    electronic resumes, 266–271
    learning, 127–130
    META tag builder, 143
    neutral background, 271
HTML Tidy Web site, 130
H.W. Wilson, 347

I

Icon Bazaar, 129
The Idaho Librarian, 363
Idaho Library Association, 339
Idaho State Library, ABLE
    (Alternative Basic
    Library Education), 198
IFLA (International Federation of
    Library Associations
    and Institutions)
    definition, 99–100
    grants, 245–246
    IFLA Journal, 81

LIBJOBS mailing list, 289
    Web site, 86, 344
Illinois Library Association, 339
Illinois State Library, 227–228, 240
Images, 128–129, 271
Index Morganagus (IM), 143,
    167–168
Indiana Library Association, 339
Indiana University
    Alumni Happenings page, 190
    School of Library and
        Information Science, 187
    SLISJobs database, 290
    student life and support, 188
Info Career Trends, 138, 233, 359
Information Outlook, 81, 349
Information Research, 154–156,
    359
"Information revolution", 125
The Information Society, 354
*Information Technology and
    Libraries*, 354
Information Today, Inc., 72,
    107–108, 113, 347
InfoToday conference, 107
Ingenta, 58, 60–61, 71
Innovative Interfaces, Inc., 108
*InPrint: Publishing Opportunities
    for College Librarians*,
    148–149, 329
Instant messaging systems, 46
International Association of
    School Librarianship
    (IASL), 294, 344
International book fairs, 248
International Coalition for Library
    Consortia, 86
International Council on Archives,
    344
*International Information and
    Library Review*, 354

International Leads, 349
Internet. *See also* Networking
    online
    accessing, 9–17
    impact on current awareness,
        53–56
    impact on libraries, 7–9
    job sites, 302–305
    recommended reading, 18–19,
        365–375
    technology, 17–19
Internet 101 Web site, 19
Internet Explorer, 46, 209, 272
"Internet-Induced Information
    Overload" (IIIO), 55
Internet Librarian conference, 107
Internet Library Association, 344
Internet Library for Librarians, 33,
    144, 327–328
Internet-On-A-Disk, 71
Internet Public Library (IPL)
    Services for Librarians,
    328
Internet Research, 354
Internet Resources Newsletter, 71
Internet Scout Project, 62, 72
Internet4-Free.net, 13
Intranet Professional, 349–350
Iowa Library Association, 339
IRC FAQ Web site, 46
IRC (Internet Relay Chat), 45–46,
    210
Ircle, 46
"Is Online Learning for Me?" quiz,
    210, 211, 213
ISIS (Information Services in
    Schools), 115–116
ISP (Internet Service Provider)
    fee-based, 11–12
    free, 12–14
    Web hosting services, 130–131

ISSN, for online newsletters, 137
*Issues in Science and Technology
    Librarianship*, 359
ITI Newslink, 72

J

JavaScript Source Web site, 130
Jenkins, Marilyn, 307
Job Hunter's Bible, 312
Job hunting. *See* Electronic
    resumes; Employment
    opportunities;
    Professional
    associations
*JoDI: Journal of Digital
    Information*, 359
Journal of Academic Librarianship,
    355, 362
Journal of Documentation, 355
Journal of Internet Cataloging, 355
*Journal of Knowledge
    Management*, 355
*Journal of Library Services for
    Distance Education*,
    359–360
Journal research, 167–169
*JOYS: Journal of Youth Services in
    Libraries*, 350

K

K12jobs.com, 293
Kansas Library Association, 339
Keeping Up Page, 70
Keirsey Temperament Sorter, 312
Kent, Peter, 128
Kentucky Library Association, 340
Keywords
    in electronic resumes, 275–276
    searching job databases,
        304–305

Klob, Priscilla, 309
KMWorld NewsLinks, 72
Kniffel, Leonard, 1
Knowledge Quest, 355
Kovacs Consulting, 228
Kurland, Ana, 212

L

L-Soft Corporation, 35, 142
LAMA (Library Administration and
    Management
    Association), 336
Laughing Librarian Web site, 122
Law Library Journal, 350
LAWLIB discussion list, 34
LearnTheNet Web site, 19
LEEP (Library Education
    Experimental Program),
    219, 220
LIANZA (Library and Information
    Association of New
    Zealand), 298, 338
LIBADMIN discussion list, 34
LIBJOBS mailing list, 289
LibLog Web site, 133–134
librarian.net, 74, 134, 135
Librarians and Library Science
    Web site, 43
Librarians Chatboard,
    teachers.net, 43
"Librarians Ignore the Value of
    Stories", 43–44
Librarians in the 21st Century, 189
Librarians' Index to the Internet,
    65, 71
Librarian's Online Warehouse, 150
Librarian's Resource Centre, 328
Librarianship. *See also* Professional
    associations;
    Professional literature;
    Publishing outlets

academic librarians, 148–149,
    290–292, 318–319
impact of the Internet, 7–9
news
    of the field, 72
    of the profession, 74
nontraditional positions,
    302–305
online presence
    advantages, 121–122
    e-mail discussion lists,
    136–142
    promoting, 142–144
    Web sites, 122–133
    Weblogs, 65, 133–136
public librarians, 292–293,
    320
recommended reading,
    365–375
reference librarians, 47
school libraries, 320–321
subject-specific positions,
    294–295
systems librarians, 44–45
Libraries and Culture, 350
Libraries Unlimited (LU), 154, 347
*Library Administration and
    Management*, 350
Library Association of Alberta, 343
Library Association Publishing,
    347
The Library Association (U.K.), 338
Library consortia, 86–87
Library E-Mail Lists and
    Newsgroups, Internet
    Library for Librarians,
    33
Library Hi Tech, 59, 355
Library Hotline, 53, 55
Library Job Hunting Web pages,
    322

Library Job Postings, 281, 282
Library Job Resources, 292
Library Journal, 65, 113, 120, 158, 292, 324, 350, 362
Library Journal Digital Web site, 74
Library journals, publishing opportunities, 149–152
Library Juice, 62, 72, 137–138
Library Literature & Information Service Online, 61, 167
Library Literature and Information Science, 168
Library Management, 59
Library Media and PR, clip art, 129
Library Mosaics, 350
Library News Daily, 134
Library of Congress
American Memory Fellows program, 244
list of state library Web sites, 149–150
Library-Oriented Lists and Electronic Serials, 143, 301
Library Philosophy and Practice, 360
Library Planet Web site, 74
"Library portals", 65, 144
Library Research Round Table, 107
Library Research Seminar II, 107
Library Research Seminar Planning Committee, 107
Library Resource List, 328
Library Resources and Technical Services, 356
Library Review, 356
Library Stuff, 134
Library Trends, 356
Librarycard.com, 65
Library_geek Web site, 134

LibraryHQ.com, 65, 74, 152, 328
LibraryJobHunt Web site, 309
Libraryplace.com, 65
LibrarySpot, 328
Libraryspot.com, 65
LIBREF-L discussion list, 34
LIBRES, 154–156
Libres: Library and Information Science Research, 360
Libr.org Web server, 131
LIBSUP-L discussion list, 34
Libweb, 14, 86, 299, 314
Link-Up, 361
LISA (Library and Information Science Abstracts), 61
Lisjobs.com, 138, 182–184, 274, 281, 283, 309, 329
LISNews.com, 65, 66–67, 134, 136
Lis.Oclc.Org, 74
The List of Library and Information Science & Telecommunications Resources on the Web, 328
LISTPROC software, 140
LISTSERV (R) software, 30, 35
Liszt discussion list, 35
LITA (Library and Information Technology Association), 63, 336
Literati Club, 248
Litwin, Rory, 62, 137
Live online reference, 47
LOEX Clearinghouse for Library Instruction, 336
Longley, Dan, 313
LookSmart, FindArticles.com, 169
L.O.S.T. (The Librarians' Online Support Team), 228–229
Louisiana Libraries, 363
Louisiana Library Association, 340

LQ: The Library Quarterly, 350, 362
LSTA (Library Services and Technology Act), 240
LTA (Library Technical Assistant) degree, 221
Lurking, 30
Lycos Companies Online, 321
Lycos Tripod, 131

M

Mach, Michelle, 304
Macromedia Dreamweaver, 127
Magazines, publishing opportunities, 156–157
MagPortal.com, 169
Mailing lists. *See also* Usenet newsgroups; Web-based discussion groups; Web-based newsgroups
 announcements, 64
 for current awareness, 73
 job ads, 291, 301
 netiquette, 31–32
 online presence, 136–142
 terminology, 30
Maine Library Association, 340
Major Orchestra Librarians Association, 336
Manitoba Library Association, 344
Manuscript queries, 159–166
Mapquest Web site, 119, 324
Mary Adeline Connor Development Scholarship, 242
Maryland Library Association, 340
Massachusetts Library Association, 340
MCB. *See* Emerald e-mail alert service
McFarland & Company, Inc., 347

MCJournal: The Journal of Academic Media Librarianship, 360
MCSE (Microsoft Certified Systems Engineer), 196–197
Medical Library Association
 awards, 242, 248–249
 conference attendance grant, 247
 Continuing Education Clearinghouse, 194
 Ph.D. programs, 241
Melton, Marissa, 313
Message boards. *See* forums
META tag builder, 143
Michigan Library Association, 89, 91, 102, 340
Microsoft FrontPage, 127, 128–129
Microsoft Office, 210
Microsoft Outlook Express, 23
Microsoft Word, 127
Milbury, Peter, 320
Mind-It Web site, 67, 74
Minnesota Library Association, 340
mIRC, 46
Miscellany newsletter, 193
Mississippi Librarian, 363
Mississippi Library Association, 340
Missouri Library Association, 340
The MLA (Medical Library Association) Style Manual, 174
MLS (Master of Library Science) degree, 201
MLS programs
 conference attendance grant, 247
 scholarships, 237–241
Modern Language Association, 174
"The Modern MLS Degree", 313

Monster.com, 275, 276, 303
Monstermoving.com, 324
Montana Library Association, 340
MOO (MUD Object Oriented)
    environment, 115–116,
    208–209, 229
Morgan, Eric, Index Morganagus
    (IM), 143, 167–168
Mountain Plains Library
    Association, 244, 297, 340
MSN Messenger Service, 46
MUD (Multi-User Dimension)
    environment, 115–116
MultiMediaSchools, 351
Music Library Association
    Joblist, 336
    Web site, 336
Music Library Association Joblist,
    295
Myers-Briggs Type Indicator, 312
Myers, Tracy, 205

N

NASIG (North American Serials
    Interest Group), 174
National & International Library &
    Information Science
    Associations, 86
National Association of
    Government Archives
    and Records
    Administrators, 336
National Association of Media and
    Technology Centers, 336
National Center for Education
    Statistics, 321
National Federation of Abstracting
    and Information
    Services, 337
National Library of Canada Web
    site, 36, 85

National Public School Locator,
    321
National Teacher Recruitment
    Clearinghouse, 294
NCATE (National Council for
    Accreditation of Teacher
    Education, 196
NCSU Libraries Web site, 47
Neal-Schuman Publishers, Inc.,
    347–348
Neat New Stuff I Found This Week,
    73
Nebraska Library Association, 341
*Nebraska Library Association
    Quarterly*, 363
NELINET (New England Library
    and Information
    Network), 83–84, 113,
    198–199
Nesbeitt, Sarah, 282. *See also*
    Library Job Postings
Net for Beginners Web site, 19
Net Happenings newsgroup, 73
Net Happenings Web site, 64, 73
Net News Today, 73
Netiquette, 30, 31–32
NetMind Web site, 67
Netscape Communicator, 23, 46,
    272
Netscape Messenger, 23
Netscape Navigator, 209
NetSurfer Digest, 72, 73
NETTRAIN discussion list, 38
Network of School Librarian Web
    Pages, 320
Network Solutions, 132–133
Networking online, 21–22. *See also*
    E-mail; Mailing lists;
    Professional associa-
    tions; Web-based dis-
    cussion groups

Nevada Library Association, 341
New England Jobline, 297
New England Libraries, 363
New England Library Association, 341
New Hampshire Library Association, 341
New Jersey Library Association, 341
New Library World, 356
New-List mailing list, 64, 73
New Members' Round Table (NMRT), ALA, 97–98
New Mexico Library Association, 341
New York Library Association, 341
New York Public Library, 316
The New Yorker, 156
Newberry Library awards, 244
NewBreed Librarian, 74, 134
Newfoundland and Labrador Library Association, 344
NewJour mailing list, 64, 73
Newlen, Robert, R., 254
NEWLIB-L, 139–140, 189
News filtering services, 68
NewsAgent for Libraries, 63, 72
NewsBlogger Web site, 136
NewsDirectory Web site, 299–300, 324
Newsgroups. *See* Usenet newsgroups
Newsletter Access Web site, 143
Newsletters, 62
NewsOne.Net, 42
Nielsen, Jakob, 130
NMRT (New Members Round Table), ALA, 114
NMRTWriter discussion list, 147, 169

Non-MLS library personnel
  continuing education opportunities, 221
  workshops, 198
Nontraditional library positions, 302–305
North American library schools, 181–182
North American Serials Interest Group, 295, 337
North American Sport Library Network, 337
North Carolina Libraries, 363
North Carolina Library Association, 341
North Dakota Library Association, 341
Nova Scotia Library Association, 344
The Nutshell, 245

O

Occupational Outlook Handbook, 312–313
Occupational Outlook Quarterly, 313
OCLC
  First Search, 168
  research grants, 243
  "visiting scholar" positions, 245
Ohio Libraries, 363
Ohio Library Association, 341
Oklahoma Library Association, 341
Olson's Library Clip Art, 129
On-ground courses, 209
Online anonymity, 283–284
Online collaboration, 172–173
Online degrees. *See* Distance education programs
Online Magazine, 351

Online Newspapers Web site, 300
Online research, 166–170
Online workshops, 115–116
Ontario Library Association, 344
Open Stacks section, 175
Oregon Library Association
    Jobline, 296
    Web site, 342
*Oregon Library Association
    Quarterly*, 364
Oryx Press, 348

P

Pacific Northwest Library
    Association, 342
Packet-switching technology, 17
PACS-L discussion list, 34
PaintShop Pro, 128
PALINET Web site, 84
PC World Web site, 23
Peer reviews, 146–147
Pennsylvania Library Association,
    342
Perl Archive Web site, 130
Personalized agents, 63, 72,
    303–305
Peterson's Education Center, 299,
    319
Peterson's Guide, 182, 192
Ph.D. programs
    conference attendance grant,
        247
    education decisions, 199–200
    scholarship information,
        241–242
Pimentel, David, 215–218
Pitas.com, 136
PLA (Public Library Association), 337
Placement firms, 301–302
Portal: Libraries and the Academy,
    356

Post MLS scholarships, 242
Posting, 30
Price, Gary, 134
Professional associations. *See also*
    Conferences; *names of
    specific professional
    organizations*, e.g., ALA
    Canadian provincial and
        regional, 343–344
    compared to library consortia,
        82–84, 86–87
    conferences, 106–107
    finding on the Internet, 84–87
    international, 344
    networking opportunities,
        79–82, 102–103
    outside the U.S., 338
    placement services, 300–301
    in the U.S.
        national, 333–337
        state and regional,
            338–343
    Web pages
        content, 87–92
        of specific organizations,
            92–102
Professional literature. *See also*
        Publishing outlets
    calls for papers, 158–159
    grants and awards, 171–172
    online collaboration, 172–173
    online research, 166–170
    publishing opportunities
        advantages, 145–148,
            171–175
        book publishers, 152–154
        electronic journals,
            154–156
        journal research, 167–169
        library journals, 149–152
        magazines, 156–157

Professional literature (*cont.*)
    query submission, 159–166
    reading online, 175–176
    reviewing opportunities, 139,
        157–158
    style guides, 174
    writing advice, 175
Professional Organizations in the
    Information Sciences,
    85–86
The Progressive Librarian, 351
PRTALK discussion list, 36
PUBLIB discussion list, 34, 293
Public libraries, 292–293, 320
Public Libraries, 351
Public Library Association, 351
Public Services Quarterly, 357
*The Publication Manual of the
    American Psychological
    Association*, 174
Publishing outlets. *See also* Books;
    Professional literature
    journals
        electronic, general, and ref-
        ereed, 358–360
        national and international,
        348–352
        peer-reviewed, with a
        print counterpart,
        352–358
        state/local, 363–364
    monographs, 345–348
    outside the library field, 381
PUBYAC discussion list, 34
"Push" services, 68

Q

Qualcomm, 23, 44–45
Quebec Library Association, 344
Query submission, 159–166
Querying employers, 306–307

R

Ramirez, Sonia, 323
Raymond Walters College, 221
RealPlayer audio/video browser
    plugin, 210
Redwood City Public Library, 133
Reed, Donna, 123
Reference librarians, 47
Reference Reviews, 362
Reference Services Review, 357
*References & User Services
    Quarterly*, 356
REFORMA (National Association
    to Promote Library and
    Information Services to
    Latinos and the
    Spanish-Speaking), 239,
    337
Reforma—northeast discussion
    list, 36
Research Buzz, 73
Research grants, 243–245
Research libraries, 290–292
Research Strategies, 357
The Researching Librarian Web
    site, 168
Reveal, from Ingenta, 58, 60–61
Rhode Island Library Association,
    342
Riley Guide, 275, 279, 302
Roberts, Beth, 38, 318
Robinson, Ann, 322
RUSA (Reference and User Services
    Association), 337
Rutgers University
    School of Communication
        Information and Library
        Studies, 224
    Youth Literature and
        Technology certificate,
        224

S

The Salary Calculator, 322
Salary surveys, 322
San Jose State University, 181
Saskatchewan Library Association, 344
Saskatchewan Provincial Library, 307
Scarecrow Press, 348
Scheiberg, Susan, 139–140
Schneider, Karen, 48
Schnell, Eric, 128
Scholarships
    continuing education, 242
    MLS programs, 237–241
    Ph.D. programs, 241–242
    researching, 236–237
School libraries, 320–321
School Library Journal, 196, 293
School library media programs, 196
School Library Media Research, 357
The School Report, 324
Scott, Peter, 134
Scout Report, 62–63, 72, 73
Searcher: The Magazine for Database Professionals, 351
"Selective dissemination of information" (SDI), 55
Self-Evaluation for Potential Online Students, 210
Seltzer, Richard, 71
SERIALIST discussion list, 35
The Serials Librarian, 357, 362
Serials Reference Services Quarterly, 357
Shapiro, Fred, 37
Shontz, Priscilla, 27–28, 123, 170, 309
The Shy Librarian, 351

Signature file, 24–25
SLA (Special Libraries Association)
    Career Information Center, 274
    Central Texas Chapter, 296
    distance learning program, 226–227
    Information Outlook, 81
    mentorship programs, 40
    online chat rooms, 47–48
    scholarships and awards, 237–238
    SLA discussion lists, 36
    SLA Salary Survey, 323
    "Virtual SLA" Web page, 294
    Web site, 101–102, 344
SLISJobs database, 290
SMILE: Studies in Media & Information Literacy Education, 360
Smith, Rebecca, 276, 279, 308
Society of American Archivists (SAA), 98, 337
Softquad, 127
SOLINET Web site, 84
Sondermann, TJ, 134
South Carolina Library Association, 342
South Dakota Library Association, 342
Southern Connecticut State University Library Jobline, 290
Southern Illinois University, Carbondale, 226
Spam, 30, 278, 283–284
Spyonit.com, 67, 74
State certification requirements, 197–199
State government Web addresses, 197
State Library of Iowa, 198

State library Web sites, 149–150
State of Florida, Florida Library
    Jobline, 296
Stenstrom, Patricia E., 52
Still, Julie, 173
Street Librarian Web site, 122
Strom, Maliaca, 231
Strunk, William (Jr.), 174
Stumpers-L discussion list, 35,
    36–37
Style guides, 174
Submit It Web site, 143
Subscribing, 30
Suburban Library System (SLS),
    227
SUNY University at Plattsburgh, 47
Switchboard, 14, 119
Synchronous communications,
    209
Syracuse University
    21st Century Librarian Award,
        249, 313
    School of Information Studies,
        189, 214–218
System certification requirements,
    197–199
Systems librarians, 44–45

T

Tables of contents (ToC) services,
    58–60, 70–71
TCP/IP technology, 17
Teacherjobs.com, 275, 293
Teachers.net, 43
*Technology Electronic Reviews
    (TER), 63, 72*
Tegler, Patricia, 52
Telementoring, 39–41
Tennant, Roy, 122
The Tennessee Librarian, 364
Tennessee Library Association, 342

Texas A&M University-Commerce,
    273
Texas Library Association
    Jobline, 296
    Web site, 342
Texas Library Journal, 364
Texas State Library Jobline, 296
Texas State University, 198
Texas Woman's University, 220–221
*T.H.E. Journal: Technical Horizons
    in Education*, 361
Theatre Library Association, 337
Theological Libraries Association,
    294
Time management, 69–70
Today's Librarian, 351–352
Tool Kit for the Expert Web
    Searcher, 52, 74
Top Ten Mistakes in Web Design,
    130
Topica mailing list, 309
Transforming Traditional Libraries,
    360
Travelocity Web site, 119
Trellix Web, 127
Tripquest Web site, 119
Tudor, Jan Davis, 55
Tutorialfind Web site, 229

U

ULC (Urban Libraries Council),
    337
*The U*N*A*B*A*S*H*E*D
    Librarian*, 352
University of Arizona (UA), 219
University of Buffalo (BU)
    Department of Library &
        Information Studies,
        187
    electronic resumes, 273
    Job Postings page, 190

Library Job Resources, 292
Resources page, 189
School of Information Studies,
224
WebBulletinBoard (WBB), 224
University of California, Berkeley
applying online, 191
School of Information
Management and
Systems (SIMS), 54–55,
181
University of Cincinnati, Raymond
Walters College, 221
University of Denver, 181
University of Illinois at Urbana-
Champaign
Graduate School of Library and
Information Science,
187, 219
GSLIS Doctor of Philosophy
Program Stages page,
200
LEEP (Library Education
Experimental Program),
219, 220
online video, 222
Ph.D. programs, 241
Self-Evaluation for Potential
Online Students, 210
University of Michigan
Finding Professional Literature
on the Net, 150
School of Information,
189–190, 274, 290
University of Missouri-Columbia,
290
University of North Texas, 220–221
University of Pittsburgh (Pitt),
FastTrack MLIS,
219–220
University of Sheffield, 185

University of Texas at Austin, 274
University of Toronto
Associations and
Organizations Related
to Information Studies,
86
JobSite, 298
Web-based continuing educa-
tion courses, 225
University of Washington
Information School, 240
list of funding resources, 236
University of Western Ontario, 298
University of Wisconsin, Madison
School of Library and
Information Studies
(SLIS), 186, 225
Scout Report, 62–63, 72, 73
student life and support, 188
Unsubscribing, 30
Urban Library Journal, 357
U.S. News & World Report, 156
U.S. News Online (USNO),
191–192
Usenet newsgroups, 33, 42, 73. See
also Mailing lists
User's group meetings. *See*
Conferences
Utah Library Association, 342

V

"Vacation message", 31
Vendors, at conferences, 108–110
Vermont Library Association, 342
Video Librarian, 362
Virginia Libraries, 364
Virginia Library Association, 342
*The Virtual Acquisition Shelf &
News Desk*, 134
Vormelker-Thomas student award,
247

VOYA (Voice of Youth Advocates), 157–158, 352, 362
VOYAGER-L mailing list, 109

W

Walsh, Joanne, 206
Washington-Centerville Public Library, 315
Washington Library Association, 343
WDG HTML Validator, 130
Web-based discussion groups. *See* Mailing lists
Web-based newsletters, 62
Web browsers
    Internet Explorer, 46
    Netscape Communicator, 23, 46
Web Design for Librarians, 128
Web Developer's Virtual Library, 128
Web editors, 127–130
Web hosting services, 130–131
The Web Resume, 279
Web sites. *See also names of specific Web sites*
    with newsworthy content, 64–67, 73–74
    update notification services, 67–68, 74–75
Web4Lib discussion list, 26–27, 35, 111
WebCT courseware, 207, 222, 225
Weblog FAQ, 133
Weblogs, 65, 133–136
Weblogs.Com, 136
WebNet Journal, 358
WebTV, 209
West, Jessamyn, 65, 74, 134, 135
West Virginia Library Association, 343

What Color Is Your Parachute?, 312
"What's New" pages, 133
Whole Internet Clipart Guide, 129
Wiegand, Wayne, 43–44
Wisconsin Library Association, 343
WNBA—Ann Heidbreder Eastman Grant, 171
Wojcik, Tim, 43, 254
The Wonderful World of Wombats: The Unofficial Stumpers-L page, 37
World List of Departments and Schools of Information Studies, Information Management, Information Systems, Etc., 185
Writing advice, 175
"Writing Effective Letters Guide", 308–309
Writing for the Web: A Primer for Librarians, 128, 130
Writing Resumes That Work: A How-To-Do-It Manual for Librarians, 254
Wu, Wei, 33
Wyoming Library Association, 343
Wyoming State Library, 193–194
WYSIWYG ("What You See Is What You Get") Web editors, 127

Y

Yahoo!, 13
Yahoo! GeoCities, 131, 273
Yahoo! Groups, 35–36, 139, 141
Yahoo! Local, 119, 299
Yahoo! Mail, 22–23
Yahoo! Messenger, 46
Yahoo! What's New, 74
Yahoo.com, 281

YALSA-L (Young Adult Library
Services Association
List), 36, 337, 350
Your Free Sources, 13
Youth Literature and Technology
certificate, 224

Z

Zagat.com, 119
Zimbabwe international book fair,
248
Zoomerang Web site, 170

More Great Books from Information Today, Inc.

Creating Web-Accessible Databases
Case Studies for Libraries, Museums, and Other Non-Profits

Edited by Julie M. Still

Libraries, museums, and other not-for-profit institutions are increasingly looking for (and finding) ways to offer patrons and the public Web access to their collections. This new book from Julie Still and her expert contributors explores the unique challenges non-profit archival institutions face in leveraging the Internet and presents a dozen case studies showcasing a variety of successful projects and approaches.

2001/200 pp/hardbound
ISBN 1-57387-104-4 $39.50

The OPL Sourcebook
A Guide for Solo and Small Libraries

By Judith A. Siess

Judith A. Siess, editor of the monthly newsletter, *The One-Person Library*, has created the definitive handbook and directory for small and one-person libraries (OPLs). Taking an international approach to reflect the growing number of OPLs worldwide, this new book covers organizational culture, customer service, time management and planning, budgeting, accounting, technology, collection development, education, downsizing, outsourcing, and many other key management issues. Includes a comprehensive directory.

2001/260 pp/hardbound
ISBN 1-57387-111-7 $39.50

Library Relocations and Collection Shifts

By Dennis Tucker

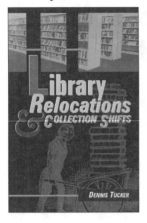

In *Library Relocations and Collection Shifts*, author, librarian, and move director Dennis Tucker explains how to develop an appropriate moving plan for a library of any type or size. A thorough revision of his classic, *From Here to There: Moving a Library*, the book provides coverage of all these topics and more:

• Appointing a move director and committee
• Moving methods and strategies
• Customizing a library moving plan
• Planning and coordinating the move
• Handling books and periodicals
• Cleaning, fumigation, and deacidification
• Working with professional movers
• Communicating with staff and the public

You'll also find information on using spreadsheets to shift periodical collections, a sample moving contract, a directory of useful resources, and suggestions for further reading.

1999/212 pp/hardbound
ISBN 1-57387-069-2 $35.00

The Evolving Virtual Library II
Practical and Philosophical Perspectives

Edited by Laverna M. Saunders

This edition of *The Evolving Virtual Library* documents how libraries of all types are changing with the integration of the Internet and the Web, electronic resources, and computer networks. It provides a summary of trends over the last 5 years, new developments in networking, case studies of creating digital content delivery systems for remote users, applications in K-12 and public libraries, and a vision of things to come. The contributing experts are highly regarded in their specialties. The information is timely and presents a snapshot of what libraries are dealing with in the new millennium.

1999/194 pp/hardbound
ISBN 1-57387-070-6 $39.50

Super Searchers Go to the Source

The Interviewing and Hands-On Information Strategies of Top Primary Researchers—Online, on the Phone, and in Person

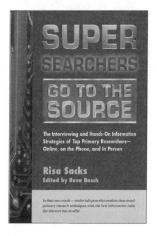

By Risa Sacks • Edited by Reva Basch

For the most focused, current, in-depth information on any subject, nothing beats going directly to the source—to the experts. This is "Primary Research," and it's the focus of the seventh title in the "Super Searchers" series. From the boardrooms of America's top corporations, to the halls of academia, to the pressroom of the *New York Times*, Risa Sacks interviews 12 of the best primary researchers in the business. These research pros reveal their strategies for integrating online and "off-line" resources, identifying experts, and getting past gatekeepers to obtain information that exists only in someone's head. Supported by the Super Searchers Web page.

2001/420 pp/softbound
ISBN 0-910965-53-6 $24.95

Introductory Concepts in Information Science

By Melanie J. Norton

Melanie J. Norton presents a unique introduction to the practical and theoretical concepts of information science while examining the impact of the Information Age on society. Drawing on recent research into the field, as well as from scholarly and trade publications, the monograph provides a brief history of information science and coverage of key topics, including communications and cognition, information retrieval, bibliometrics, modeling, economics, information policies, and the impact of information technology on modern management. This is an essential volume for graduate students, practitioners, and any professional who needs a solid grounding in the field of information science.

2000/127 pp/hardbound
ISBN 1-57387-087-0
ASIST Members $31.60 • Non-Members $39.50

Electronic Styles
A Handbook for Citing Electronic Information

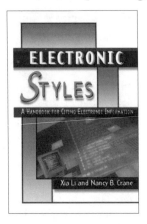

By Xia Li and Nancy Crane

The second edition of the best-selling guide to referencing electronic information and citing the complete range of electronic formats includes text-based information, electronic journals and discussion lists, Web sites, CD-ROM and multimedia products, and commercial online documents.

1996/214 pp/softbound
ISBN 1-57387-027-7 • $19.99

Intelligent Technologies in Library and Information Service Applications

By F.W. Lancaster and Amy Warner

Librarians and library school faculty have been experimenting with artificial intelligence (AI) and expert systems for 30 years, but there has been no comprehensive survey of the results available until now. In this carefully researched monograph, authors Lancaster and Warner report on the applications of AI technologies in library and information services, assessing their effectiveness, reviewing the relevant literature, and offering a clear-eyed forecast of future use and impact. Includes almost 500 bibliographic references.

2001/214 pp/hardbound
ISBN 1-57387-103-6

ASIST Members $31.60 • Non-Members $39.50